FROM HIGHER EDUCATION TO EMPLOYMENT
SYNTHESIS REPORT

ORGANISATION FOR ECONOMIC CO-OPERATION AND DEVELOPMENT

ORGANISATION FOR ECONOMIC CO-OPERATION AND DEVELOPMENT

Pursuant to Article 1 of the Convention signed in Paris on 14th December 1960, and which came into force on 30th September 1961, the Organisation for Economic Co-operation and Development (OECD) shall promote policies designed:

— to achieve the highest sustainable economic growth and employment and a rising standard of living in Member countries, while maintaining financial stability, and thus to contribute to the development of the world economy;

— to contribute to sound economic expansion in Member as well as non-member countries in the process of economic development; and

— to contribute to the expansion of world trade on a multilateral, non-discriminatory basis in accordance with international obligations.

The original Member countries of the OECD are Austria, Belgium, Canada, Denmark, France, Germany, Greece, Iceland, Ireland, Italy, Luxembourg, the Netherlands, Norway, Portugal, Spain, Sweden, Switzerland, Turkey, the United Kingdom and the United States. The following countries became Members subsequently through accession at the dates indicated hereafter: Japan (28th April 1964), Finland (28th January 1969), Australia (7th June 1971) and New Zealand (29th May 1973). The Commission of the European Communities takes part in the work of the OECD (Article 13 of the OECD Convention).

Publié en français sous le titre :
DE L'ENSEIGNEMENT SUPÉRIEUR
A L'EMPLOI :
RAPPORT DE SYNTHÈSE

© OECD 1993
Applications for permission to reproduce or translate all or part of this
publication should be made to:
Head of Publications Service, OECD
2, rue André-Pascal, 75775 PARIS CEDEX 16, France

FOREWORD

The OECD activity on Higher Education and Employment covers three discrete projects: "The flows of graduates from higher education and their entry into working life"; "The case of the humanities and the social sciences"; and "Recent developments in continuing professional education".

This report is devoted to the first of these three projects. Many Member countries submitted contributions in response to detailed guidelines prepared by the Secretariat. These contributions constitute a major conceptual effort to assemble information from many sources. They reflect the state of the art and illustrate a variety of approaches, methodologies and even philosophies.

These contributions are being published in the "OECD Documents" series. Volume I contains the contributions from Australia, Austria, Belgium (Flemish Community) and Germany; Volume II those from Canada, Denmark, Spain and the United States; Volume III those from Finland, France, Italy, Japan, the Netherlands and Norway; and Volume IV those from Portugal, Sweden, Switzerland and the United Kingdom.

This report summarises the information contained in the country contributions, although it makes use of other sources and, in particular, the OECD database on education. The intention herein is to highlight the most significant trends and the similarities and dissimilarities between these relatively diverse countries; we have sought to explain these and draw some conclusions.

It should be noted that the emphasis is on flows rather than institutions. "Higher education" is defined as the education and training experience of those who have completed upper secondary education or its equivalent. This may not coincide with the more restrictive connotation of the term in some countries.

This project was led by Eric Esnault, of the Secretariat. The views expressed in this volume, published on the responsibility of the OECD Secretary-General, do not commit either the OECD or the national authorities concerned.

ALSO AVAILABLE

Alternatives to Universities (1991)
(91 90 05 1) ISBN 92-64-13530-8   FF90 £12.00 US$22.00 DM35
Financing Higher Education : Current Patterns (1990)
(91 90 04 1) ISBN 92-64-13422-0   FF100 £12.00 US$21.00 DM39

From Higher Education to Employment

From Higher Education to Employment. Volume I: Australia, Austria, Belgium, Germany. OECD Documents (1992)
(02 92 01 3) ISBN 92-64-03524-9   FF60 £6.00 US$15.00 DM18

From Higher Education to Employment. Volume II: Canada, Denmark, Spain, United States. OECD Documents (1992)
(02 92 02 3) ISBN 92-64-03525-7   FF60 £6.00 US$15.00 DM18

From Higher Education to Employment. Volume III: Finland, France, Italy, Japan, Netherlands, Norway. OECD Documents (1992)
(02 92 03 3) ISBN 92-64-03529-X   FF60 £6.00 US$15.00 DM18

Reviews of National Policies for Education

Reviews of National Policies for Education. Higher Education in California (1990)
(91 90 02 1) ISBN 92-64-13412-3   FF140 £17.00 US$30.00 DM55

Prices charged at the OECD Bookshop.
THE OECD CATALOGUE OF PUBLICATIONS and supplements will be sent free of charge on request addressed either to OECD Publications Service, or to the OECD Distributor in your country.

TABLE OF CONTENTS

Preface 7

Part One
FLOWS OF GRADUATES FROM HIGHER EDUCATION

Introduction 13

Chapter 1
The demand for higher education: Overview 17

Chapter 2
Aspects of growth 35

Chapter 3
Outflows from higher education 57

Statistical annex 69

Part Two
ENTRY INTO WORKING LIFE

Introduction 79

Chapter 4
The general trend 81

Chapter 5
The transition conditions 103

Chapter 6
Destinations 129

Issues for the future 139

Annex
Authors of the national contributions 147

PREFACE

The OECD has undertaken a new study on the relationship between higher education and employment. The fact is that throughout the OECD area there is renewed awareness of the vital importance of education for economic and technological development; in particular, staff with post-secondary education are considered to be a strategic resource for the preservation of each country's competitiveness. While still appreciating the social and cultural functions of higher education, opinion now has a much more positive perception of its economic role, and notably its function as preparation for employment.

This study thus fits into a context very different from that of the late 1970s, a time when it was usual to speak of a "higher education crisis". Among the origins of this crisis there were of course the internal difficulties resulting from greatly increased enrolments, but also growing difficulties encountered by young graduates on entry to working life, in particular those from certain university disciplines who saw their traditional employment openings being closed.

The overall employment situation was bad, especially for young people. This was the major preoccupation at that time and unemployment among young graduates was perceived as a new and worrying development, as was the necessity for many of them to accept jobs very much below their capacities and skills. Having a degree was no longer a guarantee of a steady and well-paid job. While on the whole these graduates were in a more favourable position on the labour market than young people with more modest qualifications, their situation was bad enough for there to be a general crisis of confidence with regard to higher education. This was the subject of an OECD analysis published in 1981 under the title "Employment prospects for higher education graduates".[1]

The 1981 study shed light on a certain number of trends whose coincidence was cause for concern:

  i) the arrival on the labour market of a considerable influx of young graduates, resulting from the rapid expansion of post-secondary education, their relative weight likely to be even further increased by demographic mechanisms;
  ii) the constraints weighing on public expenditure, which limited the growth of employment in activities dependent on it, notably in public services, the main opening for those with post-secondary education, particularly women;
  iii) the saturation of certain sectors such as education and research which were among the biggest employers of people with post-secondary education and where there was no prospect of any significant upturn in recruitment for the next ten years or so;
  iv) uncertainty with regard to an upturn in the private sector, notably in industry; a possible slowdown in the expansion of activities with a high proportion of qualified staff and also the possibility of saturation or a rapid rationalisation in certain tertiary sector activities.

This diagnosis was all the more worrying in that since the beginning of the 1960s and until the mid-70s the evolution of employment structures had been very favourable to graduates. The postwar phase of industrial development had in fact been succeeded by what the report called a phase of intellectual investment, characterised by the rapid expansion of employment in teaching, research and public service management. The mere slowing of this expansion was enough to significantly change the employment opportunities for young graduates.

The diagnosis was not formulated in terms of disequilibrium or surplus. While the concept of supply is fairly clear, that of demand is to a large extent arbitrary or subjective. The report focused on the possible adjustments: in higher education, through a reorientation of demand, reinforcing the "vocational" component; in the world of work, through a redistribution of the flows of young graduates, notably from the public to the private sector, with expansion of the range of jobs sought and perhaps acceptance of jobs of a lower level. These adjustments implied a change in attitudes on both sides and were likely to come up against "social constraints", *i.e.* the difficulty of modifying ways of thinking and acting that were as firmly established in the world of work as they were in education.

This new study is concerned with a period when the climate is quite different. The vigorous growth of the early 1980s restored optimism to some extent. That optimism has no doubt been seriously tempered by the current recession, but today, despite the persistence of unemployment, there is now talk of shortages of qualified staff and concern about the consequences of demographic decline. There is now more tendency to place the emphasis on the very favourable situation for certain categories than on the difficulties that others may still encounter. On the other hand, the accelerated changes to be seen in economic life are calling into question the validity of traditional ways of thinking and the stability of the correspondences on which analyses of the relationship between higher education and employment are more or less explicitly based. The aim of this new study is thus to take stock of the situation, see whether there have in fact been adjustments between supply and demand and possibly throw light on new trends and identify as far as possible the main issues that are going to arise in the future.

It is easy to see an evolution in the nature of studies on the employment of higher education graduates. A few decades ago, the approach was mainly that of forecasting manpower requirements and corresponded to a period in which highly qualified people were relatively scarce. This approach was also well suited to evaluating the manpower needs of industry such as that for scientific and technical staff and gave rise to such concepts as that of substitution and utilisation.

Higher education then experienced a number of "fat years". Following the long phase of industrial development there was a period of intellectual investment in which young graduates from all disciplines, despite their increased numbers, were practically sure of being able to find a job and a career. This period was that of the expansion of employment in research, education, in systems management: in most countries it was also a period of substantial recruitment into the public sector, the main destination for many types of higher education. For certain categories of graduates the main preoccupation became the lower level of the job or the pay they had to accept, a natural consequence of the expansion of higher education. Corresponding quite well to this period are works on the "economics of education" and comparative studies on the "profitability" of different disciplines.

These fat years however gave way to lean years of a general regression in employment and in particular severe constraints on public sector recruitment. Attention then tended to shift to the destinations of the different categories of graduates and their situation on the labour market. While on the whole they still had an advantage over others, graduates suffered both from the difficult general employment situation and the transformation of the possibilities open to them. The emphasis was then on measuring and making known the scale of the consequences of structural adjustment and the main trends concerning global demand, *i.e.* the stock of qualified staff, in order to evaluate the implications for higher education. This was the approach adopted in the earlier OECD study.

Today it seems that the analysis is unlikely to lead to such simple and clear-cut conclusions. The general impression is that, while those emerging from higher or post-secondary education generally retain their advantage over the others as regards access to employment, we find a great diversity of situations within this group: there is a very buoyant demand for graduates in certain disciplines, while others are unable to use their qualifications or can find only insecure and badly paid jobs. It is not known whether these disparities have tended to diminish or on the contrary increase; it is not known whether the general situation has improved, as the general optimism would tend to imply, and in any event we do not have a clear idea of the scale of the adjustments that have been necessary. Present trends seem to be many and varied and hence difficult to identify. It is therefore necessary to adopt a more detailed approach. In this situation the analysis of the "flows" and the transition between higher education and employment is what will provide the most significant indications of the evolution of the relationship between them.

For this new study it is therefore proposed to concentrate attention on two particular aspects that to a large extent determine the dynamics of the change; on the supply side, the evolution of the "output" of higher education; on the demand side, the evolution of the employment of young graduates, in particular regarding the recruitment and early career of young people from different disciplines.

There are other reasons for carrying out an analysis focused on flows. First, the mere fact that higher education has expanded means that young graduates are occupying a much more diverse range of jobs than in the past. Many analyses have been based on the assumption that certain correspondences between education and employment still persist and have concentrated on the "deviations" from this implicit norm. Such correspondences may of course still exist for certain disciplines, but this is no longer necessarily the dominant situation. Young people often have to seek entirely new employment opportunities and this may modify the modalities of their entry to working life.

It is also essential to take account of the "non-university forms of higher education", something that was not possible in earlier studies because of the lack of data. It was in the late 1960s and early 1970s that efforts were made in many countries to develop this type of education with a more vocational orientation, and the OECD published an analysis at that time.[2] Since then these types of training have consolidated their position in the higher education system, to the point of bringing a redistribution of roles and functions.[3] In many countries such post-secondary education has expanded substantially and its graduates now account for a substantial share of the supply flows.[4] What is more, this post-secondary training is now itself having to compete with many other types of training, mostly the result of private initiative and very often run on a commercial basis, designed to meet the specific needs of the labour market. On both the supply and the demand sides it is therefore necessary to adopt a very broad approach.

It was in this spirit that the Secretariat first prepared an "orientation note", proposing a coherent conceptual framework for the whole of the analysis, yet taking into account the great diversity of approaches adopted in different countries to approach the problem of the relationship between higher education and employment. Pilot studies were then carried out in four countries: Germany, France, Italy and the United Kingdom, hence in very different contexts. These pilot studies were intended both to test the analytical framework proposed by the Secretariat and to give other countries wishing to participate in the project examples of the way in which the questions involved could be tackled. On this basis, interested countries were invited to prepare contributions as far as possible in conformity with the general framework and indications given by the Secretariat.

Many countries participated in this project. Most drafted substantial contributions, requiring considerable reflection and effort. These contributions, circulated by the OECD at the same time as the general report,[5] served as the basis for this report.

It must also be pointed out that in the context of the work on higher education and employment a parallel project was implemented on "the case of the humanities and social sciences". Here again, countries were invited to submit contributions on the basis of an orientation note prepared by the Secretariat. Although this project has its own aims, through analysing the role of training in the humanities and social sciences in preparation for employment, the authors of the contributions provide information of more general relevance to the definition of the relative situation of young people graduating from these disciplines. The more detailed information they give about their conditions of access to employment are all the more valuable in that it is probably in this sector that the greatest changes have taken place and where questions involving the nature of the relationship between higher education and employment continue to be the most problematic.

We were also able to draw upon various other studies by the Organisation. For Part One, devoted to the higher education "output", we were able to use the new OECD education database and in particular, thanks to the special effort made by those responsible for national statistics, the retrospective series constructed specially for the Ministerial Meeting of the Education Committee of the OECD,[6] but we should also mention other activities carried out within the Organisation for the Education Committee, the Centre for Educational Research and Innovation, and the Scientific and Technological Policy Committee.

The project was given the title "The flows of graduates from higher education and their entry into working life". This means that from the technical standpoint the objectives set were fairly ambitious, because the flow data so necessary for the analysis of trends are much more difficult to collect than data on higher education enrolments or the composition of the active population, much more generally available. Not all countries have arrangements for collecting statistics that make it possible to follow what happens to these flows. The authors of the national contributions therefore had to use very diverse and sometimes inconsistent data sources, and despite the progress made since the previous OECD study, the lack of data sometimes prevented them from dealing with certain questions, so that gaps remain, notably in the analysis of the destinations of young people emerging from higher education.

On the other hand, the rapporteurs in many cases completed their analysis with information and statistics that had not been requested in the Secretariat's orientation note, but which in fact considerably enrich the discussion. For example, in order to determine trends in the profile of exits from higher education they did not stick solely to data concerning graduates but added information on new enrolments and progress in studies, which made it possible to see the reactions of demand to changes in employment opportunities. Or again, they gave information on total employment and not solely on new entrants. These data naturally also made up to some extent for the inadequacy of the flow data. The way in which the topic is approached in each report, the lack of certain types of data or the use of other types of information, are in themselves a more general indication of the way in which the problem is perceived in each country.

It is not the intention of this report to enter into a debate on the aims of higher education or on the validity of the various theories put forward regarding its function in the preparation of young people for working life. More concretely, our aim is to take stock of the present situation on the basis of the information available and highlight the most significant trends. The report contains two parts. Part One is devoted to an analysis of the "output" of the higher education systems and the changes that may have been brought about by shifts in demand. It is mainly descriptive in nature, but it is less "neutral" than it may appear, insofar as the real profile of outflows is not known in most countries, even when the data are or could be relatively easily available. Part Two is devoted to entry into working life, the conditions of transition from education to employment and the destination of young graduates. Here the accent is on the disparities between different categories of graduates and the report takes on a more diagnostic nature, though in fact it is above all at national level that the diagnosis can be made, since an international synthesis should be limited to pointing out similarities and differences, constants and variables, in order to draw conclusions of general validity wherever possible.

Notes and References

1. Derestricted document, OECD, 1981 (out of print).
2. *Short-cycle higher education: A search for identity,* OECD, 1973.
3. *Universities under scrutiny,* OECD, 1987.
4. *Alternatives to Universities,* OECD, 1991.
5. *From higher education to employment,* country contributions, OECD, 1992
    – *Volume I:* Australia, Austria, Belgium, Germany;
    – *Volume II:* Canada, Denmark, Spain, United States;
    – *Volume III:* Finland, France, Italy, Japan, Netherlands, Norway;
    – *Volume IV:* Portugal, Sweden, Switzerland, United Kingdom.
6. *Education in OECD countries: Compendium of statistical information, 1990 Special Edition,* OECD, 1990.

Part One

FLOWS OF GRADUATES FROM HIGHER EDUCATION

INTRODUCTION

The aim of Part One is to show how the higher education "output" has evolved over the past ten years, to study the nature of the adjustments between training and employment and to see to what extent the institutional framework and higher education policies have favoured evolutions corresponding to labour market needs or employment possibilities. The difficulty of this exercise lies in the need to cover all forms of education undertaken by young people after completion of upper secondary education or post-compulsory training of equivalent level.

In the analyses of outflows from higher education, the accent was for a long time in fact solely on graduates of universities (or comparable institutions), for whom data were regularly available, while young people emerging from other types of post-secondary education and those who abandoned their studies were largely ignored. However, the expansion of higher education was in most cases accompanied, or made possible, by its diversification – this has been made abundantly clear in OECD studies. In many countries, the "output" of traditional university education does not constitute, or is no longer, the greater part of post-secondary output. It is therefore appropriate, in a study that aims to show the trend in the profile of outflows from higher education, to take account of this diversity and its impact on flows. This had not been possible in the preceding study on employment prospects for higher education graduates.

Examination of the national contributions confirms a conclusion that could be drawn from the recent study of non-university higher education,[1] *i.e.* that these other forms of post-secondary education are even today far from being as well covered by the statistics as the more traditional university courses. There are several reasons for this. The first is that data on university education have been collected for a long time and the procedures are well established. Other forms of post-secondary education often come under different authorities, statistical treatment is not always well established and, when data do exist, they are not always either standardized or centralised. Another reason is that we are seeing a proliferation of initiatives in the field of education, which is contributing to the expansion of what the study just mentioned calls the "third sector" of higher education: frequently private initiatives, run for profit, which may not appear in any of the conventional educational statistics.

Lastly, the limits of the field of higher or post-secondary education are rather vague, whereas in an analysis of flows we need to use a fairly strict definition of what we want to study even if there are gaps in the information: for example that proposed in the first paragraph above. It can be seen at once that this definition is centred on the young people themselves and not on a given set of educational institutions. Thus, forms of "post-secondary education" may be included that are neither normally nor legally considered as such, but which are in practice. An OECD study of shifts in the demand for post-compulsory education demonstrates the tendency for young people to prolong their general education and delay entry into technical and professional training and for training institutions to constantly raise their entrance requirements. The result is that certain training institutions which were once of post-compulsory level have now been officially "promoted" to the level of post-secondary establishments, so that their pupils or students should normally appear in the statistics for this level. Others however have not yet been recognised as being of this level even though they attract a substantial number of young people who have completed secondary education. According to the definition adopted here, among the pupils, students, apprentices or trainees enrolled in this type of training, those who have previously completed secondary education should logically be considered as receiving post-secondary education. This may well run counter to certain habits of thought, but it does correspond to a reality.

Another difficulty stems from the fact that the available statistics are generally compiled more from the standpoint of educational management than for the purposes of policy analysis. Thus we have a great deal of information about student numbers, less about new entrants and even less about dropouts. Similarly, the data on diplomas do not necessarily correspond to persons, which can give rise to double counting. Frequently graduates and dropouts are not broken down by sex. Lastly, and this is one of the major difficulties in the study of flows, we need to be able to distinguish between gross outflows and net outflows. Among the students completing or abandoning a programme, a certain number immediately begin another and the number of these transfers, or gross outflows, is often not known. The fact is however that in certain countries the proportion of young people who go on to other studies after obtaining a first degree or other post-secondary qualification is considerable, and often tending to rise; similarly, the number of students who abandon a course in which they are not doing well to take another is also substantial. What is more, the proportion of adult students is sometimes fairly high and it is becoming more common for people to abandon studies and then take them up again later: the very concept of ''outflows'' is becoming difficult to delimit.

For many countries it is therefore still difficult to have any precise picture of the profile of outflows from higher education. Despite the considerable progress achieved, there are still gaps everywhere, which is obviously regrettable but nevertheless interesting for the analysis. In fact, these gaps are not always simply a reflection of the inadequate development of the data collection system; they also reveal certain segmentations, certain dichotomies at the same time of a social and cultural nature. These segmentations are comparable to those found at post-compulsory level between general, technical and vocational education[2] and are situated differently depending on the country. For example, certain countries make a clear distinction between higher education, which covers universities and establishments assimilated to them, and post-secondary education or courses not leading to a university qualification; analyses and data relating to this latter sector are often relatively scarce. Other countries include courses of very different levels and very different types under the heading of higher education. The limits of ''higher education'' often correspond to those of the statistical coverage. It would appear that in several countries a considerable effort has been made in the course of this project to gather the necessary information and to at least sketch the profile of outflows from higher education.

While the efforts of the rapporteurs have not always made it possible to directly answer the questions asked in the initial orientation note, the majority of them took the initiative to complete the data on flows from higher education by providing information on such things as the trend in the demand for it as indicated by the data on transfer rates from secondary to higher education and on new entrants to the various higher education programmes; information concerning a number of parameters indicating the way studies proceed: dropout and success rates, proportion of part-time students, repeats, duration of studies, etc. In some cases this initiative was intended to compensate for the gaps in the data on outflows, but often the field covered was deliberately expanded to give a more complete view of the process and the evolution of behaviours. The relationships between this evolution and that of employment prospects are often quite striking and the topics thus raised will be returned to later in this report.

We must not let ourselves be diverted from the central theme of the relationships between higher education and employment, however. If we take the trouble to bring together all the information on new entrants, taking advantage of the new OECD data bank and the information contained in the country reports, this is not in order to compete with other more descriptive statistical studies, but in order to enrich the discussion of demand reactions and the evolution of behaviours and to draw conclusions in terms of outflows. As regards the data by sector and level, this approach could lead to the establishment of flow diagrams showing what becomes of young people leaving secondary education.

The description by level and sector, proposed in the orientation note, nevertheless tends to schematise the profile of outflows. It is well suited to systems where there are clearly distinct levels and sectors with respect to which it may be possible to situate types of training with less sharply defined contours, but this is not necessarily true for all countries. Very often, alongside a number of clearly, or even rigidly, defined institutions and programmes there is often a great diversity of courses whose level may be difficult to determine precisely, for example to be able to say whether a given course is higher or lower than a first degree; some of these courses can be taken after or at the same time as some other training. University courses themselves, once so monolithic, are tending to become segmented and multifaceted. With the delayed entry to training preparing for a job, general and technical education is occupying a growing share of post-compulsory education, so that the diversity characteristic of this level is tending to shift to post-secondary level and the diversity of courses here will no doubt go on increasing. Examination of the country reports nevertheless suggests that identification by level and sector remains useful and practicable even if the ISCED classification is not always the most appropriate, notably to take account of the diversity of employment prospects.

As regards data by field of study, discipline or vocational orientation, certain similarities between the classifications used in different countries are immediately apparent, but closer examination reveals differences of greater or lesser significance. Some differences appear in the attribution of a given discipline in one group or another, while others concern the groups of disciplines themselves. This should not be regarded simply as a difficulty of statistical classification or comparability: it often turns out that these differences concern disciplines or groups of disciplines which, in the present context, are by no means certain to lead to a job.

At university or equivalent level (ISCED 6), the groupings are made on the basis of disciplines. There are some minor divergencies, for example in the classification of biology or pharmacy courses, sometimes put with the medical disciplines, sometimes with the pure sciences; or information technology, sometimes classified with mathematics or the engineering subjects; or again with the physical sciences which may be found grouped with the arts. The main difficulties however concern two major groups: the educational sciences and the social sciences. In a certain number of countries, teacher training at this level does not constitute a separate category, future teachers receiving first a training in their discipline and then more specific pedagogical preparation, while in others there is a separate group of future teachers receiving integrated training, and in others again, both paths exist in parallel. In a period in which recruitment into teaching has considerably declined, the analysis of job opportunities for arts graduates, for example, will be very different according to whether teacher training is separate or not. The second difficulty is concerned with the social sciences. In certain cases this term applies only to ''academic'' disciplines such as sociology, while in others more vocationally oriented courses such as law, management and finance and even accounting are included, and in one case even physical education. This difficulty is not simply of concern from the descriptive standpoint, but is a real problem here because the employment prospects are very different according to the discipline. In the discussion it is necessary to distinguish at least between the two major orientations: academic and vocational. Fortunately, the country reports provide a great deal of information on these questions, as do those prepared for the complementary project on the humanities and social sciences.

In the case of short-cycle post-secondary education (ISCED 5), the groupings used tend to be more according to vocational orientation, which is not surprising as courses at this level are, but for a few exceptions, characterised by their vocational aims and close relationships with the world of work. Here again, teacher training, training for social work and the paramedical professions occupy an important place, notably for women, and the trend in job opportunities in these fields greatly influences the overall trend for this level. In some cases fairly precise information is available about some of these courses, for example primary school teaching. On the other hand, information relating to this level is often rather vague and aggregated at a fairly high level so that we have to make do with much less detailed data than in the case of university courses.

Lastly, as regards what has been called the ''third sector'' of higher education, we have, one might almost say by definition, only sparse data. It is generally thought that this type of training is very vocationally oriented, centred on a very precise occupation or speciality, such as computer programming, but we have little information about the flows concerned or the job opportunities, which may range from the excellent to the non-existent.

Notes and References

1. *Alternatives to Universities,* OECD, 1991.
2. *Pathways for learning. Education and training from 16 to 19.* OECD, 1989.

Chapter 1

THE DEMAND FOR HIGHER EDUCATION: OVERVIEW

Access to post-secondary education remains one of the prime concerns of the political authorities. The nature of the preoccupation may vary from one country to another, however, and the country reports even suggest that views as to what is cause for concern may be quite contrary.

Some countries are worried about the demographic trend and its possible repercussions on student numbers in higher education establishments.[1] The fall in the birth rate, after having affected primary and secondary education, is now starting to affect the post-secondary level. In most countries, funding for higher education establishments and the possibilities for innovation and research are directly linked to student numbers and it is feared that the rapid fall in the size of generations will not be compensated by a sufficient increase in the number of young people qualified for higher education. This fear no doubt partly explains the interest in various countries in recruiting foreign students or expanding the opportunities open to adults. It would be simplistic to say that the fear is that there will be an excess of higher education supply; it is more probably an expression of concern about the vitality or even the survival of certain establishments in their present form due to the possible shrinkage of their traditional recruitment base and competition from other training centres that are more flexible, more modern and more in tune with market needs.

Other authorities are concerned for quite opposite reasons. They note the generalisation of post-compulsory education and the constant increase in the role of general education that traditionally leads to higher education. They believe that the effects of the present reforms of upper secondary education, the aim of which is to stimulate increased schooling at this level will result in a concomitant increase in the number of young people qualified for entry to higher education. Their fear is therefore the contrary, one of a considerable increase in demand pressure.[2] More specifically, they are concerned about whether present higher education structures are capable of meeting a further increase in demand and responding to changing requirements on the labour market. This problem obviously tends to appear more in countries where education is the least diversified and where, besides the traditional university courses, there is only a short-cycle post-secondary education sector that is little developed and as yet not firmly established.

The policy-makers must not only take account of school demography however; they must also more or less explicitly take account of employment prospects. The country reports show that employment considerations often play a determining role, whether it is a matter of meeting increased demand in certain sectors or specialities or putting a brake on expansion where the employment opportunities have been reduced and reorienting demand.

Their answers to these problems may be very different. Their main concern may be with all entries to higher education and their distribution, or with the future of certain institutions, or with how to make education more "vocational". In the case of Yugoslavia, for example, the policy of opening up access to higher education had disastrous consequences for graduate employment and the policy finally had to be completely reversed. In the case of Sweden, admissions policy imposed a generalised quota system.[3] Even though this system corresponds to a substantial proportion of each generation, there is now concern about its consequences on skilled human resources during the present decade and the early years of next century. In Australia, the former teacher training colleges have been transformed and now offer courses more oriented towards management. In France efforts have been concentrated on the "vocationalisation" of university education.

All this means that we cannot be satisfied with policies based mainly on the satisfaction of social demand; the criteria that should be adopted depend on both the monitoring and detailed analysis of the social mechanisms that determine demand for higher education on the one hand and structural changes in employment on the other.

In the Preface we outlined the analysis of employment that will be carried out in this report, and to which Part Two will be devoted. In this chapter, before presenting an overview of the trend of entries to higher education on the basis of data contained in the new OECD databank, we shall make a few comments about factors currently affecting the demand trend. We shall examine the main aspects of growth in more detail in Chapter 2, on the basis of the various data presented in the country reports.

I. DEMAND FACTORS

The factors determining demand for higher education have been the subject of many analyses: all demonstrate the diversity of the motivations involved, but also the importance of employment considerations. It will be useful to consider the form now being taken by these motivations and their foreseeable consequences.

A. Increased demand pressure

A first set of factors is of a social nature. So long as higher education remained the preserve of an elite, the prestige and social status conferred by the diploma was sufficient in itself to increase demand. It was generally a matter of a university degree or a diploma awarded by institutions of equivalent prestige. This motivation still remains, especially in countries where only a minority of young people go on to higher education, but it is tending to diminish in importance as higher education becomes more generalised. Only certain institutions and some very selective disciplines have retained their prestige. Among other factors, this generalisation is not unconnected with the crisis of confidence experienced by higher education during the 1970s and early 1980s, which in some cases caused a reduction in the number of enrolments. Confidence now seems to have returned, perhaps with an overall impression of a better match between the orientation of courses, the needs of society and employment prospects, but also with the feeling that modern society requires a higher general level of education.

With the generalisation of post-compulsory education, a new form of social pressure is being created. In certain countries and in certain social groups the majority of young people continue their studies after completion of secondary schooling and proceeding to higher education is becoming the norm. This trend is reinforced by the internal dynamic of secondary education systems and the ever increasing attraction of general education preparing people for higher education without really leading to any qualification that can be used for access to a skilled job; the young people emerging from this type of secondary education have scarcely any choice but to continue their studies.

This means that young people who have neither the same aptitudes nor the same motivations as their predecessors are being brought to the threshold of higher education. Their profile does not always correspond to the requirements of higher education establishments – the argument is scarcely new, but it has not lost any of its relevance, quite the contrary. This new clientele attaches much more importance than the old to the employment prospects opened up by higher education and to the risk of failure associated with it, notably if the duration of study is long. For these people, the alternative therefore depends on personal circumstances – the results obtained at school, the family background, and possibly financial resources – but also on the diversity of higher education supply and selection mechanisms which may significantly reduce the choice open to them.

Employment considerations are also taking a new form. The idea is spreading in the majority of OECD countries – though it is not new in the United States, Canada or Japan – that those who have ''only'' a qualification at post-compulsory level no longer have much of a chance of obtaining a really skilled job. Vocational post-compulsory training, which even quite recently was thought should be given to all those who did not go on to the upper technical or general secondary education, is often no longer of the level required in the speciality and very often leads only to semi-skilled jobs; technical education itself now leads but rarely or indirectly to employment at technician level, which now requires more advanced training. It is also immediately obvious that in the present employment situation the risk of unemployment is often very high for those with secondary education qualifications only. For all these reasons we must therefore expect an increase in demand pressure.

B. Choice of orientation

The transformation of the ''output'' of higher education depends to a large extent on the reorientation of demand on the part of students. But demand is very sensitive to the trend in employment opportunities. The accent has often been placed on the time necessary for the output of higher education to adjust to changes in employment prospects, but in fact we often have the impression that changes in demand have anticipated them. Young people sometimes demonstrate a perspicacity that surprises even the best analysts.[4] In some countries, admission to the various courses is regulated according to trends in employment opportunities: this is the case in

Sweden, for example, where it is noted that the orientations given by the planning system correspond fairly closely to those of student demand, which frequently precedes them.[5]

Students do not have very complete information about the job opportunities opened up by the various post-secondary courses at any given moment, and even if they did it would not necessarily be of much use to determine an individual choice. In most cases it is a matter of diffuse information. When a publicity campaign attracts attention to the needs of a particular sector, or conversely to the risks associated with certain types of training, it may thus bring about an exaggerated response.[6] The choice of an orientation to take account of the employment prospects is thus in itself far from being a simple problem for the student who does not have access to elite training paths. But he is also faced with other difficulties.

A first difficulty stems from the very diversification of higher education. When it was reserved to a small number of people, it was enough to apply to a particular institution and a particular faculty. The path was already traced and well known, including the job opportunities at the end of it. The multiplication of training paths, the fragmentation of courses and above all the number of possible combinations impose the choice of a *strategy* involving the evaluation of costs, the career prospects and also the risks. It is possible, for example, to embark on accounting training on the understanding that a diploma in applied mathematics will also be obtained, or in management training provided a diploma in tax law or financial sciences will be obtained. Such diversity was no doubt not sought in the past; universities and colleges offered students ready-made courses, with just a few options. Today the need to vocationalise education has led to this diversity and it is up to the student to design his own course.

At the same time, the notion of *risk* is becoming increasingly important. This applies to study programmes where there is a high probability of failure. In France, less than half of the new medical students get beyond the second year, but here the selection is explicit and concentrated on the first two years. Engineering training in Spain is another example of extreme selectivity. It is thus risky to embark on such studies (which are generally long courses) for those who are not sure of their aptitude or motivations or for those for whom these studies represent a major financial sacrifice, which is often the case with those who form the "new clientele" of higher education. In this connection, the concept of "the most accessible objective" was developed in another study for the young people who form this new clientele, and who only a few years ago would not have dreamt of embarking on higher education. If they do so today they generally do not try to enter the most selective, longest and most risky courses, but turn rather towards more modest, more certain and more accessible ones. What is more, it is well known that it is now often possible, on completion for example of a short course, to go to studies at a higher level. A safety-first strategy may therefore be to undertake such short courses and then go on to university studies while already holding a diploma that can be used on the labour market. Girls in particular may adopt such a strategy.

Other difficulties are created by admission policies however. Certain sectors are more open than others, which leads to a distortion of choices and often, unfortunately, to "negative selection". The situation varies greatly from one country to another, but there are probably examples everywhere of students starting on courses that correspond neither to their first choice nor to a field in which they have the best chances of success. Two cases of a paradoxical nature are often cited. First, that of more restricted admission to courses where the job opportunities are most favourable, thus forcing many students into other sectors where employment prospects are often poor (notably towards the social sciences). Then the case of students not admitted to short-cycle training, where access is often fairly restricted, who have to turn to long courses (it is sometimes more difficult to become a nurse than a doctor).

These are well known examples of dysfunctions in the admission system. In this study it is no doubt also necessary to draw attention to the global effect of the selection process, which comprises a certain number of more or less visible phases, involving different actors, each of them applying different criteria. Among the least visible are the selection processes in secondary education, which prevent certain candidates who would no doubt have the necessary abilities from entering higher education. In this respect, the case is often cited of mathematics teaching, of a very academic character, which dissuades many pupils from continuing their studies, notably in the sciences, whereas they would in fact have the ability to do so.

II. OVERVIEW

For this overview we use the new OECD data bank which contains annual statistical information as from 1983/84. In addition, in preparation for a meeting of OECD Ministers of Education, reconstituted data conforming to the new definitions were prepared by Member countries for the years 1975 and 1980. Generally speaking, the data in the OECD data bank are intended to be published in the *Compendium of statistical information.* However, certain more detailed data that are used here have not so far appeared in this publication. It was therefore considered useful to complete the more synthetic tables given in the text by various other tables in an annex to this Part One.

The data on entries to higher education are not without certain difficulties of definition, which means that they do not correspond exactly to the flow data. What is more, the data by programme level use the international ISCED classification which does make useful distinctions between programme levels, but it is the individual countries who decide whether certain types of training belong to ISCED 5 level (short-cycle) or ISCED 6 (university, first degree). In some cases much could be said about this attribution. Here we shall limit ourselves to identifying the general trends: in what follows we shall refer to the national data, which naturally best show the trends particular to each country.

A. Increases in flows

1. New enrolments

Table 1 shows that during the 1980s the total number of new entrants to higher education continued to increase at a rapid rate. There were exceptions however. In the United States the number of entries has declined since 1980, although these figures do not cover all new enrolments (see Note *c* to Table 1). In Japan, after some weakening in the late 1970s, expansion resumed at the beginning of the 1980s. In the countries for which we have data for 1980 and 1988, it can be seen that there was an increase over the period ranging from 14 per cent in Italy to 220 per cent in Turkey.

Table I–1. **Annual rates of increase in the number of new enrolments in higher education (all levels)**

1980-84 and 1984-88 except where otherwise indicated

	Total		Women	
	1980-84	1984-88	1980-84	1984-88
Australia	–	6.22	–	8.63
Austria	5.93	0.23	6.90	–0.51
Belgium	–	10.26[a]	–	8.44[a]
Denmark	3.71	4.55	3.48	4.62
Finland	3.01	7.10	3.37	8.01
France	–	9.32	–	9.42
Germany	2.26	2.43	1.79	5.99
Greece	14.93	–2.20[b]	17.47	–1.04[b]
Ireland	3.97	4.89	5.21	4.73
Italy	0.96	2.44	2.49	3.28
Japan	2.53	3.86	1.16	5.61
Netherlands	10.53	2.19	12.45	3.48
New Zealand	6.10	6.83[b]	8.00	6.00[b]
Norway	1.40	–1.98[b]	1.93	–3.75[b]
Portugal	5.46	–	7.67	–
Spain	5.37	6.43[b]	–	7.33[b]
Sweden	2.98	3.48[b]	1.95	4.01[b]
Switzerland	–	2.63	–	4.95
Turkey	24.31	9.80	28.29	12.19
United Kingdom	–	1.75	–	4.84
United States[c]	–2.30	0.30	–2.32	0.75
Yugoslavia	14.51	–3.92[b]	–	–18.32[a]

a) 1985-87.
b) 1983-87.
c) Prior to 1987, the US did not calculate new enrolments for all tertiary institutions, but only traditional academic enrolments in four-year bachelor and two-year associate degree programmes. As of 1987, the formula changed to include post-secondary vocational enrolments. Had the post-secondary vocational programme enrolments been counted prior to 1987, it is probable that the average annual rate would have increased every year rather than decreased. Between 1987 and 1988, for example, the rates of increase would have been +5.92 per cent (total) and + 6.58 per cent (women). The percentages shown above, therefore, do not reflect the total initial enrolment activity in past years.
As stated in the report for the United States (Volume II), the demographic decline during the 1980s has been offset by the increased participation of women and adults; in the 1990s the effects of the economic recession, combined with those of a falling birth rate, are producing an absolute decline in initial enrolment rates.

Sources: *Digest of Education Statistics 1991,* Washington, US Government Printing Office, 1992, Table 169. Data derived from the IPEDS ''Fall Enrolment Survey'', National Center for Education Statistics.
OECD Databank, except for the United States.

This overall balance conceals very different trends however. Of the 15 countries for which we have data for the periods 1980-84 and 1984-88, and which all showed increases over the period 1980-84, eight saw the upward trend accelerate over the period 1984-88; in three countries, Austria, Netherlands and Turkey, the rate of increase slowed considerably and in three others, Norway, Greece and Yugoslavia, the trend was reversed. It was in Turkey (14.5 percentage points), Greece (17) and Yugoslavia (18.5) that the variation was greatest. In the Netherlands it was only 8 percentage points and in Austria only 6.

If we examine the annual variations more closely, we see that the growth was by no means always regular. We in fact see fluctuations in Japan, Netherlands and Italy. In Japan there was a decline until 1985, followed by a marked revival. In the Netherlands, the revival dates from 1987 and continued at the high rate of over 10 per cent a year. In Italy, the number of new enrolments declined until 1986 and then rose at the rate of 6.3 per cent. In Norway the trend is confused: after various fluctuations, there was a positive growth rate of 1.42 per cent between 1987 and 1988, while the overall balance for 1983-87 is negative (–2 per cent). We can also speak of fluctuations in Austria, where the annual average rate is slightly positive, 0.2 per cent, but where the most recent trend is downwards (–4 per cent between 1987 and 1988).

We have mentioned three countries where the change was very marked, Turkey, Greece and Yugoslavia. In Turkey the rate of growth has slowed greatly but remains in the order of 10 per cent a year, which is still very high – the only countries to reach a comparable rate were Belgium, between 1985 and 1987, and the Netherlands, between 1980 and 1984. On the other hand, the rates of increase became negative in Greece and Yugoslavia. In Greece, the average rate for the period 1983-87 was –2.2 per cent. After a period of strong growth there was a rapid decline after 1984, at a rate of about 10 per cent a year. In Yugoslavia, after a period of strong growth, the average growth rate over the same period fell to –3.92 per cent, while after 1986 there was a fall of over 50 per cent in a single year. In both cases this was the result of a policy decision. In Greece, it was more the result of over-population in higher education establishments, while in Yugoslavia, it was imposed by the very unfavourable situation of young graduates on the labour market.

As regards girls, similar trends are found. In the majority of countries there has been a regularly rising trend and rates are generally higher than those for total new enrolments, sometimes very much higher. Over the period 1980-84 lower rates are found for Denmark, Germany, Japan and Sweden, but it can be seen that these differences were compensated in the following period by rates higher than the average. Conversely, in New Zealand, the slightly lower rate in 1984-88 compensated the markedly higher rate in the earlier period. A lower rate is found for 1984-88 in Belgium too, but we do not have information for the preceding period in the database.

We have mentioned fluctuations in Austria and Norway: these were more disadvantageous to the girls than the boys, but it may be considered that this was partly compensated by higher rates of growth in the preceding period. The same remark applies to Greece. In Yugoslavia on the other hand the girls were greatly penalised by the reform in admissions policy. Over the period 1984-88, the average annual rate of increase was –4 per cent for total enrolments but –18 per cent for girls. However, by and large it can be said that in the case of girls the number of new enrolments is increasing faster, or falling more slowly, than the total number.

Tables 2 and 3 show the trend in the number of new enrolments in training classified as ISCED level 5 (not leading to a university degree or equivalent) and 6 (first degree or equivalent).

Internationally comparable data concerning ISCED level 5 are less readily available than those relating to university courses. In the countries where data do exist, the situations vary far more than when we simply examine the figures for total new enrolments. For the period 1980-84, two countries have a negative growth rate: Italy and the United States. In the United States we have already noted a reduction in the total number of new enrolments (covered by the surveys prior to 1987). In Italy, where the total number shows fluctuations, at ISCED level 5, we see a slightly negative rate (2.4 per cent, but this figure is not significant in view of the small number of students recorded). In the other countries the sector sometimes shows fairly strong growth, as in Austria (10 per cent), Greece (18 per cent) and Yugoslavia (13 per cent). In these three countries the growth rate is far higher than that of total new enrolments. Conversely, in the Netherlands it is very much lower (1.2 as against 10.5 per cent).

Over the period 1984-88, the growth rate in Italy remained slightly negative as it did in the United States (in both countries, however, the figures do not cover every type of programme). The growth rate increased sharply in the Netherlands while the overall rate fell in about the same proportion. In some countries, such as Finland, France, Germany and Japan the trend is continuing and matches that of the total number of new enrolments. In Greece and Yugoslavia there is a much more marked fall than in total enrolments; in Greece from +18 to –18 per cent and in Yugoslavia from +12 to –37 per cent. We have already spoken of fluctuations in Austria as regards total numbers; at ISCED 5 level the case is similar to that of Greece with the rate falling from +10 to –2 per cent. In Denmark, while total numbers have constantly increased, there is a significant fall at ISCED 5 level, and the

Table I–2. **Annual rates of increase in the number of new enrolments in higher education (ISCED 5)**

1980-84 and 1984-88 except where otherwise indicated

	Total 1980-84	Total 1984-88	Women 1980-84	Women 1984-88
Australia	–	5.45	–	8.06
Austria	10.08	2.49	6.20	–3.05
Belgium	–	5.18[a]	–	–4.31[a]
Denmark	5.30	0.06	4.39	–1.97
Finland	2.94	3.82	2.51	9.13
France	–	11.46	–	14.11
Germany	0.77	1.23	1.81	–2.11
Greece	17.67	–18.50[a]	22.55	–25.76[a]
Italy	–2.39	–0.48	2.14	–0.10
Japan	0.36	4.74	0.53	5.08
Netherlands	1.21	8.3	3.02	4.97
Sweden	–	–1.34[b]	–	–0.69[b]
Switzerland	–	3.63	–	7.94
Turkey	–	8.61	3.36	10.19
United Kingdom	–	6.63[b]	–	4.37[b]
United States[c]	–3.04	–1.29	–	–
Yugoslavia	12.62	–37.15[a]	–	–31.32[a]

a) 1985-87.
b) 1986-88.
c) In the case of the United States, no correspondence has yet been established with the ISCED levels. The author of the US report has used data for enrolment in programmes of less than 4 years (Community and Junior Colleges, and vocational/technical schools).
As with Table I-1, prior to 1987 data were collected only for enrolment in academic programmes leading to an Associate degree, which is not all that sought after in the United States. The figures reflect reality to an even lesser degree than those in Table I-1. When enrolment in vocational programmes (by far the largest category at this level) was included in 1987/88, the rate of increase jumped to +7.93 per cent. Were complete data available for previous years, they would probably reflect annual increases rather than decreases.
Source: OECD Databank, except for the United States (see sources to Table I-1).

Table I–3. **Annual rates of increase in the number of new enrolments in higher education (ISCED 6)**

1980-84 and 1984-88 except where otherwise indicated

	Total 1980-84	Total 1984-88	Women 1980-84	Women 1984-88
Australia	–	7.19	–	9.32
Austria	4.84	1.02	7.09	0.27
Belgium	8.85	–	–	–
Denmark	2.82	7.04	2.66	9.81
Finland	3.09	9.44	4.32	6.09
France	–	7.89	–	6.59
Germany	3.12	3.07	1.77	4.29
Greece	13.83	–4.52[a]	14.40	0.28[a]
Italy	1.09	2.54	2.72	3.42
Japan	0.20	3.45	2.18	6.41
Netherlands	4.01	5.15	7.52	6.94
Portugal	10.46	–	–	–
Spain	5.54	5.99[a]	7.40	6.70[a]
Sweden	–	–0.15	–	1.20
Switzerland	–	0.17	–	0.96
Turkey	–	7.53	–	9.97
United Kingdom	–	–2.88[a]	–	–0.79[a]
United States[b]	–1.42	2.03	–	–
Yugoslavia	15.29	–20.38[a]	–	–14.86[a]

a) 1985-87.
b) The figures here refer to initial enrolment in 4-year programmes leading to a Bachelor degree. The broadening of the statistical coverage in 1987 had little effect on these figures.
Source: OECD Databank, except for the United States (see sources Table I–1).

situation is comparable in Sweden. We can sum up by saying that in certain countries the trends at ISCED 5 level and total enrolments are in parallel, either upwards (Germany, Finland, France, Italy, Japan), or downwards (Greece, Yugoslavia), while pointing out that the fall is much more marked at ISCED 5 level. In several other countries however the trends, notably in the second half of the decade, bear no resemblance to one another and often move in opposite directions. At a later stage we shall have the occasion to describe the structural effects that explain these differences.

In the case of the girls, we see that the trends are generally in the same direction as for the total new enrolments at ISCED 5 level, but they are frequently more marked. In the positive direction, in Finland for example, where the overall rate for the periods 1980-84 and 1984-88 are 2.9 and 3.8 per cent respectively, for girls they are 2.5 and 9.1 per cent. Conversely, in Greece total new enrolments at this level for the two periods were +18 and –18 per cent and for girls +23 and –26 per cent. There are exceptions however. In the case of Germany and Italy, the two trends run in opposite directions, but it seems to be a case of fluctuations. In the Netherlands, the variations are of the same sign but are less marked in the case of the girls. Without trying to systematise too much, we can say that for the girls the trend is comparable to that of total new enrolments, which may reflect in particular a greater proportion of girls at this level. There are also differences however, which may be explained by the structural effects mentioned above.

As regards ISCED 6 level, the results can be expected to be complementary to those given above. We shall simply point out that over the period 1980-84 all rates were positive (except in the United States) for total new enrolments and for girls, and were particularly high in Portugal (10.5 per cent), Greece (13.8 per cent) and Yugoslavia (15.3 per cent). The lowest figures are for Italy and Japan. With the exception of Denmark and Germany they are higher for girls than for boys.

For the period 1984-88 the situation is less homogeneous. While in several countries the trend remains positive and even considerably accelerates, as in Finland and Denmark, there are negative rates in a number of other countries. In Sweden and the United Kingdom they are only slightly negative and in fact a positive trend has recently been resumed, while in the United States the trend reverses and the rates become positive once again. In Greece and Yugoslavia we find the expected fall, but it is less marked than at ISCED 5 level, notably in Greece where there is an average rate of –4.5 per cent. Generally speaking, more girls than boys enrol in ISCED 6 courses and with but few exceptions the variations are greater than for the total of new enrolments.

2. *Proportion of new enrolments in level 5*

Examination of new enrolments at ISCED 5 level as a percentage of total enrolments gives a cross-sectional view that completes the above analysis. We see first of all, in Table 4, fairly substantial differences in the proportion of the flows entering courses at this level, from 3 per cent for Italy (the true figure is much higher) to 71 per cent for Sweden. In broad terms it can be said that this level attracts two-thirds of the flow in three countries: Sweden, Switzerland and the Netherlands. In three other countries (United Kingdom, France, Finland) they represent a little under half; in four others (Germany, Australia, Japan, Denmark) they attract one-third, and in Austria, Turkey and Yugoslavia the proportion is roughly one-fifth.

As regards the girls (Table 4b), it can be seen that the picture is much the same and the same grouping of countries can be made. There are however two exceptions: Switzerland, where the proportion of girls is significantly lower (which may mean that they are more inclined to go to university) and above all Japan, where on the contrary the proportion rises from one-third of the total to almost two-thirds of the girls (for whom there is scarcely any access to the university). Another point is that the percentages of girls, apart from these two exceptions, are generally either close to or more often higher than those of total new enrolments. This is notably the case in Australia, Austria, Denmark and Germany (and naturally also in Japan). The result is that the girls are significantly more dependent on the trend in job opportunities on completion of these courses. Table A4 shows the proportion of girls entering courses at ISCED levels 5 and 6.

3. *Proportion of a generation entering higher education*

While the trend in the number of new enrolments (and, more directly, of graduates) is of interest to the labour market, the study of the proportion of a given generation entering higher education is more closely connected with the evolution of social attitudes. In the numerator the risk of double counting is the same, but is of more significance because we are now referring explicitly to actual persons. In the denominator the numbers chosen reflect certain hypotheses regarding the age of entry to higher education (see the remarks on methodology in the *Compendium of statistical information*). Despite the resulting possible bias, this is an interesting indicator.

Table 5 shows the importance that post-secondary education has now taken on for young people. With the exception of Sweden and Australia, whose figures are surprising (for Australia one could perhaps refer to the

Table I–4. **New enrolments in level 5 as a percentage of total new enrolments**
Total

	1975	1980	1984	1986	1987	1988
Australia	..	..	44	..	33	32
Austria	..	19	22	19	19	19
Belgium	..	..	..	..	52	..
Denmark	..	35	37	32	32	31
Finland	47	52	51	57	53	45
France	..	..	39	39	42	42
Germany	45	37	35	36	34	34
Greece	29	45	..	..	42	..
Italy	3	4	4	4	3	3
Japan[a]	30	31	31	33	32	32
Netherlands	..	64	45	54	..	65
New Zealand	..	..	29	..	..	..
Portugal	..	..	11	..	..	..
Spain	..	1	0	0	..	..
Sweden	..	..	69	72	80	71
Switzerland	..	..	61	..	..	65
Turkey	..	..	18	18	18	18
United Kingdom	..	..	..	47	47	49
United States[b]	54	54	53	50	48	49
Yugoslavia	30	30	28	22	20	20

a) *Senshu Gakko* excluded.
b) The figures for 1975 to 1987 cover only Associate Degree programmes. The smallness of the increase between 1987 and 1988, despite the inclusion of vocational programmes, is due to the sharp decline in enrolment in Community and Junior Colleges over recent years.
Source: OECD Databank, except for the United States (see Table I–1).

1984 figure; for Sweden the country report gives a figure of 40 per cent for all post-secondary education),[7] it can be seen that the proportions range from 15 per cent for Turkey to 50 per cent for Finland and 63 per cent for the United States (1986). In France, Belgium and Denmark, the proportion is respectively 44, 45 (1986) and 48 per cent. Several other countries have a proportion of between 30 and 40 per cent: Switzerland and New Zealand (3 per cent), Japan and the United Kingdom (37 per cent), the Netherlands (36 per cent), Germany and Ireland (32 per cent), Spain (30 per cent in 1986). Then come Yugoslavia (27 per cent), Italy (26 per cent in 1986) and Austria (24 per cent). We can summarise by saying that in the majority of OECD countries, the proportion of a generation entering post-secondary education is between one-third and one-half. Certain countries have already exceeded the 50 per cent level and a few others remain at about one-quarter.

In the majority of the 22 countries for which we have data, more girls than boys enter post-secondary education. The difference is frequently fairly marked, the figure being over one-quarter higher in countries like Portugal, New Zealand, Sweden, Denmark, France, Finland and Norway. On the other hand there are several countries in which the proportion of girls entering higher education is lower than that of boys: Germany, Ireland, Greece, Italy, Japan, the Netherlands, the United Kingdom and it is very much lower in Switzerland and Turkey.

The OECD data bank does not yet contain information making it possible to calculate the proportion of new enrolments in each generation for all Member countries. On the basis of the existing data it is nevertheless possible to determine the relative importance of ISCED levels 5 and 6 for girls and boys in a certain number of countries.

We shall consider first the countries where more girls than boys enter higher education. There are nine countries for which we have data for 1988 or for earlier years. In just one country, Yugoslavia, the predominance of girls is due solely to their higher participation in university courses at ISCED 6 level. In France, the proportion is higher in courses of both levels but the predominance of girls is above all due to their higher participation in level 6 courses. In the seven remaining countries (Australia, Austria, Denmark, Finland, New Zealand, Portugal and Sweden) it is enrolment in ISCED 5 level courses that is the determining factor, especially in Austria and Finland where the proportion of girls at ISCED 6 level is lower than that of boys.

Of the countries for which we have data, there are eight where the proportion of girls in a generation to enter post-secondary education is lower than that of boys. It will be noted that in three of them the proportion of girls entering ISCED 5 courses is higher than that of boys, so that their "disadvantage" is explained solely by their lower proportion in university courses at ISCED 6 level. In Italy, the difference is not great. Neither is the overall difference very great in Germany but there is a marked "university deficit" for girls and they have a very much

Table I-4. **New enrolments in level 5 as a percentage of total new enrolments** *(Cont'd)*

	1975	1980	1984	1986	1987	1988
a: men						
Australia	..	..	40	..	29	28
Austria	..	9	16	14	13	13
Belgium	..	..	..	..	42	..
Denmark	..	21	24	24	24	24
Finland	47	50	52	56	54	36
France	..	..	43	44	48	42
Germany	37	29	25	29	28	28
Greece	30	48	..	..	47	..
Italy	3	3	3	3	3	3
Japan	9	8	8	8	7	8
Netherlands	..	62	43	50	..	64
New Zealand	..	..	25	..	..	..
Portugal	..	..	2	..	..	..
Sweden	..	..	67	70	78	70
Switzerland	..	..	66	..	..	69
Turkey	..	..	18	17	19	19
United Kingdom	..	..	..	45	46	49
Yugoslavia	..	..	..	..	20	21
b: women						
Australia	..	..	49	..	37	36
Austria	..	28	27	23	25	24
Belgium	..	..	..	..	61	..
Denmark	..	47	48	39	38	37
Finland	46	53	51	58	52	53
France	..	..	35	35	37	42
Germany	55	47	47	45	42	42
Greece	27	42	..	..	38	..
Italy	4	5	4	4	4	4
Japan	61	63	61	62	61	60
Netherlands	..	68	48	60	..	67
New Zealand	..	..	32	..	..	..
Portugal	..	..	18	..	..	..
Sweden	..	..	70	73	81	72
Switzerland	..	..	50	..	..	57
Turkey	..	.	16	18	16	17
United Kingdom	..	..	..	49	48	50
Yugoslavia	..	..	..	..	20	20

Source: OECD Databank.

higher proportion in level 5 courses. The most striking case is the well known one of Japan, where girls have a virtual monopoly of ISCED 5 level, but are little represented in the universities. In the five other countries (Greece, Netherlands, Switzerland, Turkey and the United Kingdom), the proportion of girls entering higher education is lower at both levels 5 and 6. In Switzerland it is in fact in level 5 courses that the deficit is greatest and determines the overall proportion. In the other four countries, it is mainly in the universities that the proportion of girls is lower and it is this deficit that determines their relative position. This clarifies the conclusions drawn from Table 4.

It is interesting to compare the trends in terms of new enrolments and the proportion of a generation. We can expect to find similar trends when growth rates are high, but the influence of the demographic trend might give rise to different results. If we consider all higher education (ISCED 5 and 6) and compare Table 1 and Table A7, we do in fact see such divergencies. The most striking case is that of Japan where Table 1 shows positive rates of increase for 1980-88, whereas in fact the chances of entering higher education regularly diminished until 1986. Since the chances of the girls regularly increased, it can be seen that as a result those of the boys diminished, at a rate of −1.04 per cent between 1980 and 1984, and −1.94 per cent over the period 1984-88. Conversely, the negative rate of increase between 1984 and 1988 for new female enrolments in Austria corresponds to an increase of +2.62 per cent in their chances of access to higher education. Two changes of sign are found for Norway and there are a few other differences of this type. The reductions concern mainly boys: in addition to Japan, Italy, the

Table I-5. **Proportion of a generation entering post-secondary education, 1988**

Per thousand

	Level 5			Level 6			Total		
	Men	Women	Total	Men	Women	Total	Men	Women	Total
Australia[a]	145	224	184	337	369	353	519	621	569
Austria	31	60	45	198	194	196	229	254	241
Belgium[b]	..	..	..	..	..	..	406	487	446
Denmark[c]	100	201	149	319	337	328	419	539	477
Finland[d]	159	306	231	279	259	269	449	572	509
France	165	208	186	223	291	256	388	498	442
Germany[e]	96	119	107	248	174	212	344	294	320
Greece[f]	125	93	..	134	130	..	250	223	242
Ireland[g]	..	..	..	..	..	..	339	310	325
Italy[h]	8	16	..	259	242	..	267	252	260
Japan[i]	29	215	120	348	144	249	376	360	368
Netherlands	244	224	234	146	115	131	383	336	360
New Zealand[j]	68	114	..	164	133	..	268	361	313
Norway[k]	..	..	..	..	..	..	159	198	178
Portugal[l]	3	31	..	118	138	..	121	169	145
Spain[m]	..	..	..	292	316	..	292	316	304
Sweden[n]	482	652	565	197	250	223	693	902	795
Switzerland	350	148	251	156	110	134	507	258	384
Turkey[o]	36	17	27	154	86	121	191	103	148
United Kingdom	190	179	185	202	176	189	392	356	374
United States[p]	..	..	..	..	..	..	576	680	627
Yugoslavia	56	56	56	209	228	218	265	284	274

a) Students enrolled for the first time in a course at a given institution, even if they have already been enrolled in another course or at another institution. TAFE (Technical and Further Education) students excluded.
b) 1986 data.
c) Data for level 6 and the total include level 7.
d) Full-time students only.
e) Data for level 6 and the total include level 7.
f) 1980 data.
g) Full-time students only.
h) 1986 data. Data for level 5 do not cover all types of post-secondary courses (see the Italian report, Volume III).
i) Data for level 5 do not cover all types of post-secondary courses (*Senshu Gakko* excluded, see the Japanese report, Volume III).
j) 1986 data.
k) 1986 data for level 6 only.
l) 1984 data.
m) 1984 data.
n) First-year students in each study programme (including adults). A number of very short courses are classified under ISCED 5. The corresponding rates are therefore not comparable to those in other countries.
o) Full-time students only.
p) The author of the United States report prefers to use the ratio of new entrants (in October 1988) to the number of high school graduates over the last 12 months. The figures are 570 (men), 608 (women), 589 (total). Source: *Digest of Education Statistics 1991, op. cit.*, Table 172.

Source: OECD Databank.

Netherlands (1984-88), Norway (1980-84), the United Kingdom (from 479 per 1000 in 1980 to 392 in 1988). The opportunities for girls are increasing everywhere, except in Italy where they are stationary.

A number of impressions arise from this survey. First, but for a few countries there has been a considerable increase in the volume of flows of new enrolments, corresponding to an increase in the proportion of young people entering higher education. As compared with the late 1970s and early 1980s, this reflects a return of confidence in this type of training. In most countries, between one-third and one-half of young people go on to higher education and the proportion is even higher in some countries: it is to be expected that in a few years' time the post-secondary system will receive over half of each generation. In the context of this growth it can be seen that the position of level 5 education tends to remain stationary, which is important to the extent that these courses play a determining role for girls. Since the number and proportion of girls is generally increasing more rapidly, this may imply a shift to university education. At this level of aggregation it can be considered that these trends are in line with employment prospects.

B. Breakdown by field of study

We shall again rely here on the OECD database on education. This uses the ISCED classification by field of study, which is fairly detailed. The first question that arises is therefore to define the groupings of disciplines to be used.

A first idea is to distinguish between two broad categories: first, the humanities and social sciences, taking these in the broad sense to include economics, management and law; second the pure and applied sciences, technology and medicine. This distinction is behind the parallel OECD project devoted to the case of the humanities and the social sciences. This is based on two considerations. The first is that the sector made up of this group of disciplines is often the one that has had to absorb the increase in demand for education. The second is that young graduates from this sector are those for whom access to employment presents the greatest difficulties. It is defined as the "vulnerable sector" of higher education.

This distinction is of all the more interest in that it draws attention to a group of disciplines that is often neglected in the policy analyses, which tend to put the accent on the scientific and technical disciplines. However, it would seem that a finer breakdown is necessary. Medicine, both as a personal orientation and a sector of employment, is clearly distinct from the other sciences. Within the very broad group of humanities and social sciences, the distinctions may sometimes be more difficult to make. Taking account of the groupings generally used in OECD countries and by the authors of the country reports, as well as those inspired by the discussion of employment prospects, we have been led to adopt four categories for this study (see Chapter 5) giving the term "social sciences" a more restricted sense by excluding economics, management and law:

i) ST: Science and Technology;
ii) HS: Humanities and Social Sciences;
iii) BL: Business and Law;
iv) MD: Medicine.

1. *Breakdown of flows by discipline*

Table 6 shows the breakdown of new entrants by group of disciplines for the whole of higher education (ISCED 5 and 6). Here there are fairly big differences between countries. If we could speak of an "average" for the eighteen countries for which we have data, it would be around 30 per cent for Science and Technology (ST), 40 per cent for Humanities and Social Sciences (HS), 20 per cent for Business and Law (BL) and 10 per cent for Medicine (MD) (it should be borne in mind that Japan does not distinguish between groups HS and BL, so the figure of 40 per cent is somewhat over-estimated). In practice, most countries, perhaps with the exception of Spain, depart significantly from this average. (Note that the United States is not included in this table. The reason for this is that students initially undertake general courses and specialise only at a later stage. This means that in the United States the breakdown of flows can be analysed only on the basis of data for graduates).

We can nonetheless try to establish a typology, while bearing in mind that the distribution evolves over time and that we shall no doubt find intermediate or less clearly defined cases. On the basis of Table 6 however, we can identify different models:

i) *A model where ST dominates,* typically represented by Germany and Finland, with 42-43 per cent of new enrolments in this group of disciplines. It can be seen that in these two countries the medical group also absorbs considerable flows: 17 per cent in Germany and 26 per cent in Finland. To these two countries we should add Yugoslavia, which receives 48 per cent in the ST group, but a very low percentage in Medicine. In these three countries the HS group receives no more than 33 per cent of new entrants (23 per cent in Finland) and the HS + BL aggregate account for 45 per cent in Yugoslavia, 40 per cent in Germany and 31 per cent in Finland.

ii) *An HS dominant model* that may apply in the case of Australia and Italy and very certainly Japan, the Netherlands, Portugal and Turkey. In these countries the HS group receives 45 per cent or more of the new entrants (60 per cent in Turkey) and the HS + BL aggregate absorbs 66 per cent or more of the flows (70 per cent in Japan and Turkey). The result is that the entire group of scientific disciplines (including Medicine) occupies at most one-third of the total and that the size of the ST group will vary as a function of that of the medical group between 25 and 30 per cent of the total flow.

iii) *A more homogeneous group, HO,* closer to the "average", to which the other countries belong. There are of course differences between these countries. The most significant difference seems to be in the proportion of new entrants in the HS + BL aggregate. In one group of countries there are proportions in the order of 61-63 per cent: Austria, Canada, Spain, Switzerland; and in another totals in the order of 53-54 per cent: Greece, Sweden, New Zealand. Belgium and Denmark occupy an intermediate position.

Table I–6. **Relative weights of groups of disciplines as a percentage of the number of new enrolments in higher education, by level of programme**

A. Total

		Men and women				Women			
		ST	HS	BL	MD	ST	HS	BL	MD
Australia	1988	25	44	22	10	13	57	16	14
	1985	25	48	21	6	14	63	15	8
Austria	1988	30	37	26	7	17	50	24	9
	1985	24	39	28	10	12	52	24	13
Belgium	1987	29	28	30	13	14	35	33	18
Canada	1984	28	38	24	10	13	47	24	15
Denmark	1988	29	41	16	14	15	52	12	22
	1985	27	41	16	16	12	53	10	26
Finland	1988	42	23	8	26	18	31	8	43
	1985	43	24	9	23	17	35	9	39
Germany	1988	43	32	8	17	17	42	9	32
	1985	39	33	7	21	14	42	8	36
Greece	1987	34	33	20	13	20	43	20	17
	1985	31	36	20	13	18	47	19	16
Italy	1988	29	47	19	5	18	57	20	5
	1984	28	46	18	8	18	56	18	8
Japan	1988	23	— 72 —		5	5	— 88 —		7
	1985	24	— 70 —		6	5	— 88 —		8
Netherlands	1987	29	47	19	6	15	56	12	7
	1985	30	45	19	5	15	56	21	8
New Zealand	1983	35	28	26	11	20	40	23	17
Portugal	1984	26	46	21	8	17	57	16	9
Spain	1987	29	39	24	8	16	48	25	11
	1984	29	40	22	9	16	52	20	12
Sweden	1988	31	35	18	16	14	45	17	24
	1986	31	35	19	15	14	45	17	24
Switzerland	1988	34	32	29	5	12	53	26	9
	1985	34	32	30	4	11	57	24	8
Turkey	1988	23	61	10	6	17	64	11	9
	1985	26	56	12	7	17	62	13	8
Yugoslavia	1987	48	33	12	6	36	46	11	8
	1983	48	34	12	6	..	..	..	..

ST = Science and Technology.
HS = Humanities and Social Sciences.
BL = Business and Law.
MD = Medicine.

It is interesting to note that there does not seem to be a link between the model that applies in a given country and the proportion of a generation entering higher education (see Table 5 above). The ST model corresponds to countries whose entry rates range from 28 (Yugoslavia) to 50 per cent (Finland). The HS model applies to countries whose rates range from 15 per cent (Turkey, Portugal) to 40 per cent (Netherlands, Japan, Australia). The HO model applied to countries whose rates range from 25 per cent (Austria) to 50 per cent (Denmark, Sweden). Neither does there seem to be any connection between the model and the proportion of girls in higher education, this proportion ranging from 45 to 55 per cent in the ST model, from 34 to 54 per cent for the HS model and from 33 to 55 per cent for the HO model. Knowing that the figures of 33 and 34 per cent correspond to rather particular cases, we can in fact not detect any difference.

If we examine the distribution of girls in higher education, we can make two general observations: first, the proportion of girls is always highest in the HS group and second, it is always lowest in the ST group (it may be pointed out that the proportion of girls in this group in Yugoslavia is far higher than anywhere else).

These two general trends result in certain shifts in the distribution of entries to higher education. If we apply the previous criteria (45 per cent or over), the majority of the countries examined would fit the HS model as regards girls in higher education. The exceptions are Finland (31 per cent), Belgium (35 per cent), Germany (42 per cent) and New Zealand (40 per cent). If we take the HS + BL aggregate, the criterion being 66 per cent or over, the exceptions would be Finland (39 per cent), Germany (51 per cent), Yugoslavia (57 per cent), then Sweden, Greece and Denmark. It is in fact possible to see certain groupings:

  i) *ST model:* Germany and Finland, with a reduction in flows in the ST group, show a significant increase in the proportion of girls in the MD sector, in fact a bipolarisation in the HS and MD sectors. Yugoslavia, where the medical group is small, shows a bipolarisation on the HS and ST groups. The proportion of girls in the HS group ranges from 31 to 46 per cent, and in the HS + BL aggregate from 39 to 57 per cent.
  ii) *HS model:* as we have pointed out, in the countries that fit this model as regards total new enrolments, this is even more the case with the girls. The HS group no longer represents 45 per cent or more of the entrants, but 56 per cent or more (with the minimum rising from 66 to 73 per cent for the HS + BL aggregate).
  iii) *HO model:* we have pointed out that the countries that fit this model are more or less close to the HS model. In the first sub-group of countries, Austria, Canada, Spain and Switzerland, the proportions in the HS group range from 47 to 57 per cent and in the HS + BL aggregate between 71 and 79 per cent. In the second sub-group the proportion is 62 or 63 per cent. As regards the HS + BL aggregate, Belgium and Denmark are in an intermediate position with 64-68 per cent.

Bearing in mind the general trends identified above, the models remain but are evolving. The position is shown in Table 7, which clearly shows that there is little overlapping.

The total number of new enrolments is by definition the sum of new entries to courses at ISCED levels 5 and 6, but there may be very different configurations according to level. The question is therefore to know whether the models outlined above have and maintain significance for each of the two levels.

As regards ISCED 6 level, it can be seen that the models remain significant, but that some countries may shift from one category to another (Table 8):

  i) *ST model:* Germany, Finland and Yugoslavia continue to fit this model, these three countries being the only ones to have ST flows higher than 43 per cent. On the other hand, in Germany and Finland there is a noticeable reinforcement of the HS group (in 1985, one may have hesitated to include Finland). This corresponds to a reduction in the medical group in these two countries. The HS group represents 30 to 44 per cent and the HS + BL aggregate 43 to 53 per cent.
  ii) *HS model:* Italy, Japan, the Netherlands and Turkey remain in this group, which loses Australia and Portugal, more homogeneous at this level, and gains Switzerland and Greece. The shifts are between HS and HO, if we stick to the criterion of 45 per cent in the HS group. On the other hand, if we consider the HS + BL criterion, the changes of category are less clear: with a range of 66-75 per cent (66-69 if Turkey is excluded), Australia has 67 per cent and Portugal 69. On the other hand, Greece and Switzerland have 65 and 62 respectively. In view of the fluidity usual with this type of breakdown, it may even be considered that this model is retained also.
  iii) Since it is what remains we can conclude that the *HO model* keeps its relevance. Within this group we make a distinction between two sub-categories. We see that two countries move into that where the group HS + BL predominates, Greece and New Zealand, both through the expansion of the arts group: the HS + BL aggregate increases from 53-54 to 63-65 per cent, a level still below that of the previous model.

Table I–7. **Different models of higher education : distribution of new entrants ISCED 5 and 6**

For both sexes and for women only, percentage ranges

	Total			Women		
	ST	HS	HS+BL	ST	HS	HS+BL
HS model	23-29	44-61	66-72	5-18	57-88	73-78
HO1 model	29-35	32-39	61-63	12-17	48-53	73-79
HO2 model	31-25	28-35	50-54	14-20	40-45	62-63
ST model	42-48	23-33	31-45	18-36	31-46	39-57

Table I-8. **Relative weights of groups of disciplines as a percentage of the number of new enrolments in higher education, by level of programme**

C. ISCED 6

		colspan="4"	Men and women	colspan="4"	Women
		ST	HS	BL	MD	ST	HS	BL	MD
Australia	1988	27	41	26	6	17	54	21	8
	1985	29	43	24	4	17	59	19	5
Austria	1988	32	34	28	7	19	46	27	8
	1985	26	34	30	10	15	47	26	12
Belgium	1987	35	30	28	8	19	39	32	10
	1984	33	30	23	13	20	37	26	17
Denmark	1988	32	40	21	8	20	50	18	12
	1985	32	40	20	9	18	52	15	14
Finland	1988	46	38	12	4	24	58	12	6
	1985	34	43	16	7	20	56	14	10
Germany	1988	43	44	9	4	22	62	11	5
	1985	44	44	8	4	23	62	10	5
Greece	1987	30	51	14	6	18	62	15	5
	1985	31	43	17	8	22	53	18	8
Italy	1988	29	46	20	5	18	56	20	6
	1984	28	45	18	8	18	56	18	8
Japan	1988	27	— 68 —		5	8	— 85 —		8
	1985	27	— 67 —		6	8	— 83 —		9
Netherlands	1988	30	47	19	5	15	56	22	7
	1985	30	45	19	6	15	56	21	8
New Zealand	1983	34	36	27	3	21	53	23	3
Portugal	1984	27	38	31	4	22	51	21	6
Spain	1986	29	39	24	8	16	48	25	11
	1984	29	40	22	9	16	52	20	12
Sweden	1988	31	27	28	14	16	37	27	20
	1986	38	35	17	10	21	48	18	12
Switzerland	1988	29	51	11	9	16	59	13	12
	1985	30	49	10	11	16	58	4	15
Turkey	1988	19	67	8	6	17	69	7	8
	1985	24	60	9	8	21	61	9	9
Yugoslavia	1987	50	30	13	6	39	41	12	8
	1983	50	30	13	7	..	..	..	..

As regards ISCED 5 level, we must expect a more convoluted picture in view of the very different role played by this type of training in different countries (Table 9).

 i) *ST model:* if we retained the criterion of 42-43 per cent, this group would no longer include Germany, having recently lost Finland and Yugoslavia. If the threshold is reduced to 38-40 per cent (which could have been done for ISCED 5 and 6 without changing the distribution), this group would retain Finland, Germany and Yugoslavia and be joined by Greece, New Zealand, Switzerland and Turkey. The next country, Sweden, is far behind with 31 per cent. It is interesting to note the very marked bipolarisation ST + MD in Germany and Finland, where the HS + BL aggregate is only 6-9 per cent. The percentage in the medical group is also considerably higher in Greece (24 per cent).
 ii) *HS model:* Australia, Italy and Japan remain and are joined by Austria, Denmark and Spain. The high proportion of new enrolments in the medical group is to be noted in Spain.
 iii) *HO group:* here there remain only Belgium and Sweden, where the distribution is not very different from that seen for ISCED 6 or 5 + 6.

The much more marked differences reflect the specialisation of training at ISCED 5 level. The countries in the HS group (or those that have joined this group) are those where primary teacher training occupies a

Table I-9. **Relative weights of groups of disciplines as a percentage of the number of new enrolments in higher education, by level of programme**

C. ISCED 5

		colspan="4"	Men and women	colspan="4"	Women
		ST	HS	BL	MD	ST	HS	BL	MD
Australia	1988	17	51	14	18	7	60	8	24
	1985	18	58	14	10	7	69	9	14
Austria	1988	22	55	14	8	8	65	14	13
	1985	14	60	18	9	3	67	15	14
Belgium	1987	24	26	32	18	10	32	35	23
	1985	13	32	37	17	6	38	34	22
Denmark	1988	23	44	6	27	5	54	2	38
	1985	18	44	9	30	3	53	2	42
Finland	1988	38	6	3	53	14	7	4	76
	1985	51	9	4	36	14	16	5	65
Germany	1988	45	2	4	49	7	3	3	87
	1985	31	12	6	50	4	18	5	74
Greece	1987	41	6	29	24	22	8	30	40
	1985	30	29	25	24	15	43	21	21
Italy	1988	19	81	–	–	13	87	–	–
	1985	20	80	–	–	13	87	–	–
Japan	1988	13	— 81 —		6	3	— 91 —		6
	1985	15	— 79 —		6	2	— 91 —		7
New Zealand	1983	40	8	23	29	18	10	25	47
	1984	–	–	.	100	–	–	.	100
Spain	1986	–	58	–	42	–	54	–	46
	1984	–	46	–	54	–	32	–	68
Sweden	1988	31	38	15	16	13	48	14	25
	1986	29	35	19	17	12	44	16	27
Switzerland	1988	38	21	38	3	8	47	36	8
	1985	37	22	41	1	6	56	36	2
Turkey	1988	41	29	24	6	15	38	34	13
	1985	36	37	25	3	11	54	30	5
Yugoslavia	1987	40	46	8	6	25	60	6	9
	1983	43	41	11	6	..	..	..	..

determinant position (except in Japan, with the case of the Junior Colleges, and Italy where the percentage is not significant). In certain countries medical sector training dominates (100 per cent in Portugal).

It is therefore not surprising when examining the distribution of girls at this level to see much more marked profiles on top of the general trends pointed out above. In Germany and Finland, for example, we no longer see a bipolarisation but a polarisation on the medical group (76 per cent in Finland, 87 per cent in Germany and also 54 per cent in Spain, 47 per cent in New Zealand and 38 per cent in Denmark). For the HS group, we see 60 per cent in Australia and Yugoslavia, 65 per cent in Austria, 87 per cent in Italy and 91 per cent in Japan. On the other hand, there are very few girls in scientific and technical disciplines except in Greece and Yugoslavia.

2. Trend in the breakdown of flows

On the basis of Tables 6, 8 and 9 we can make some observations about the trend in the distribution of flows over time. It should be pointed out however that here we are considering only the breakdown by level. A variation of the percentage within a given level may correspond to a transfer from one level to the other, or with a constant distribution within a given level there may be a different distribution between levels. Lastly, the stability of flows in a given group may conceal *internal transfers* between disciplines within the group (for example from science to technology). The tables, using figures from a recently established data bank show the variations over only a short period; we shall obtain more detail about the variations through examining the country reports.

As regards the total of new enrolments, the most striking feature is the stability of the distribution, for both sexes together and for the girls. Among the countries for which we have data, the majority have retained virtually identical distributions, though it is true we have data only for the short period of 2 to 4 years. Where there are differences they amount to no more than 5 or 6 percentage points. There is above all a tendency towards a *reduction in flows in the HS group* (4 percentage points in Australia, 3 in Greece), with the exception of Turkey. This reduction is more frequent and more marked for the girls (6 percentage points in Australia, 4 in Finland, Greece, Spain and Switzerland). The reduction is not compensated everywhere in the same way, particularly as there are *opposing trends in the MD group* (+4 percentage points in Australia, +3 in Finland, –3 in Austria, –4 in Germany, the corresponding figures for girls being respectively +6, +4, –4, –4 and also –4 in Denmark). The flow data available indicate a *slight increase in flows in the ST group,* notably in Austria (6 percentage points overall and 5 for the girls), Denmark (2 and 3 points respectively), Germany (4 and 3) and Greece (3 and 4). Except in Spain there is *no substantial transfer to the BL sector,* though there is a general, but modest, upward trend.

At ISCED 6 level the stability of the distribution is even more striking. Otherwise, there are no coherent trends, but rather isolated cases. The proportions in the ST group vary in only three cases: up 6 percentage points in Austria (4 for the girls), 12 in Finland (4 for the girls) but down 7 points in Sweden (4 for the girls) and 4 in Turkey (identical for the girls). The HS group rose 7 percentage points in Turkey and Greece (7 and 9 respectively for the girls) but fell by 5 and 6 points respectively in Finland and Sweden (2 only for the girls in Finland but 11 in Sweden). The BL group increased only in Belgium and Sweden (5 and 11 percentage points, 14 and 11 for the girls); it fell by 4 points in Finland and 3 in Greece (same figures for the girls). Despite these divergencies, a slight upward trend can be seen. With the exception of Australia and Sweden, the MD group is declining. It is not easy to identify the direction of transfer; quite often a significant variation in one area is explained by the combination of three smaller variations. In Austria there seem to be compensations between the basic sciences; in Spain, for girls, between HS and BL. There is the sum of these two movements in Finland and Sweden. The case of Turkey is probably explained by the more rapid expansion of the HS sector, the compensation being only apparent.

At ISCED 5 level, where the variations are more marked, we can see some interesting trends and above all transfers. We have seen that in many countries the HS group is declining. In Australia (and in Spain by force) the flows are heading towards the medical sector. This same transfer is found in Finland and Germany for the girls only. In Germany and Greece flows of both sexes are moving towards the ST sector. In Greece we have the sum of these two transfers in the case of girls, and in Turkey for the total and for the girls. In Denmark and Finland there are two transfers in opposite directions between ST and MD. Lastly, in Austria and Belgium the increase in the ST group is fed by both the HS and BL groups. There is no notable transfer towards the BL group, except perhaps in Greece, and above all for the girls. Bearing in mind the methodological reservations mentioned above, there seems to be considerable adaptability of flows.

3. Orientations within generations

As has been pointed out, while the flows are of interest to the labour market, the orientations taken by students within each generation more closely reflect social realities. Through relating the distribution of flows to the average size of the generation, we obtain an indicator of more direct interest, showing for example that if

Table I–10. **Germany**

Orientations in higher education, by sex, as a proportion of a generation (1985-88)

Per thousand

		Men Total	ST	HS	BL	MD	Women Total	ST	HS	BL	MD
ISCED 5	1985	73	51	4	6	12	116	4	21	6	85
	1988	96	77	0	5	14	119	8	4	4	103
ISCED 6	1985	198	113	63	14	7	136	81	84	14	7
	1988	248	140	80	20	9	174	39	107	19	9
Total	1985	271	164	67	20	19	252	35	105	20	92
	1988	344	217	80	25	23	294	47	111	23	112

Source: Calculated on the basis of the OECD Databank.

Table I-11. **Finland**

Orientations in higher education, by sex, as a proportion of a generation (1985-88)

Per thousand

		Men Total	ST	HS	BL	MD	Women Total	ST	HS	BL	MD
ISCED 5	1985	185	163	5	0	14	230	38	37	11	150
	1988	159	129	8	0	21	306	42	21	12	232
ISCED 6	1985	159	80	44	29	6	187	37	105	26	19
	1988	279	185	53	34	6	259	61	150	31	16
Total	1985	344	243	49	29	20	418	71	146	38	163
	1988	449	314	61	34	27	572	103	177	46	245

Source: Calculated on the basis of the OECD Databank.

4 young people out of 10 enter higher education, 1 boy out of 10 takes a short-cycle technical course and 1 girl in 10 embarks on nursing training.

In this short section we shall not try to give a systematic picture of the orientations of each generation, but simply to show the value of this type of data. A first reason is that the OECD database is still fairly recent and does not always contain the necessary data for all countries and all years. Above all however it is not certain that using the ISCED classification (notably as regards programme level) is appropriate, to the extent that the approximations implied are contrary to the impression of "truth" that may be given by these figures. It would be possible to try the exercise and compare the results with what would be given by using national data.

Here we shall therefore limit ourselves, using Tables 6, 7 and 8 and the educational enrolment figures in the Statistical Annex, to giving two examples concerning the orientation of boys and girls in Germany and Finland (Tables 10 and 11). Table 10, relating to Germany, shows for example that in 1988 1 girl in 10 embarked on university studies in humanities or social sciences and another 1 in 10 in post-secondary training in the paramedical sector. All other forms of training together receive only 1 girl in 10. In Finland (Table 11), where higher education is more generalised, almost 6 girls out of 10 enter higher education, 4 of them heading either towards university arts courses or short-cycle training in the paramedical sector.

As in the comparison between the trend of flows of new entrants and the proportion of a generation embarking on higher education, we find contradictory trends, which is perhaps less surprising in this case in view of the "abstract" nature of the distribution of flows. This comes about when there are fairly rapid variations in the distribution or in enrolments. We see such differences in Germany in scientific disciplines at level 6: a slight fall in terms of distribution corresponds to a big increase in terms of the generation. Similarly, in Finland at level 6 we find a fall in economics and law in terms of distribution, but also a significant increase in terms of generations.

Notes and References

1. R. Pearson, *The IMS Graduate Review 1991*, Institute of Manpower Studies, Report No. 206, Brighton, United Kingdom, 1991. See also Mr. Tessaring, Germany, Volume I. *Note :* Data on Germany refer to the period before its reunification; or later to the corresponding Länder.
2. K. Schedler, Austria, Part II. R. Pearson, *op. cit.*, p. 5.
3. S. Fornäng, Sweden, Volume IV.
4. M. Tessaring, Germany, Volume I.
5. S. Fornäng, Sweden, Volume IV.
6. M. Tessaring, Germany, Volume I.
7. S. Fornäng, Sweden, Volume IV.

Chapter 2

ASPECTS OF GROWTH

As pointed out in the Preface, the intention of the Secretariat was to present in Part One an analysis of the outflows from higher education, something we do not have a very clear idea of in the majority of countries. Such a balance sheet is not only of descriptive interest: it also constitutes a diagnosis of the functioning of higher education. We thus thought of devoting a first chapter to entries to higher education, a second to the progress of studies, dropouts, repeats, transfers and a third chapter to outflows proper. In fact, the country reports in some cases give information on new enrolments or first-year students, sometimes on student numbers or graduates. It thus seemed more realistic, after the overview in Chapter 1, to devote this chapter to a presentation of the major trends using the data available, notably in the country reports.

I. STRONG GROWTH

In the previous chapter we presented the broad lines of development of higher education. Bearing in mind the possibility of differences in classifications or statistical coverage, we should find the same trends if we turn to national sources.

In fact, Table 12, based on the country reports for this project, shows the same general trend of vigorous expansion for a period running generally from 1980 to 1988. There is however a divergence for Belgium: the negative balance for the period 1982-89 is due primarily to the decline in numbers of students in universities and short-cycle non-university training, followed by a strong revival, whereas the OECD database covers only the most recent period.

It is interesting to examine how the countries explain this expansion, while several of them feared the consequences of the demographic decline and, what is more, there was talk at the beginning of the 1980s about a crisis of confidence in higher education, which again threatened to result in a reduction in the level of demand.

In this discussion it is perhaps appropriate first of all to consider those countries where there are restrictions on access to higher education, or where such restrictions have recently been introduced (as in Greece and Yugoslavia). It is obvious that if there is a significant difference between the number of people qualified for entry and the number of places available, the influence of demographic or other factors will probably hardly be felt at all. Similarly, if there are many adults among the new entrants, the effect of demographic variations will be cushioned or spread over time.

In Sweden, where all admissions are subject to quotas we can in fact see that the demographic trend and other factors had no effect other than on demand pressure. It is also pointed out that the proportion of young people choosing pre-university courses in upper secondary considerably increased during the 1980s, a factor that contributed to the growing mismatch between the number of people qualified and the number accepted. Normally, this "reserve" should compensate the effects of the demographic trend.[1] Similar remarks are formulated in the Danish contribution, whose author points out that the number of applicants refused a place has significantly increased, amounting to almost one-third of the total number in 1990, with the result that the number of places available has recently been increased.[2] The Austrian contribution also stresses the increase in the number of young people qualified for entry to higher education, notably due to the expansion of pre-university secondary courses; it also points out the poor employment prospects for the young people emerging from these courses, which forces them to go on to higher education. The author concludes that the present system, insufficiently diversified, will not be able to deal with this increase in demand.[3] In Yugoslavia, where we know that considerable restrictions were placed on admissions to courses during the 1980s, this argument about the lack of employment possibilities for people with secondary education only being a demand-strengthening factor is also mentioned.

Table I-12. **Trend in the number of new entrants in the different types of institution during the 1980s**[a]

Thousands

Country[b]		U	C	T	Total
Germany[c]	1980	138.3	54.2	48.0	241.0
	1987	158.4	71.3	47.0	276.7
		+14.6	+30.3	−2.1	+14.8
Australia[d]	1979				316.4
	1989				441.1
					+39.4
Austria[e]	1977	5.449	5.685		11.134
	1987	8.305	4.551		12.856
		+52.4	−19.9		+15.5
Belgium[f]	1982	10.732	4.624	24.120	39.476
	1989	10.868	6.983	19.584	37.435
		+1.3	+51.0	−23.2	−5.5
Canada[g]	1981	401.9	273.4	−	675.3
	1989	515.0	317.3	−	832.3
		+28.1	+16.1	−	+23.2
Denmark[h]	1982	13.152	8.480	12.565	34.197
	1988	17.377	12.661	12.222	42.260
		+32.1	+49.3	−2.7	+23.6
Spain[i]	1982	510.383	128.093		638.476
	1987	696.673	264.263		960.936
		+36.5	+45.4		+38.8
United States[j]	1980	1.183	1.405	n.d.	
	1988	1.209	1.170	n.d.	
		+2.2	−16.7	n.d.	
France[k]	1980	805.026	94.805	121.141	
	1988	956.158	143.987	231.256	
		+18.8	+52.4	+90.9	
Italy[l]	1982	70.244	25.458	6.129	101.831
	1987	74.085	21.280	16.082	111.447
		+5.5	−19.6	+162.4	+11.2
Japan[m]	1980	1.742	366	338	2.446
	1989	1.929	456	522	2.907
		+10.7	+24.6	+54.4	+18.8
Norway[n]	1980	76	42		118
	1989	122	58		180
		+60.5	+38.1		+52.5
Netherlands[o]	1980	26.896	48.345		75.241
	1987	35.079	50.169		85.248
		+30.4	+3.8		+13.3
United Kingdom[p]	1979	98	388	222	708
	1987	123	471	288	882
		+25.5	+21.4	−29.7	+24.6
Sweden[q]	1980	10.0	26.4	6.3	42.7
	1988	12.1	27.5	6.4	46.0
		+21.0	+4.2	+1.5	+7.7
Yougoslavia[r]	1980	310.026	101.149		411.175
	1988	291.019	48.560		339.677
		−6.8	−52.0		−21.1

a) The orientation note prepared by the Secretariat as a guideline for the authors of country reports did not contain a section on new enrolments. We have therefore had to present data on total numbers or even on graduates in the case of certain countries.

b) In the majority of countries there are more than two types of institution, so that the ISCED classification used in the overview is very simplificatory. We consider here that three categories make it possible to give an adequate picture of any changes under way. The three letters U (universities), C (colleges), T (technical) are used just to give a general idea. The institutions to which they correspond are detailed in the notes below.

c) U = Universities
   C = *Fachhochschulen*

T = *Fachschulen*
Source: M. Tessaring Table 6.
d) Total numbers:
Source: B. Williams, contribution to the project on the humanities and social sciences, Table 2.
e) Graduates:
U = Universities
C = Non-university
Source: L. Lassnigg, Tables 1 and 2.
f) First-year higher education in Flanders:
U = Universities
C = Non-university long-cycle higher education
T = Short-cycle non-university higher education
Source: A. Bonte, Table 1.1.
g) Full-time students in post-secondary education:
U = Universities
C = Community Colleges, CEGEP, etc.
Source: R. McDowell, Figure 1.
h) U = Universities LVU
C = Colleges MVU
T = Vocational courses KVU
Source: H. Traberg, Table 3.
i) Total numbers:
U = University faculties and higher technical colleges
C = University schools (technical and non-technical)
Source: A. Casanueva, Table 7.
j) New entrants:
U = Four-year programme
C = Two-year programme
T = Other vocational courses (no data available)
Source: *Digets of Education Statistics 1991, op. cit.,* Table 169.
k) Numbers per category of establishment:
U = Universities (excluding IUT)
C = Engineering and commercial schools, preparatory classes
T = Higher technical training and university institutes of technology (IUT)
Source: A. Pottier and A. Charlot, Table 1.
l) Graduates (net exits):
U = University (laurea)
C = "Institutional" short-cycle training: university diplomas, special-purpose schools, level II regional vocational training
T = Short-cycle post-secondary training in secondary establishments, private courses
Source: F. Bussi, Table I/2.
m) Total numbers:
U = University (4-year courses)
C = Short-cycle training (2-year courses, junior colleges, predominantly girls)
T = "*Senshu gakko*" (special vocational schools)
Source: M. Kaneko, Tables A9, A10 and A12.
n) Total numbers:
U = Universities
C = Regional colleges
Source: P. Aamodt, Figure 1.
o) First-year full-time students:
U = Universities
C = Higher technical training (HBO)
Source: I. Coppens, Table 1.1.
p) Total numbers, full and part-time:
U = Post-graduate courses
C = First degree
T = Sub-degree courses
Source: J. Tarsh, Table 3.
q) U = Universities and equivalent institutions *(fackhögskola)*, courses of at least three years
C = College programmes and short courses in universities and equivalent institutions
T = Municipal colleges (nurses)
New entrants, see Note g, Table 5.
Source: UHA, Dan Andersson.
r) Total numbers:
U = University courses (at least 4 years)
C = "Advanced" schools (2 to 3-year courses)
Source: H. Hanic, Table 1.

In Japan, at least as regards the universities, the admission restrictions have brought a slight reduction in the chances of access to university education, notably for boys, compensated, in terms of flows, by the development of the "*senshu gakko*".[4] Spain is manifestly a country where, to judge by the successive selection processes to which young people are subject, the supply of higher education is considerably lower than demand;[5] the number of places offered was increased by 9 per cent between 1989 and 1990. In France, university growth continued at a lower rate during the 1980s, but with the increase in the number of *baccalauréat* holders, a period of renewed growth is expected.[6]

We have seen that in Belgium,[7] at least at the beginning of the 1980s, the increase in secondary education was not enough to compensate for the demographic downturn, at least as regards the universities and short-cycle education.[8] The author nevertheless points out that the decline was only of 9 per cent, whereas the size of the cohorts fell by 14 per cent. There was also concern about the consequences of the demographic trend in several other countries. This was notably the case in Germany, Canada, the Netherlands and the United Kingdom, but the fact is that no such effects were observed in these countries. It is interesting to see the reasons put forward to explain this situation.

The Canadian report points out on one hand the increase in the participation of women and adults and the development of part-time studies, and on the other the improvement in the chances of being recruited into "professional" and management jobs. These two factors made it possible to compensate for a reduction of over 10 per cent in outflows from secondary education between 1980 and 1987.[9] The Netherlands report also points out the increase in female participation and the influence of employment requirements, but also the policy of expanding higher education. The United Kingdom report points out among other things that the demographic decline hardly affected the social categories that supply the highest proportion of flows of new entrants.[10] In Norway, the interesting argument is put forward that parents who benefited from the expansion of higher education during the 60s have a greater tendency to encourage their children to continue their studies.[11] This argument is quoted in Canada to explain the increase in female participation.[12] It has also been borne out by research in the United Kingdom. In Norway unemployment is considered as one cause of the extension of studies, whereas in Germany a contrary reaction is demonstrated. Obviously, in the case of Norway it is a matter of unemployment in general and, as in the countries mentioned above, the difficulty of finding a job on emerging from secondary education, whereas in Germany it is a matter of graduate unemployment.

The German report stresses the fact that young people's desire to continue their studies on completion of secondary education is closely linked to the employment trend. The author points out that in the early 1970s, almost 90 per cent of them had the intention of continuing their studies, but by the end of the 1970s this proportion had fallen to 70 per cent and as far as 62 per cent for the girls. After a slight increase in the early 1980s, the proportion reached a minimum of 67 per cent for the boys and 50 per cent for the girls. These variations closely follow those of the economic situation and the employment level. In the late 1980s, the economic upturn brought an immediate increase in the percentage intending to continue their studies.[13] The "economic rationale" of these choices is obvious; it takes precedence over another motivation, which is to consider the continuation of studies as a refuge when the employment situation is unfavourable. We shall find this ambiguity again later on.

II. GROWTH POLES

The overall growth in fact conceals very different trends according to the category of the educational establishment. The breakdown adopted here, which comprises three categories instead of two is somewhat closer to the national realities and makes it possible to detail, and above all explain, the trends observed on the basis of ISCED data.

Table 12 shows that there are only three countries in which the highest growth rate was in university education: Austria, Canada and the Netherlands. In view of the earlier observations, it may be considered that in Canada it is a matter of a natural tendency towards prolonging studies, explaining a shift from the colleges to the universities. In Austria, on top of this factor there is a noticeable reduction in outflows from non-university education, connected with the disappearance of some traditional employment outlets: this explains over one-third of the university expansion. In the Netherlands, a variety of factors are quoted, more particularly the increased demand from women and also measures designed to promote the expansion of higher education. In Norway, following a lengthy period during which the focus was on the development of regional colleges, the authorities are once again placing the emphasis on the expansion of universities. It can also be seen that in Yugoslavia, restrictions recently imposed on admissions have concerned above all the "advanced schools", and that by contrast the university sector has been less penalised.

It is interesting to note that not only is it in the non-university sector that we generally find the highest growth rates, but also the biggest differences. A certain number of factors obviously have to be taken into account, but the influence of employment prospects seems to be the determining factor here. In a number of countries we have seen in particular a sharp fall in the recruitment of primary teachers, in the paramedical sector and social service careers, and this has had an immediate effect on the corresponding training courses. The most striking case is that of Italy: in Table 12, we combined the "institutional" short-cycle courses, which fell overall by almost 20 per cent between 1982 and 1987 and "non-institutional" courses which grew by over 160 per cent over the same period. These latter courses include private courses and those set up by secondary education establishments, notably the technical institutes, both types of course very closely linked to labour market requirements, but not leading to a recognised diploma (hence the term used by the Secretariat) [it is interesting that one such establishment has obtained authorisation for its students to receive a diploma from a French university institute of technology (IUT)]. In the case of France, there was a fall of almost one quarter in non-university paramedical training over the period 1980-88, but on the other hand an increase over the same period of almost 90 per cent in the combined figure for the university institutes of technology (+25 per cent) and above all the higher technician level section in the secondary technical education establishments (+143 per cent).[14]

The cases of France and Italy also constitute interesting examples for another reason. We can in fact establish a parallel between the strong growth of the "higher technician sections" (STS), despite the fact that they were programmed to disappear when the university institutes of technology were created, with the "post-diploma" courses in the Italian technical institutes, which have no institutional basis. One of the factors for their success pointed out in both reports is their *proximity:* after obtaining their secondary education certificate, students do not have to change establishment and above all move to another town, which is necessary with most other choices. It should also perhaps be pointed out however that a good proportion of this type of training is oriented towards tertiary sector jobs, therefore requiring relatively low investment, but financially or politically profitable. On the whole this type of training gives rapid access to employment.

Conversely, it should be pointed out that the success of certain non-university sectors is connected with the employment difficulties encountered by young university graduates, a good proportion of whom used to find jobs in the public sector and teaching. This is no doubt the case in Belgium, where university education grew by only a little over 1 per cent (over a period in which there was initially a net reduction, as pointed out above), while at the same time long-cycle non-university courses expanded by over 50 per cent. It is also the case in Germany, where holders of the *Abitur* have for the past 10 years or so become increasingly numerous to head not toward the university, but to the *Fachhochschulen,* formerly intended for young people completing apprenticeships. In this respect we should also point out the increasing number of *Abitur* holders who enter apprenticeships or vocational schools. Various reasons have been put forward to explain such a choice and the fact that a good number of them (30-40 per cent) subsequently enter a university or *Fachhochschule.* Assuming a constant proportion of one-third going on to university or FHS, it can be estimated that for 3.2 per cent of *Abitur* holders in 1975, apprenticeship represented *terminal* post-secondary training. This proportion had risen to 12 per cent by 1985: apprenticeship, to say nothing of the vocational schools, is thus becoming a post-secondary training, with university or FHS being a direct or indirect destination for only 33 per cent of *Abitur* holders.[15]

III. ORIENTATION OF STUDIES

As regards the choice of the field of study, the main question is of course to find out what orientations were taken by the type of student who previously headed for teaching or the public service. We have collected some relevant data in Table 13. As in the case of Table 12, we have to use very heterogeneous information, covering new enrolments, first-year students, total numbers or graduates, which introduces substantial bias. What is more, in Table 12 we used three categories of establishment, which was already a simplification. Here, in order not to make the table too complicated we have selected one particular category of establishment or made certain aggregations. Lastly, we again encounter the same difficulties as in the overview: first the fact that teacher training is not always a separate category and then the fact that we do not always know the breakdown of the very large field of "social sciences". Table 13 is thus presented more by way of illustration than of evidence. It can nevertheless serve as a basis for discussion and at the same time suggest improvements that could be made in the statistical information.

Because of the heterogeneity of the data and the time differences between information concerning new enrolments or graduates, we shall not make any comparison between this table and Tables 6, 7 and 8 of the overview. We can nevertheless see that the analysis given in this overview is confirmed in its broad lines, whether it is a matter of national configurations or their evolutions. Table 13 (and of course the country reports), nevertheless highlight very clear trends that the overview was unable to show.

In this table we should first of all distinguish between those countries that break down the social sciences to separate economic and legal studies and those that do not. In the latter case, it is in fact not possible to determine the volume of transfers between the humanities and social sciences in the restricted sense and teacher training on the one hand and more "vocational" training on the other. Among these countries, two show a positive, though

Table I–13. **Evolution of student orientations, by group of disciplines***

		Ed	H	SS	HS	B	L	BL	S	T	ST	MD
Germany[a]	1975	24.2	13.5	–	37.7	–	–	23.1	10.6	24.9	35.5	3.5
	1988	7.6	15.9	–	23.5	–	–	31.9	14.3	25.5	39.8	4.7
Australia[b]	1979	25.0	25.7	–	50.7	15.8	2.9	18.7	13.3	9.2	22.5	6.2
	1989	16.5	23.0	–	39.5	20.8	2.7	23.5	13.6	9.7	23.3	10.5
Austria[c]	1977	29.3	9.4	3.5	42.2	12.0	8.3	20.3	3.6	16.5	20.1	17.4
	1987	19.6	10.2	5.3	35.1	15.0	11.3	26.3	3.0	15.1	18.1	19.9
Belgium[d]	1982	–	19.6	12.2	31.8	13.2	14.6	27.8	13.1	9.6	22.7	17.7
	1988	–	11.5	10.9	22.4	23.4	17.0	40.4	8.9	13.0	22.9	15.3
Canada[e]	1975	22.7	12.3	27.7	62.7	–	–	–	8.1	9.0	17.1	6.3
	1988	15.6	11.8	37.7	65.1	–	–	–	10.4	11.1	21.5	7.1
Denmark[f]	1982	25.8	19.4	22.0	67.2	–	–	–	6.1	12.5	18.6	14.1
	1988	12.2	16.5	32.4	61.1	–	–	–	5.8	20.91	26.7	12.2
Spain[g]	1983	–	25.0	7.4	32.4	7.5	12.2	14.7	10.0	7.7	17.7	30.1
	1987	–	33.8	5.6	39.4	10.2	17.2	27.4	12.3	5.3	17.6	16.4
United States[h]	1977	15.6	11.5	17.9	45.0	16.4	–	–	9.7	6.1	15.8	–
	1987	8.8	9.4	14.0	32.2	24.3	–	–	7.5	13.3	20.8	–
Italy[i]	1979	–	25.1	5.2	30.3	4.8	10.0	14.8	16.2	18.2	34.4	20.5
	1988	–	20.9	4.8	25.7	12.7	14.3	27.0	14.2	17.2	31.1	15.8
Japan[j]	1980	–	17.6	40.5	58.1	–	–	–	3.1	22.9	26.0	15.9
	1989	–	19.0	39.4	58.4	–	–	–	3.3	23.1	26.4	15.2
Norway[k]	1980	–	14.4	9.0	23.4	9.8	10.9	20.7	–	–	32.7	17.3
	1987	–	7.6	9.2	16.8	16.8	10.5	27.3	–	–	34.0	15.9
Netherlands[l]	1980	–	18.5	19.2	37.1	9.0	16.0	25.9	10.9	16.5	27.4	9.9
	1988	–	16.8	15.5	32.3	16.8	16.0	32.5	10.5	17.4	27.9	7.2
Sweden[m]	1981-85	32.2	9.9	4.8	46.9	12.3	2.7	15.0	2.3	11.0	13.3	24.5
	1986-90	25.7	11.6	3.3	40.6	12.4	2.6	15.0	2.7	17.3	20.0	25.0
Yugoslavia[n]	1980	–	–	–	63.1	–	–	–	3.1	24.4	27.5	9.4
	1988	–	–	–	40.9	–	–	–	5.9	38.5	44.4	14.7

* Ed : education; H: humanities; SS: social sciences (in the restricted sense);
   B : economics and management; L: law;
   S : sciences; T: technology;
   MD : medicine.
a) New enrolments (universities and *Fachhochschulen*).
   Source: M. Tessaring, Figure 12 and Table A7. b.
b) Total numbers.
   Source: B. Williams, Table 1 (see also Table 5 for the period 1967-89).
c) University graduates.
   Source: L. Lassnigg, Table 1 (see also Table 2 for non-university courses).
d) Number of first-year students in Flemish universities. Educational sciences, psychology, political science and social sciences classified SS.
   Source: A. Bonte, Table 2.1 (see also Table 3.1, ESNUL, and Table 3.3, ESNUC).
e) First degrees: The social sciences include law and economics; The category "agriculture and biology" has been divided evenly between S and T.
   Source: A. McDowell, Table 3a (see also Table 2 for the Community Colleges).
f) Number of graduates from long and medium-cycle courses, MVU and LVU: Psychology is grouped with education; the social sciences include law and economics.
   Source: H. Traberg, Table 7.
g) Number of students having completed their studies in universities and higher technical colleges. Teachers for basic general education are trained in university colleges, not included in these figures.
   Source: A. Casanueva, Table XI.
h) Bachelor Degrees. Theoretical Economics is included under Social Sciences. There are no courses in Law or Medicine at this level.
   Source: E.S. Hunt, United States report, Table II–5.
i) Number of university graduates.
   Source: F. Bussi, Table I–7.
j) Number of university students: The social sciences include law and economics.
   Source: M. Kaneko, Table A9 (see also Table A10 for junior colleges and A12 for *Senshu gakko*).
k) University graduates The source does not distinguish between science and technology.
   Source: P. Aamodt, Table in Section 3.4.
l) New enrolments in universities only.
   Source: I. Coppens, Table 1.2.
m) Average numbers of graduates from the higher education system over two 5-year periods, 1981-85 and 1986-90.
   Source: S. Fornäng.
n) Number of first-year students. The report does not indicate the breakdown of the social sciences. The medical and "biotechnical" sectors have been merged.
   Source: H. Hanic.

modest, trend for the HS group: Japan and Canada. In the case of Japan, we in fact see remarkable stability, the HS group having declined very slightly from 61.1 to 58.1 per cent between 1960 and 1980, to subsequently increase marginally to 58.4 per cent in 1989. This stability does not exclude some shifts within the category, but these are again very moderate; the humanities for example represented 15.4 per cent in 1960, 12.7 per cent in 1970 and 15.1 per cent in 1989; the social sciences fell only very slightly from 41.1 per cent to 39.4 per cent over a period of almost 30 years.[16] In Canada, the HS group increased slightly from 62.7 to 65.1 per cent between 1975 and 1988, but there was a sharp fall in the education category from 22.7 to 15.6 per cent, and a slight fall in the humanities, while the social sciences category increased by 10 percentage points.

In Denmark we also see a slight fall in the HS group, but above all a very sharp fall in the education category which more than halved from 25.8 to 12.2 per cent in the short period from 1982 to 1988. There was a slight fall in the arts and a very marked increase in the social sciences, where long and medium-cycle courses taken together increased from 27.2 to 37.7 per cent. This aggregation conceals a drop of 60 per cent in medium-cycle teacher training.[17] In Yugoslavia, where there is no detail for non-scientific training, we should point out the sharp fall in HS + BL from 63.1 per cent in 1980 to 40.9 per cent in 1988. The restrictions on access during the 1980s severely affected the HS group, while the scientific group grew considerably in relative terms (from 27.5 to 44.4 per cent) and in absolute numbers, the number of first-year students rising from 113 000 to 151 000.

Among those countries that make a distinction between social sciences and courses in economics and law, Spain is the only one that shows an increase in the HS group, this being due to the humanities category. This did not prevent a strong increase in the BL group, from 19.7 to 27.4 per cent, fed by the sharp reduction in the medical group. These conclusions need to be qualified however, because breakdowns may be modified by differences in growth rates. The absolute number of medical graduates nevertheless fell by 35 per cent in the four years from 1983 to 1987, while this number more than doubled in philosophy and the arts. These figures refer to universities and higher technical colleges. At the level of "university schools" we see a marked reduction in the training of teachers for basic education, down 18 per cent in four years, which boosted nursing training (up 13 per cent) and above all management training (up 41 per cent). There was also a marked increase in technical training (up 21 per cent) at this level, whereas at the higher level it grew by less than 5 per cent.[18]

All the other countries saw the relative weight of the HS group decline, sometimes very substantially. The fall ranges from 5 to 6 percentage points in the Netherlands, Sweden, Norway and Italy to 11 in Australia and 14 in Germany. Because of the heterogeneity of the data, too much importance should not be attached to these figures, but there was nevertheless a marked downward trend, sometimes over a very short period, almost 9 percentage points in six years in Belgium, for example. This confirms that higher education reacted rapidly to the reduction of job opportunities in the public sector and teaching.

The dominant trend was the reduction of flows in teacher training. This is naturally more visible in those countries where this constitutes a separate training path. The differences are considerable, except perhaps in Sweden (no doubt partly because of the quality of planning, but mainly due to the comparison of *average* values for data that are already very aggregated). It is not surprising to see a difference of only 7 percentage points in Canada and the United States, where teacher training is of lower relative weight because of the very high rate of participation in higher education which means that variations in categories are damped down. In percentage terms, there was a fall from 29 to 20 per cent in Austria, from 25 to 16 in Australia, while the biggest fall was in Germany, down from 24 to 8 per cent. In the Netherlands, teacher training takes place in the non-university sector, so the figures do not appear here. In the HBO sector they represented 31 per cent of enrolments in 1975 and only 16 per cent in 1987.[19] In Belgium, there was a fall of 45 per cent in short-cycle teacher training between 1982 and 1989.

These figures are given by way of illustration. To follow trends in teacher training a much more detailed analysis would be required and this lies outside the framework of this report. It should be pointed out however that there are still shortages of teachers in certain disciplines, notably scientific subjects, and certain countries report a revival of recruitment, including in arts subjects and history, due to the generalisation of schooling at upper secondary level.[20]

Table 13 also enables us to see where the flows thus released headed for, plus those corresponding to growth. It is not impossible that a small proportion headed towards the humanities: there was an increase here in Germany (from 13.5 to 15.9 per cent between 1975 and 1988), in Austria, up from 9.4 to 10.2 per cent and in Sweden up from 9.9 to 11.6 per cent. In Germany, the humanities (at university level) are presented as an alternative for young people who are not attracted by mathematics or technology.[21] The social sciences in the restricted sense scarcely attracted any additional students, though there was an increase of 2 percentage points in Austria. In all the other countries that the table enables us to say anything about there was a reduction; 1 percentage point in Belgium, Italy and Sweden, 2 in Spain, 4 in the Netherlands. For the most part, these flows were in fact directed to the BL group, which grew everywhere, except apparently in Sweden. This shift is one of the features of the decade.

Law was far from being the prime beneficiary: an increase is seen only in Austria and Belgium (about 3 percentage points), Italy and Spain (5 points). There is scarcely any change to be seen in the other countries. It was thus a group comprising economics, commercial subjects, accounting and management in general that saw the greatest increases. While in Spain and Austria the increase was only of 3 points, it was 7 in the Netherlands and Norway, 8 in Italy and 10 in Belgium. In those countries that do not distinguish between the social sciences and courses in economics and law it is difficult to derive any figures. The increase of 10 percentage points in Canada is no doubt explained to a large part by this shift, if we assume that the trend in the universities was parallel to that in the Community Colleges, where there was an increase in social sciences from 5 500 to 8 500 graduates between 1976 and 1988, but a doubling from 8 000 to 16 000 in management and commerce.

In Australia, management student number increased by over 80 per cent between 1979 and 1989.[22] In Austria, the humanities and social sciences are also presented as a replacement for teacher training; the Table shows that in fact the disciplines concerned are mainly law and management. The increase in management studies had not been foreseen.[23] In Belgium the same advance is found in the three levels of training: an increase of 152 per cent in nine years in the universities, 189 per cent in long-cycle non-university courses and 35 per cent only in short-cycle.[24] In Canada, the social sciences, *i.e.* mainly economics and law represent almost 40 per cent of the first degrees awarded; in the Community Colleges, management is now the biggest single sector (16 per cent of graduates).[25] In Denmark, the ministry's policy has been to limit admissions to the humanities and medicine and to promote training leading to private sector employment and to encourage the non-university sectors. The social sciences thus increased by about 50 per cent between 1982 and 1988.[26] In Spain, law and the economic sciences at university level expanded even more rapidly than the humanities, the number of graduates more than doubling in just four years.[27] In the United States, the number of business graduates rose from 16 per cent in 1977 to 24 per cent in 1987. In France, the management schools have experienced ''exponential'' growth since 1979 (up 88 per cent between 1980 and 1988, student numbers tripled between 1975 and 1988).[28] In Italy, in the ''post-diploma'' and private courses, which have expanded very rapidly as we have seen, it is estimated that over half are concerned with management, commerce, banking, etc.; in the universities, the number of *graduates* more than tripled between 1979 and 1988 (the word graduate is underlined because there are many drop-outs in economics).[29] In Japan, we have noted the apparently great stability at university level, but in the *senshu gakko* the number of management students increased by 155 per cent between 1980 and 1988.[30] In Norway, the number of graduates in management and economics increased by 84 per cent over the same period and the author points out that in addition many young Norwegians follow management courses abroad, notably in Switzerland and the United States. They are no doubt more numerous than those who obtain their qualification in Norway.[31] In the Netherlands, it is pointed out that this rapid expansion in management training was particularly marked in the period 1975-85, with new enrolments increasing from 8 to 13 per cent of the total in the universities and from 8 to 27 per cent in the HBO sector, and the growth is still continuing.[32] In the United Kingdom there is a similar situation, with the decline in teacher training and the development of management training dating from the second half of the 1970s and the early 1980s. At non-university level (''sub-degrees''), management represents over 40 per cent of the graduates.[33] It has been pointed out that if the number of people qualifying in accountancy continued to increase at the present rate, the whole United Kingdom population would have an accounting qualification by the beginning of the next century.

This description is however insufficient to give a real idea of the extent of ''vocationalisation''. The fact is that in many countries there has been diversification or transfer *within* each group of disciplines. We may take the example of France, where new diplomas and new study paths have been created and shifts have been encouraged from the sciences towards technology, from theoretical economics towards commerce and management, from traditional humanities towards ''applied'' humanities and the communications professions. The results have not been very encouraging in the field of humanities, notably with the revival of the recruitment of teachers in the traditional discipline, but the other initiatives have been very successful, especially in the field of economics.[34]

These rapid changes give rise to two questions. The first is whether these reactions to demand (or these policy actions) have been sufficient, or, on the contrary, excessive (something we shall examine in Part Two). The second concerns the factors involved: the two main ones are no doubt demand pressure and the evolution of employment prospects, even when it is a matter of the simple possibility of *access* to employment and not of career prospects. The difficulty of orienting and channelling this demand can easily be seen, the measures taken (or not taken), being capable of causing great shortages or surpluses.

IV. SCIENCE AND TECHNOLOGY

The majority of countries hope to see the flows of graduates in 5the scientific and technological fields expand, and several have made this a priority. We must therefore study developments in this field. As in the case of teachers, a more detailed, in-depth study is really required, but this would go beyond the framework of the present report. Here we shall limit ourselves to gathering some information, using the OECD database and the country reports.

In the overview, we have already given certain indications on the place of the ST group in each country on the basis of the statistics in the OECD database. In addition, by way of illustration, Tables 10 and 11 have demonstrated the value of statistics showing orientations within each generation. On the basis of the same sources, Table 14 has given more detailed indications concerning new enrolments in science and technology as a proportion of a generation. It is regrettable that at present this table can be compiled for only about ten countries as several Member countries, and not the smallest, give information on this breakdown only occasionally if at all. It is again necessary to treat the figures with caution because of differences in definition and classification. It is nevertheless possible to make some interesting observations.

With the exception of Turkey (one-quarter of whose higher education system is devoted – like that of Japan – to scientific and technical training, but which as yet accepts only 10 per cent of a generation, a proportion that tripled during the 1980s), we see that in several countries the proportion of young people heading for these disciplines is in the order of 7 to 8 per cent of a generation: Austria, Italy and Japan. In Germany, Australia, Denmark and Switzerland, the proportion ranges from 10 to 15 per cent, while in Finland it is over 20 per cent. As we have pointed out, the figures for Sweden are not strictly comparable, but this country is certainly at a high level. The Italian figures are underestimated, as has been shown for level 5, a large proportion of which is not recorded in the statistics. By and large, the figures show that in most countries one or two young people out of ten enter post-secondary scientific or technical training.

If we now turn to the country reports, we see fairly contrasting situations and points of view. In certain countries the policy is one of strong expansion of scientific and technical training and demand, influenced by the economic revival and increasing needs in this area, is increasing at the same time. Table 15 shows the example of the trend in intentions to pursue studies in the ST field in Germany.

In France, Sweden and Denmark, for example, we see high growth rates. In Sweden, admissions were increased by 50 per cent during the 1980s in order to meet the requirements of the economic boom and the demands of employers who stressed the danger for the Swedish economy of a shortage of engineers. The rate of this expansion is shown in Table 16, which shows the figures for graduates. France has a similar policy: the schools of engineers saw their student numbers increase by 43 per cent between 1980 and 1988.[35] In the case of university-level science courses, the rate of growth in enrolment has risen from zero per cent for the period 1971-1976 to 5.5 per cent for 1976-1981 and 7.3 per cent for 1981-1986; there has, however, been a slight slackening in this growth rate over the past three years (4.2 per cent). Table 17 shows the equally rapid expansion in the number of scientific and technical graduates in *Denmark.*

In other countries the volume of flows in the science and technology field is stable or even falling. In Japan, at least as regards the universities, there was an increase of 12.5 per cent in student numbers in the ST sector between 1980 and 1988, as against 10.8 per cent for total student numbers (and we know that this corresponds to a reduction in terms of the proportion of a generation, as shown in Table 14). This is probably due to the admissions policy of the universities or the relative weight of national universities and private universities, the former having only 27 per cent of their students in the humanities and social sciences, the others 67 per cent.[36] In Norway there was net growth in the universities and regional colleges until 1985/86, then a levelling off in the number of graduates. The report indicates that between 1975 and the mid-1980s the policy was to give priority to vocational training in management and technology, but it was then considered that perhaps the move had gone too far in this direction and it was time to give more place to other sectors like education and health. Another reason may be the change in Norway's economic situation, which hit engineers and technicians in particular (see Chapter 5). However, since the figures refer to *graduates* it would appear that demand anticipated the change.[37]

In Canada and Belgium, where access is more flexible, there was also a period of growth followed by some decline. In Canada it should be recalled that student numbers in all forms of higher education grew strongly until 1985 and then there was a slight fall in the following period. Technical training in the period to 1985 developed very rapidly, the number of graduates more than doubling between 1976 and 1985, but the trend was then reversed. The report puts forward the hypothesis that the strong demand for technical qualifications at the beginning of the decade has been satisfied and that the market is now saturated.[38] These trends are shown in Table 18.

Table I-14. **New enrolments in scientific and technical courses as a proportion of a generation**

Per thousand

			Level 5			Level 6			Total		
			M	F	T	M	F	T	M	F	T
Australia	1985-88	S	6.3	3.2	4.8	38.7	29.7	34.5	45.0	32.9	39.3	73.5
		T	41.2	14.2	27.6	86.1	25.2	56.7	127.3	39.4	84.3	55.2
		ST	47.6	17.4	32.4	125.1	54.9	91.2	172.7	72.3	123.6	128.7
Austria	1985-88	S	—	0.6	1.0	23.7	15.0	17.5	23.7	15.0	17.5	28.6
		T	8.9	4.2	8.7	43.4	11.3	24.9	52.3	13.3	30.7	43.8
		ST	8.9	4.8	9.7	67.1	26.3	42.4	76.0	28.3	48.2	72.4
Denmark	1983-88	S	—	0.0	0.0	34.3	14.5	25.0	34.3	14.5	25.0	39.0
		T	29.9	5.6	17.3	63.9	17.4	42.0	93.8	23.0	59.3	100.6
		ST	29.9	5.6	17.3	98.2	31.9	67.0	128.1	37.5	84.3	139.6
Finland	1985-88	S	28.1	13.6	20.3	29.4	23.6	25.3	57.5	37.2	45.6	67.4
		T	134.7	19.6	77.8	50.2	14.0	31.0	184.9	33.6	108.8	145.1
		ST	162.8	33.2	98.1	79.7	37.6	56.3	242.4	70.8	154.4	212.5
Germany	1985-88	S	—	0.8	1.4	34.6	16.6	25.9	34.6	16.6	25.9	34.5
		T	51.2	7.4	47.0	78.5	14.1	47.2	129.7	18.3	76.9	104.5
		ST	51.2	8.2	48.4	113.1	30.7	73.1	164.3	34.9	102.8	139.0
Italy	1984-88	S	3.3	1.4	1.8	30.7	25.5	28.1	34.0	27.2	29.9	30.0
		T	—	—	—	66.8	17.8	42.4	66.8	17.8	42.4	44.9
		ST	3.3	1.7	1.9	97.5	43.3	70.5	100.5	45.0	72.3	74.9
Japan	1983-88	S	0.0	0.2	0.1	13.6	3.7	8.8	13.6	3.9	8.9	8.1
		T	21.6	4.2	16.8	112.6	6.4	61.9	134.2	10.6	78.7	72.6
		ST	21.6	4.4	16.9	125.8	10.1	70.7	147.8	14.5	87.6	80.7
Netherlands	1983-88	S				14.5	5.0	33.3		3.9		
		T				31.9	7.1	67.0		10.6		
		ST				46.2	12.1	100.3		14.5		
Spain	1984-87	S				39.6	14.8	34.5				
		T				76.1	7.3	46.7				
		ST				115.4	22.1	81.2				
Sweden	1986-88	S	49.7	29.3	40.0	40.8	21.1	30.0	90.5	50.5	70.3	75.7
		T	164.8	39.7	106.8	68.9	23.8	45.7	233.7	63.5	152.5	169.8
		ST	214.5	69.0	146.8	109.7	44.9	69.8	324.2	113.9	222.8	245.5
Switzerland	1983-88	S	118.3	4.5	56.8	27.6	19.7	18.5	145.9	24.2	75.3	19.4
		T	44.7	1.4	21.4	26.6	12.5	16.4	71.3	13.9	37.8	114.6
		ST	163.0	5.9	78.2	54.2	32.2	34.9	217.3	38.1	113.1	134.0
Turkey	1983-88	S	0.1	0.2	0.5	7.3	4.3	6.2	7.4	4.4	6.3	8.1
		T	13.5	1.7	7.2	30.0	7.5	19.2	43.5	9.2	26.4	26.3
		ST	13.6	1.8	7.3	37.3	11.8	25.4	50.9	13.6	32.7	34.4

Source: Calculated on the basis of information in the OECD Databank.

Table I–15. **Germany**

Intention to pursue studies in the scientific or technical fields among final-year secondary pupils

Percentages

	1975	1980	1985	1989
Mathematics, sciences	13.3	13.4	14.4	15.3
Technology	22.9	21.6	25.0	26.3

Source: M. Tessaring, Table 5.

Table I–16. **Sweden**

Growth in the number of science and technology graduates in three successive five-year periods

	1981-85 a	1986-90 b	1991-95 c	b/a %	c/b %
University engineers	2 060	2 620	3 180	27.2	21.4
College engineers	150	700	3 960*	366.7	465.7
Scientists	640	740	820	15.6	10.8
Total	3 800	5 440	9 600	43.2	76.5

* Including integration in the post-secondary level of long-cycle secondary technology courses.
Source: S. Fornäng.

Table I–17. **Denmark**

Increase in the number of science and technology graduates, 1982-88

	1982 a	1985 b	1988 c	b/a %	c/b %
Technology:					
Long-cycle	904	991	1 255	+9.6	+26.6
Medium-cycle	649	1 107	1 355	+70.6	+22.4
Short-cycle	1 180	1 057	1 577	–10.4	+49.2
Science	759	741	730	–2.4	–1.5

Source: H. Traberg, Table 7.

Table I–18. **Canada**

Number of science and technology diplomas awarded in the Community Colleges and Universities (first degree)

Thousands

	1975	1980	1985	1988
Universities				
Mathematics, physical sciences	4.2	4.4	7.6	7.2
Technology	4.8	7.3	8.4	8.0
Colleges[a]	7.0	11.0	16.0	14.0

a) The data for the Comunity Colleges are for 1976, 1981, 1984 and 1989.
Source: R. McDowell, Tables 2 and 3.

Table I–19. **Belgium**

Trend in the number of first-year science and technology students in higher education (Flemish Community)

	1983	1988	1989	1988/83	1989/88
Universities					
Science	1 471	939	970	–36.2	3.3
Technology	1 081	1 266	1 417	17.1	11.9
HENU long cycle	2 785	3 892	3 612	39.7	–7.2
HENU short cycle	2 210	2 583	2 294	16.9	–11.2

Source: A. Bonte, Tables 2.1, 3.1, 3.3.

In Belgium, where the flows entering higher education tended to fall throughout the 1980s, there was a similar fall for technical and scientific courses taken as a whole, as shown in Table 19. The report points out that in general demand is strongly linked with the evolution of job opportunities and it is thus surprising to see engineering training become less attractive and above all to see a fall in demand for mathematics and information technology, which declined by half in five years. The explanation put forward in this latter case is that the demand shifted to the engineering faculties. As regards the sector as a whole however the question remains open. There was nevertheless an overall increase of 14.4 per cent over the period 1982-88, whereas the total number of first-year students in higher education fell by 6.3 per cent.

Other countries seem to be concerned with the need for an increased number of scientists and engineers but find at the same time that the number of new enrolments or of graduates remains steady or is even falling. In Australia it can be seen that the debates on the need for engineers and scientists does not seem to have much effect on demand for training in this sector and the government intends to take measures to stimulate this demand. Student numbers increased by 50 per cent between 1979 and 1989, *i.e.* at a slightly higher rate than for all subjects, but as a percentage of the whole they remained virtually identical. It should be pointed out however that the market is to a large extent supplied by immigration.[39] In Italy, where employment prospects for engineers are very good, it can be seen that the proportion of engineers in total graduates fell from 15.8 to 13.6 per cent over the period 1979-1988; in absolute figures this corresponds to a fall of 8 per cent, while the total grew by 6.7 per cent. The number of scientists fell by 6.5 per cent. In Spain, we have already seen that the number of graduates from the higher technical schools increased by only 4.8 per cent and from university technical schools by 21.3 per cent, with an overall increase of almost 29 per cent. In Austria, we see that there is no solid proof of a shortage of engineers (*Techniker Mangel*), but in any case it has not been possible to stimulate demand for such training.[40] At university level, the sector grew by only 3.3 per cent, as against 52 per cent for all subjects (Table 20). In the United Kingdom there is concern about the fact that while the total number of graduates is expected to rise by 37 per cent by 1993, that of engineers will increase by only 9 per cent.[41]

In the Netherlands it can be seen that the number of new enrolments has not increased as might have been expected in view of the needs of the society. In particular, there is decline in the percentage of new enrolments in

Table I–20. **Austria**

Trend in the number of science and technology graduates

	1977	1987	1987/77
University			
Technology	713	1 049	47.1
Science	438	243	–44.5
Non-university	320	522	63.1

Source: L. Lassnigg, Tables 1 and 2.

Table I–21. **Netherlands**

Trend in the number of first-year science and technology students

	1975	1980	1988	1988/75
University				
Science	2 893	2 932	3 707	+28.1
Technology	2 643	3 362	5 120	+93.7
HBO	14 792	14 939	12 492	–15.5

Source: I. Coppens, Tables 1.1., 1.2, 1.3

technology in the non-university sector (HBO), which the increase in entries to the universities has not been able to compensate. Since 1985 however there has been a very positive trend in absolute numbers, including in the HBO (see Table 21). In addition, it is intended in the Netherlands to take measures to increase the number of teachers in scientific and technical subjects.[42]

It can be seen that the growth rate was different according to the type of training. In many cases it was not university technology courses that were the main growth poles. This was the case in the Netherlands and Belgium (particularly if we consider the recent trend) and very often it was on the contrary *non-university training* which experienced the most rapid expansion, sometimes at a spectacular rate. This was the case in Sweden, Denmark and also Japan: while there was no growth at university level, it was spectacular in the *senshu gakko* where numbers increased overall by 54 per cent between 1980 and 1988, but by 127 per cent in technology. There are also differences within the non-university sector itself. This is notably the case in Belgium, where short-cycle training grew only very slightly as compared with long-cycle.

On the other hand, in a number of other countries it was the sciences whose student numbers increased only slightly or even fell during the 1980s. This was the case of Austria (Table 20), Belgium (Table 19) and Denmark (Table 17). It may be thought that this weakening is connected with the reduction of recruitment into teaching, which in the European countries used to be the main outlet for science graduates; this explanation implies influence by the general context, since while there was indeed an overall reduction, there has always been a shortage in scientific and technical subjects. What is more likely is that young people who feel they have an aptitude in this field are now much more attracted by engineering careers. This would mean a double shift: at the entry to higher education demand moves towards technology courses and at the exit – as we shall see in Part Two – science graduates prefer a private sector career to teaching. The Netherlands is not the only country to be concerned about the recruitment of science teachers in the years to come.

In the United States, a twofold trend is apparent. The popularity of science programmes has been declining for ten years (which is not due to any substantial increase in participation rates and thus to an inflow of new categories of students); the popularity of technology courses is far greater, but seems to have been tailing off since 1981 (Table 22). Looking at the numbers of graduates (Table 23) there has in fact been a noticeable decrease in the number of science graduates and, at the same time, a marked shift away from short courses towards four-year university programmes. The number of Bachelor Degrees awarded in technology increased by

Table I–22. **United States**

Percentage of all full-time first-year students indicating an interest in science and technology fields, 1977-87

	1977	1981	1985	1987
Science	10.6	8.9	8.4	7.7
Technology	14.1	20.3	18.2	16.0
Total	24.7	29.2	26.6	23.7

Source: E.S. Hunt, Table II–3.

Table I-23. **United States**

Number and proportion of science and technology graduates by level of education

	1984	1987	Var. %
Vocational certificates			
Science	202	132	−35%
Percentage	0.2	0.1	
Technology	16.328	14.875	−9%
Percentage	13.1	13.5	
Associate degrees			
Science	4 869	3 633	−25%
Percentage	1.2	0.9	
Technology	63 586	58 702	−8%
Percentage	14.0	13.4	

	1977	1981	1987	Var. %
Bachelor's degrees				
Science	90.298	78.246	74.577	−5%
Percentage	9.7	8.4	7.5	
Technology	55.690	90.121	132.278	+47%
Percentage	6.1	9.7	13.3	

Source: E.S. Hunt, Tables II–1, II–2, II–5.

47 per cent between 1977 and 1987, with degrees in science and technology accounting for about 21 per cent of the total in 1987 compared with under 16 per cent in 1977.

In most countries therefore there is a desire to see the flows of scientists and engineers increase and much discussion about the reasons for what is considered to be insufficient growth. Several are put forward, for example:

   i) The nature and form of science teaching at secondary level, which excludes a good number of pupils from this path at an early age and probably unjustifiably: this is notably the case with girls;

   ii) In the United Kingdom it has also been noted that young people from a lower social class are less inclined to choose the scientific streams at university, so that the vigorous expansion expected in the next few years will not be accompanied by a corresponding increase in the output of engineering graduates.[43] Another study, covering higher education as a whole, shows that differences in social class have little or no effect in the case of women. On the other hand, although working class adolescents tend to a greater extent to choose science subjects, the expected expansion over the coming years will come from the middle classes, adults and women, all of whom are less attracted by these disciplines;[44]

   iii) The selection and orientation mechanisms at secondary level and at entry into higher education and sometimes even later on, are based on criteria which may be excellent when considered in isolation (capacity of the establishments, quality of applicants, quality of teaching), but which taken together have quite detrimental effects. We may mention the case of the higher technical schools in Spain, which have been criticised for their "Malthusianism",[45] but which are not solely responsible for the selection;

   iv) The image of scientific and technical careers, very positive in many countries, is less attractive in others; this image is linked with that of manufacturing industry, which remains fairly negative, or there may be social and professional structures where the technical component is not valued very highly, except at the highest hierarchical levels, as has been pointed out in Spain.[46] An examination of all these data suggests however the existence of a fairly strong demand pressure, which has difficulty in expressing itself in the context of existing institutions and capacities: as soon as new possibilities open up we see impressive rates of growth, as in Japan, Italy, France, Sweden, etc. The impression is also that, despite the tendency for the prolongation of schooling and hence towards training at higher levels, it is in the short or medium-cycle non-university level that demand is greatest: the ease to access to employment on exit from these courses is likely to increase demand even further, all the more so because the expansion of management and commerce training is likely to lead to disappointment.

V. WOMEN IN HIGHER EDUCATION

From the point of view of education as from that of employment, the increased participation of women in higher education is one of the major aspects of its development. Several country reports stress the fact that the 1980s were marked by *catching up* on the part of women, who now occupy a place comparable to and sometimes higher than that of men in higher education as a whole. We do not propose to present a monograph on this theme, but will simply illustrate this development and try to see to what extent this trend corresponds to the evolution of employment requirements.

The French and Japanese reports present graphs showing in dramatic fashion how female participation has caught up with, and in the case of France passed, the level of men.[47] The Canadian report adds that it is thanks to increased female participation that it has been possible to compensate for the effects of the demographic decline.[48] This gives the general tone. Certain countries are of course further advanced than others along this path, and while Spain is already well beyond the 50 per cent mark, other countries such as Germany, Denmark and the Netherlands have not yet reached it.

The fact is that in the majority of cases, the global data may conceal fairly big differences in situation between men and women when we look at particular aspects. The author of the Canadian contribution reports for example that the duration of schooling has long been identical for males and females in this country, but this a false equality due to the fact that the girls generally complete their secondary studies, whereas the boys either leave earlier or continue them at post-secondary level. A similar situation is found in higher education. The phenomena are widely known and abundantly documented; we shall limit ourselves here to data relating to the level of training and the field of study insofar as these are connected with the general theme of this report.

1. Level of studies

We shall start on the basis of the data provided by the Canadian contribution. The proposition is simple: the higher the level of study, the lower the proportion of women. The proportion of women graduates falls from 56 per cent in the Community Colleges to 54 per cent of first degrees, 45 per cent for Masters and 31 per cent for doctorates. If we examine the figures for France, we see a comparable situation: 56 per cent of first-cycle student numbers, 55 per cent at second, 39 per cent in the third cycle of university studies. The percentages among higher level technicians (60 per cent) and in the engineers' schools (18 per cent) only go to reinforce the diagnosis; however, there is already an exception to the rule with the Institutes of Technology, where the proportion of girls is only 37 per cent. If we look at Japan, we of course see the general rule confirmed with a very low percentage of women in the universities (27 per cent), but a majority of women in the junior colleges (91 per cent) and the *senshu gakko* (53 per cent).

If we admit that we have here a general rule, it is changing rapidly. In Table 24 we present some data taken from the country reports. For the university sector, these show very rapid change, the percentages rising for example from 22 to 37 in eight years in Norway and from 28 to 43 per cent in the Netherlands (though over a longer period, from 1973 to 1988). Such figures justify the idea of "spectacular catching up", but this general impression needs some qualification.

The fact is that when we examine entries to the different categories of higher education establishments in greater detail (and Table 24 gives only a very incomplete idea of this), we see that the situation is not so simple. In several countries, for example Germany, Denmark and France, girls are not so well represented in certain non-university courses of a very good level, vocationally oriented and for which there are good labour market openings. On the other hand, they are much more numerous in short-cycle training where the job opportunities are sometimes not so good. This is the case in Belgium with short-cycle higher education, France (with higher technician sections of the tertiary sector type leading to fairly low level service sector jobs), of Denmark with short-cycle courses and of Spain with the non-technical university schools. It is naturally the case with the Junior Colleges in Japan. The dominant impression is that such short-cycle training, often belonging to the field of social sciences in the broad sense, serves as much to absorb the demand for higher education as to prepare students for specific types of job and of a level corresponding to those open, for example, to people graduating from the same type of training, but in a technological field. It can in fact be seen in France that the proportion of women dropping out of short-cycle studies is particularly high.

It is clear that this situation, where women are often more numerous at the beginning, more numerous at the exit from ISCED 3 or 5, but less well represented in outflows at a higher level, is connected with the subject orientations. The effect of this factor is however more complex: part of the female demand for short-cycle training is diverted, either because of limited capacities in the establishments concerned or because the job opportunities on completion of such courses are mediocre or poor, to longer-cycle university studies. We may cite the case of Spain, where the number of teachers trained in non-university colleges greatly diminished between

Table I-24. **Proportion of women in higher education by type or level of establishment**
Percentages

		U	C	T	Total
Germany[a]	1975	41.0	24.00	–	–
	1987	43.6	32.5	–	–
Belgium[b]	1989	49.5	34.1	60.7	–
Canada[c]	1975	45.0	58.0	–	48.6
	1988	54.0	56.0	–	54.3
Denmark[d]	1980	38.1	43.1	76.5	47.8
	1987	43.0	42.7	70.3	48.6
Spain[e]	1982	48.7	8.1	71.7	53.7
	1986	55.0	12.8	73.6	56.8
United States[f]	1980	49.5	54.8	–	52.3
	1988	52.2	57.2	–	54.0
France[g]	1983	44.5	60.9	–	54.8
	1989	49.1	58.8	–	54.3
Italy[h]	1981	43.9	–	–	–
	1988	47.4	–	–	–
Japan[i]	1989	26.9	91.2	53.4	–
Norway[j]	1980	21.8	34.7	64.8	–
	1988	37.2	51.5	67.3	–
Netherlands[k]	1974	29.0	37.0	–	–
	1989	43	48	–	–
United Kingdom[l]	1982	40.4	40.8	60.2	42.8
	1988	43.6	46.3	58.7	46.9
Sweden[m]	1980	43.0	62.9	84.6	61.4
	1988	46.4	57.0	1984.4	58.1

For more details see Table I.12.
a) New entrants. No data available on the *Fachschulen* (T).
   Source: M. Tessaring, Table 11.
b) First-year students (Flemish Community).
   Source: A. Bonte, Tables 2.3, 3.2, 3.4.
c) Graduates
   U : First degrees only
   C : Vocation programmes in the colleges.
   Source: R. McDowell, Figure 8.
d) Enrolments.
   Source: H. Traberg, Table 13.
e) Graduates
   U : University faculties
   C : Higher technical schools
   T : Non-technical university schools.
   Source: A. Casanueva, Table 16.
f) Enrolments
   U : 4-year programmes
   C : 2-year programmes.
   Source: Digest of Education Statistics 1991, Table 167.
g) Net outflows (with a degree or other certificate)
   U : Levels 1 and 2 of the French classification (universities, *grandes écoles*)
   C : Level 3 (*instituts universitaires de technologie, sections de techniciens supérieurs*).
   Source: A. Charlot, F. Pottier, Table 8.
h) University degrees.
   Source: F. Bussi, Table I-10.
i) Enrolments.
   Source: M. Kaneko, Tables A5B, A6, A7.
j) Graduates
   U : Second university cycle
   C : First university cycle
   T : Regional colleges.
   Source: P. Aamodt, Table 8.
k) First-year students
   U : Universities
   C : HBO
   Source: I. Coppens, Table 1.1.
l) First degrees
   U : Universities
   C : Polytechnics
   T : Colleges (teacher training excluded).
   Source: J. Tarsh, Table 7.
m) First-year students.

1983 and 1987. Part of the demand was switched to nursing training and management courses, but the overall reduction in outflows from these types of course over the period suggests that part of the diverted demand went to contribute to the growth of university studies in philosophy and the arts.[49]

Another question that would merit further consideration in a more detailed study is that of the strategies pursued by women in higher education. We suggested above that they often adopt a "safety-first strategy", through fixing a clearly accessible initial objective, for example a vocational qualification from a short-cycle course, then a higher objective, for example university studies (where they qualify for admission). It would be necessary to analyse in detail the rates of transfer and of dropouts and see whether these behaviours could be linked to employment considerations. In fact, the argument of "proximity" used to explain the rapid growth of training courses organised by secondary schools themselves, notably in France and Italy, which makes it possible to pursue higher level studies without changing establishment, and above all town, probably also has a great influence.

2. Orientation of studies

The baseline situation is well known: in higher education, the women are concentrated in the more literary and artistic subject areas, in courses leading to traditionally female jobs such as teaching, para-medical and social work careers, secretarial work, accounting and documentation. Models and social attitudes continue to play a major role here and are one of the factors tending to keep women within these types of training.[50] However, the earlier school subject orientation, no doubt less directly connected with such attitudes, plays an equally important role: it is possible to analyse the succession of choices that from a very early age progressively lead women away from scientific and technical studies.[51]

Looking at the country reports however, we have the feeling that this image is to a large extent outmoded, the progress of girls in types of training "traditionally dominated by men" is just as spectacular. We have collected some data to illustrate this progress in Table 25.

In Germany there is an increase in female participation in all sectors of higher education, though this increase remains modest in science and technology. On the other hand there is a clear advance in medicine from 34 to 45 per cent between 1975 and 1988 and also in the economics and social sciences group. Women were represented above all in the social sciences, but there has more recently been a boom in management studies, both in the *Fachhochschulen* and in the universities since 1988.[52] In Austria, there has also been a marked advance in law and management, which increased from 18 to 30 per cent between 1977 and 1987, but the proportion of women in science and technology remains stagnant. In Belgium, the girls are "occupying the last male bastions of the university one by one". They are already in the majority in law, medicine, veterinary science and chemistry. The proportion of women in civil engineering courses is fairly low (16.3 per cent), but this is double the figure recorded at the beginning of the decade; the advance is even more striking in non-university long-cycle training where the proportion of women has increased from 5 to 16 per cent. In Canada, 53 per cent of university diplomas go to women and there is an advance in all fields. At first degree level women are in the majority everywhere except in science and technology, but in this last field the proportion doubled between 1978 and 1988. At doctorate level on the other hand, they are in the majority only in the educational sciences. In Denmark, the traditional pattern is being left increasingly far behind. Women are now in the majority among the new enrolments in medicine, theology and law, but there are still only a few in the technical fields. The government has been trying to increase their representation here with a certain amount of success as shown in Table 26, and women are already in the majority in chemical engineering.

In Spain, it is pointed out that while the number of women has increased in the humanities and social sciences – which is probably the dominant trend – the proportion of women in engineering courses has also increased, rising from 11 to 15 per cent in the higher technical schools. Table 27 shows that technology is the field where the number of female graduates is increasing most rapidly.

In the United States, the percentage of women among those graduating with Bachelor Degrees is increasing in all fields, but most dramatically in technology and business management, with the figure rising between 1977 and 1987 from 6 to 19 per cent in technology, and from 23 to 46 per cent in business management. In France, in the first university cycles the women are in the majority everywhere except in science (36.3 per cent): in the engineers schools they make up only 18 per cent of the students, but in the big commerce and management schools they have reached the level of 43.4 per cent. In Italy, while the women are not yet in the majority among university graduates, their proportion is increasing in all fields, notably in medicine (up from 29 to 38 per cent between 1981 and 1988), but also in law and management. Women still make up only 17 per cent of the engineers, but they are very much in the majority in the sciences (56 per cent in 1988, 62 per cent in 1984). In Japan, the increase in female participation took place above all before 1975 in the junior colleges and since 1977

Table I-25. **Proportion of women in universities by field of study**[*]
Percentages

		Ed	H	SS	HS	B	L	BL	S	T	ST	MD
Germany[a]	1985	58.8	54.5					30.0	29.1	7.8		34.5
	1988	71.6	65.2					39.5	32.5	10.8		44.8
Austria[b]	1977	64.4	72.9	46.6		18.0	18.9		8.7	7.7		28.5
	1987	75.7	75.7	53.8		31.7	29.9		9.7	8.7		42.1
Belgium[c]	1989	73.8	68.1	50.4		39.9	55.8		51.3	16.3		54.4
Canada[d]	1978	65.0	58.0	–	57.0				2.5	7.0		57.0
	1988	70.0	63.0	–	67.0				2.0	13.0		67.0
Denmark[e]	1980									6.0		
	1987								50.0	23.0		
Spain[f]	1982				(100)				(100)	8.1	(100)	(100)
	1986				(140)				(137)	12.7	(160)	(106)
United States[g]	1977	72.2	59.3	44.4	–	23.4	–		33.1	6.1	–	–
	1987	76.2	64.6	51.7	–	46.5	–		39.9	19.3	–	–
France[h]	1988				70.9	47.3	54.7				16.2	46.5
Italy[i]	1981	–	79.1	39.4		26.1	37.3		51.9	14.3		28.6
	1988	–	81.5	45.8		33.4	45.8		55.7	16.9		38.4
Japan[j]	1980	59.9	64.5	34.3		6.1	8.0		17.2	1.2		38.7
	1987	54.3	63.2	32.6		6.0	10.9		19.8	3.1		38.8
Norway[k]	1980		38.3	32.9		10.3	21.3			13.3		32.8
	1988		44.2	47.9		14.9	47.0			26.0		45.2
Netherlands[l]	1975		(17.2)	(32.6)		(1.0)	(16.0)		(8.7)	(1.4)		(19.6)
	1987		(29.6)	(30.3)		(2.6)	(14.9)		(6.8)	(2.4)		(10.0)
Sweden[m]	1981	63.5	44.6	48.4	48.0	–	–	–	43.9	14.7	16.8	50.1
	1989	69.4	60.3	56.0	56.7	–	–	–	46.6	23.1	24.7	50.0
Yugoslavia[n]	1978			51.9					54.6	18.7		65.8
	1988			55.7					60.1	27.8		66.9

[*] For the abbreviations, see Table I-13.
a) BL includes law, economics *and* social sciences (new enrolments).
  Source: M. Tessaring, Figure 16.
b) Ed: language teaching; H: languages; graduates.
c) H: philology of Western languages; S: chemistry only; MD: medicine only (first year students, Flemish Community).
  Source: A. Bonte, Table II-3.
d) SS includes law and economics.
  Source: R. McDowell, Figure 11.
e) T: chemistry (student numbers).
  Source: H. Traberg, Table I-14.
f) ST: graduates from higher technical schools and universities: *per cent;* other categories: *indices* of student numbers, 1982 = 100.
  Source: A. Casanueva, Tables I-14 and I-16.
g) Bachelor degrees.
  Source: E.S. Hunt, Table II-6.
h) Student numbers, second cycle university.
  Source: A. Charlot, F. Pottier, Table I-7.
i) Graduates.
  Source: F. Bussi, Table I-10.
j) Student numbers.
  Source: M. Kaneko, Table A-11.
k) Student numbers.
  Source: P. Aamodt, Table I-9.
l) Graduates, *percentage breakdown* by field of study.
  Source: I. Coppens, Table I-7.
m) Graduates, universities and university-type institutions (excluding Doctorates). H : include Fine Arts; SS : include Law and Economics
  Source: Additional data from Dan Andersson, NBUC.
n) University graduates only.

Table I–26. **Denmark**

Percentage of women in higher technical education

	1980	1987
Short-cycle	9	15
Medium-cycle	3	13
Long-cycle	6	23

Source: H. Traberg, Table I–11.

in the *senshu gakko*; they are concentrated in the traditional disciplines, though there is a certain progression elsewhere, for example in law and science.[53]

In Norway, it was during the 1980s that the proportion of women in higher education passed the 50 per cent mark. They have today reached this level in university disciplines such as medicine and law and there is also a rapid increase in technology where women now make up 25 per cent of the students. In the Netherlands, the overall proportion has not yet reached 50 per cent, notably in the universities. There is however a certain time lag. The proportion of women among engineering graduates remains low and it is in the field of management, above all in the HBO sector, that the advance is greatest. In the United Kingdom, women are not yet in the majority among new university and polytechnic enrolments, but they do make up 43 per cent of the entries in management, 16 per cent in physics and 9 per cent in mechanical engineering.[54] In Yugoslavia, women make up over 60 per cent of the first-year students in science and mathematics, 64 per cent in medicine and 30 per cent in technology. Certain commentators point out the dynamic of female participation, but at the same time stress that there is no reciprocity, *i.e.* the men are not turning more towards the fields "traditionally reserved" to women. It should be noted however that in present circumstances these are the fields of studies for which subsequent employment is most problematical, so that there is scarcely any incentive to do so. There is reason to ask what forces are at the origin of this dynamic. There is a tendency to examine the question above all from the scholastic (and egalitarian) standpoint, considering for example that women "should" make up between 40 and 60 per cent of enrolments in all fields. The preceding paragraphs suggest in fact that there is a very strong demand pressure which has led women to "occupy the bastions" of higher education, but this does not exclude a certain economic rationale: given the trend in job opportunities, many women have left the field of education, for example, to head for other sectors, the most important of which is no doubt management and commerce. The author of the Italian report in fact points out that when we examine the trend of new enrolments, the movement is much more marked than when we consider the outflows of graduates. Women thus now have the same economic behaviours as men, which will further contribute to reducing the specificity of their distribution. The fact remains that careers such as teaching did represent for women a privileged path to social promotion and entry to professional life. The reduction of teacher recruitment has caused a substantial reduction in intentions to continue studies in Germany: it has been more difficult for women than for men to redeploy towards private sector jobs.

Table I–27. **Spain**

Trend in the number of female graduates by field of study

Indices

	1982	1986
Total	100	139.7
Humanities and social sciences	100	147.7
Exact and natural sciences	100	136.5
Health	100	106.1
Technology	100	160.1

Source: A. Casanueva, Table XIV.

Notes and References

1. S. Fornäng, Sweden, Volume IV.
2. H. Traberg, Denmark, Volume II.
3. K. Schedler, Austria II, Volume I.
4. M. Kaneko, Fig. 2, Volume III.
5. A. Casanueva, Spain, Volume II.
6. F. Pottier and A. Charlot, Volume III.
7. Whenever the term "Belgium" is used hereafter in this report, by this is meant solely the Flemish Community (comprising about 60 per cent of the population) to which Professor André Bonte's report refers.
8. A. Bonte, Belgium, Flemish Community, see Note 8.
9. R. McDowell, Canada, Volume II.
10. R. Pearson, *op. cit.*, p. 11.
11. P. Aamodt, Norway, Volume III.
12. R. McDowell, Canada, Volume II.
13. M. Tessaring, Germany, Figures 10*a* and 10*b*, Volume I.
14. F. Pottier and A. Charlot, Table 1.
15. M. Tessaring, Germany, Figure 11, Volume I.
16. M. Kaneko, Japan, Table A9, Volume III.
17. H. Traberg, Denmark, Table 7, Volume II.
18. A. Casanueva, Spain, Table XI, Volume II.
19. I. Coppens, Netherlands, Table 1.3, Volume III.
20. M. Tessaring, Germany, Volume I; A. Charlot and F. Pottier, France, Volume III.
21. M. Tessaring, Germany, Volume I.
22. B. Williams, Australia, Table 1, Volume I.
23. L. Lassnigg, Austria I, Volume I.
24. A. Bonte, Belgium, Tables 2.1, 3.1, 3.3, Volume I.
25. R. McDowell, Canada, Tables 2 and 3*a*, Volume II.
26. H. Traberg, Denmark, Volume II.
27. A. Casanueva, Spain, Table XI, Volume II.
28. F. Pottier and A. Charlot, France, Table 1, Volume III.
29. F. Bussi, Italy, Volume III.
30. M. Kaneko, Japan, Table A.12, Volume III.
31. P. Aamodt, Norway, Volume III.
32. I. Coppens, Netherlands, Tables 1.2 and 1.3, Volume III.
33. J. Tarsh, United Kingdom, Table 4, Volume IV.
34. F. Pottier and A. Charlot, "Dix ans d'insertion des diplômés universitaires", in *Formation-emploi No. 25.*
35. F. Pottier and A. Charlot, France, Table 1, Volume III.
36. M. Kaneko, Japan, Volume III.
37. P. Aamodt, Norway, Table 6, Volume III.
38. R. McDowell, Canada, Volume II.
39. B. Williams, Australia, Volume I.
40. L. Lassnigg, Austria I, Volume I.

41. R. Pearson, *op. cit.*
42. I. Coppens, Netherlands.
43. R. Pearson, *op. cit.*, pp. 5 and 39.
44. J. Tarsh, contribution to the OECD project on Access and Disadvantage, 1991.
45. A. Casanueva, Spain, Volume II.
46. A. Moncada, quoted in A. Casanueva.
47. M. Kaneko, Japan, Volume III, Figure 2. F. Pottier and A. Charlot, France, Volume III, Figure 20.
48. R. McDowell, Canada, Volume II.
49. A. Casanueva, Spain, Table XI, Volume II.
50. F. Pottier and A. Charlot, France, Volume III.
51. R. Pearson, *op. cit.*, p. 47.
52. M. Tessaring, Germany, Table 16, Volume I.
53. M. Kaneko, Japan, Table A.11, Volume III.
54. Universities Central Council on Admissions.

Chapter 3

OUTFLOWS FROM HIGHER EDUCATION

In this chapter we intend to identify and present various factors concerned with the output of higher education and which for this reason can constitute a balance sheet or diagnosis of its operation.

This chapter will therefore be brief. In the previous chapters we discussed the main trends, globally and individually. In addition, in Chapter 2 we had to use fairly heterogeneous data sources, sometimes concerning entries to, sometimes outflows from (and even student numbers in) higher education. We shall therefore not be able to compare entries and outflows or to demonstrate the period required (delay in the reactions of demand or institutions, length of studies) for the output of higher education to adapt to changes in employment requirements, possibly giving some examples of the delay in adjustment and others where demand has clearly anticipated the change. We shall thus have to limit ourselves to results.

I. THE PATTERN OF STUDIES

The country reports provide interesting indications on the progress of studies, dropouts, repeats, extension of studies, etc. In order to establish the profile of outflows in each country it would of course have been desirable to have information making it possible to determine the net losses, for example, but this has generally not been possible. On the other hand, these indications do bring out the influence of several factors, including employment prospects.

A. Dropouts

A first observation is that the proportion of dropouts often seems to be very high. However, the figures are often over-estimated in so far as we generally know only the gross exit figures. What is more, in countries like Norway and Sweden, where students may enrol for a short course, interrupt their studies and then take them up again later, it is difficult to make any calculations if we have no time series for real cohorts. It should also be pointed out that the discussion loses part of its significance in such systems; however, the Swedish reform in the admissions regime suggests that there is cause for concern about the overall effectiveness of higher education courses.

Table 28 gives indications of the rates of success through showing dropouts by type of institution for selected countries. It can be seen that in three countries, Germany, Denmark and Canada, the percentage of dropouts is highest in long university studies, the Netherlands being an exception here. The case of Spain is different: it is the higher or medium-level technical schools that have the highest failure rates; as regards other courses, it is the universities that have the highest number of dropouts. However, these dropouts do not necessarily constitute net outflows, and it is estimated that in the Netherlands two-thirds of those who drop out of university training and half of those who drop out of an HBO course take up other studies, while in Denmark most of those who drop out of one course undertake another and complete it (perhaps an over-optimistic assessment). The same is true for France where over half of those leaving first-degree university programmes switch to advanced short technical programmes where they have a good chance of obtaining a diploma. In fact, in France the proportion of students obtaining a degree or diploma three years after entering higher education is very much the same in the case of those enrolling directly in a university or those enrolling in a type of higher education with more selective entrance requirements.

The overall "yield" of higher education is probably fairly low in many countries. In Italy, it is estimated that only 37 per cent of students obtain the university diploma and in Spain a little over half. A Yugoslav study (Novi Sad) gives a figure of 30 per cent. Few countries give any indication of the trend. In Germany (as regards

Table I–28. **Dropout rate[a] in higher education in selected countries by type of institution**

Percentages

		U	C	T
Germany[b]	(1987)	29.3	4.5	10.0
Denmark[c]	(1987)	51.3	39.0	24.1
Spain[d]	(1987)	55.8	88.0	46.0
France[e]	(1986)	44.0	28.0	–
Italy[f]	(1986)	63.0	–	–
Norway[g]	(1988)	47.0	–	–
Netherlands[h]	(1990)	36.0	43.0	–
Sweden[i]	(1985)	34.9	22.7	9.0
Yugoslavia[j]	(1989)	70.0	–	–

a) Percentages: the figures are generally gross outflows (see the country reports).
b) U: University; C: *Fachhoschschulen*; T: *Fachschulen*.
   Source: M. Tessaring, Table I–6.
c) U: LVU; C: MVU; T: KVU.
   Source: H. Traberg, Table I–6.
d) U: University faculties; C: Approximate average, higher technical colleges and university schools; T: Non-technical university schools.
   Source: A. Casanueva, Table XII.
e) U: Universities, 1st degree level; C: Higher technical training and university institutes of technology.
   Source: A. Charlot and F. Pottier, Table I–3.
f) Source: F. Bussi.
g) Estimate based on actual cohort.
   Source: P. Aamodt, p. 12.
h) U: Universities; C: HBO. Estimates on the basis of actual cohorts.
   Source: I. Coppens, p. 22.
i) UCT: See Table I–5, excluding courses taken in isolation. Dropouts: 1st-year students in 1979 who had not graduated and were no longer enrolled in the same programme in 1985.
j) Novi Sad students.
   Source: H. Hanic.

universities), Italy and Spain (for the whole of the system), the tendency is for the proportion of dropouts to increase. In Germany the ratio of the number of dropouts to that of new entrants (fictive cohorts) increased from 10 to 30 per cent between 1980 and 1987 and the proportion of dropouts to total outflows from 15.6 to 35.3 per cent.[1] In Spain (estimate based on actual cohorts) the proportion of dropouts increased from 55.1 to 57.4 per cent between 1984 and 1987. This trend is not due to university faculties and university technical courses, but to the higher technical colleges, whose yield fell from 30 to 23 per cent and non-technical university courses where it fell from 66 to 54 per cent.[2] In Italy, the annual average rate (number of dropouts as a percentage of total enrolments for the previous year) increased from 15.4 to 17.6 per cent, which is a significant increase in the overall rate (12.15 per cent). Several countries point out that dropouts occur mainly in the early years. In this connection the author of the Italian report notes that the first year dropout rate has fallen significantly, from 29 per cent in 1980/81 (and as much as 32 per cent in 1981/82) to 24 per cent in 1986/87.[3] In the United States, the only data available at the moment come from a 1972 longitudinal study on new university entrants. In 1984, 12 years later, only 14.6 per cent had obtained a Bachelor Degree.

If we examine the dropout data by field of study, the first thing we see is the great diversity of situations between countries, but it nevertheless still seems possible to formulate a few general remarks. Table 29 shows data that are not strictly comparable, except as regards ranking.

Three general remarks can be made in fact: the first, rather surprising, is that medicine is the discipline where the losses are least; the second is that the humanities, economics and above all the social sciences, and in the Netherlands law too, are the fields where the dropout rates are the highest; the third is that the ranking of engineering training varies greatly from one country to another. The other national reports give concordant indications. The *Canadian report* cites two studies: in Quebec, the dropout rate in the CEGEP (ISCED 5) ranged from 49 per cent in the applied arts to 25 per cent in biotechnology, while in Ontario, the dropout rate in the Community Colleges (ISCED 5) were higher in applied arts, commerce and technology than in paramedical studies. In *Denmark,* it is pointed out that the dropout rate is particularly high in the humanities, sciences and above all social sciences. In *Spain,* we have already pointed out the very high dropout rate in the higher technical colleges. In *Norway,* the dropout rates are very high in science and mathematics, but above all in the humanities and the social sciences, while 90 per cent of the engineering students successfully complete their studies in the

Table I-29. **Dropout rate, by field of study**

Percentages

	Germany[a]	Austria[b]	Italy[c]	Netherlands[d]	Sweden[e]
Medicine	6	40	16	13	17
Law	7	43	27	35	51
Agriculture	7	50	27	18	32
Science	8	46	27	25	54
Humanities	10	44	31	31	61
Economics	10	54	30	36	43
Social sciences	10	63	37	29	35
Arts	11	–	–	–	39
Technology	12	44	24	32	26

a) Total number of dropouts in 1985 among students obtaining a secondary qualification in 1976 who entered universities or *Fachhochschulen*. M. Tessaring, Table I-7.
b) Estimate: ratio of dropouts to total outflows, expressed as a percentage. L. Lassnigg, p. 11.
c) First-year dropouts. F. Bussi, Table I-4.
d) Proportion of students not having passed the first-year university examinations after two years. I. Coppens, Table I-5.
e) Dropout: see note to Table I-28. Universities and equivalent institutions, courses lasting 3 or more years. D. Andersson.

normal time (which suggests a dropout rate of less than 10 per cent). In *Yugoslavia* on the other hand, it is the engineering schools that have the biggest proportion of dropouts.

Various reasons are put forward in the different countries to explain first of all the level of dropout rates and then the differences according to the type of institution and the field of study. The high level is probably connected with the expansion of higher education, but the reasons are formulated differently according to the country: some put the accent on the lack of preparation of the students entering higher education, others on the level demanded by higher education establishments (the two proportions are not identical). In Austria and Italy it is considered that the dropout rate, notably in first year, is mainly due to free access to the university. A second reason often put forward is also concerned with admission and selection procedures and hence student motivation. The fact is that students are often forced to undertake studies that do not correspond to their first choice, either because of admission mechanisms or because they are eliminated by selection procedures. The author of the Italian report for example makes a correlation between first-year dropout rates and the proportion of graduates who started their studies in another discipline and finds that the highest change of orientation rate is in the social sciences, which appear to be an alternative solution after failure in another discipline. He also correlates these rates with the frequency of part-time work undertaken by students and the proportion of repeats, thus describing a set of behaviours: the comparison of the rankings is striking (Table 30). The highest failure rates in the (long) engineering courses are explained mainly by the high demands of this type of training, or the fact that students often underestimate them. Apparently this reasoning does not apply to medicine.

Table I-30. **Italy**

Proportion of dropouts[a], changes of orientation[b] and students who worked part-time during their studies

	Per cent			Ranking		
	DO	CO	PT	DO	CO	PT
Science	27.0	11.0	18.6	5	4	7
Medicine	16.2	3.9	11.6	8	8	8
Technology	24.1	9.8	35.0	7	5	3
Agriculture	27.4	11.8	27.1	4	3	6
Economy	30.1	6.7	31.3	3	6	4
Social science	37.5	20.6	58.5	1	1	1
Law	26.7	5.4	31.3	6	7	4
Humanities	31.4	9.6	49.4	2	2	2

a) First-year dropouts.
b) Percentage of graduates having started their studies in another faculty.

The dropout rate is also very much connected with the trend in employment prospects. In this connection, the reaction to poor prospects of getting a job can be very different: it could be thought that in this case students may be well advised to remain as long as possible at university and complete their studies: or quite the contrary, since these studies give them no advantage from the standpoint of subsequent employment, to drop them or to refrain from starting. Very detailed analyses would be necessary to explain individual strategies. It seems in fact that while in the 1970s the first tendency was dominant, leading commentators to speak of the "custodian function" of higher education establishments, it is today the second that is very largely dominant. This is perfectly in line with the reduction in the first-year dropout rate in Italy (and the increase in the university dropout rate in Germany) and with the respective rankings of the different disciplines: the highest dropout rates are in courses "of a very general nature, not leading to precise jobs". Taking all these parameters into account (dropouts, changes of course, repeats, working at the same time as studying), the author of the Italian report speaks of the "rationalisation" of behaviours.

B. Duration of studies

The prolongation of the duration of studies is a question that comprises different aspects which it is not always easy to distinguish and analyse. Neither is it easy to determine exactly the reasons for this prolongation or to say whether it is positive or negative from the standpoint of employment. Here we shall simply present some information.

If we ignore the prolongation of studies simply due to the increased participation in higher education or the deliberate extension of the normal duration of studies in a given establishment (for example extension of the study cycle from 2 to 3 years), there are two main dimensions.

  i) *increase in the time necessary to obtain a given diploma:* this notion is only relatively clear because the increase may be explained by a constant increase in the content of the course, the admission of new clienteles whose earlier training is not the same, etc. It is therefore difficult to determine what is "pathological" about this trend. There are two aspects that give rise to concern: the increased cost of studies for the authorities and the age at which graduates enter working life.
  ii) *embarking on another course after obtaining an initial diploma:* this second notion is much more complex, as it is difficult to know whether this second course will be useful in the subsequent career or is simply an escape from the difficulties of access to employment. The student's age and the level of the qualification do not necessarily constitute a criterion if we think, for example, to specialist studies in medicine. What is more, students may be working at the same time as taking this second course, so that they do not necessarily delay their entry into working life.

The extension of the duration of study has long been cause for concern in Germany and the Netherlands. In Germany, there has been a constant increase in this duration: between 1977 and 1986 it increased from 6.1 to 6.9 years in the universities (from 3.7 to 4.5 in the *Fachhochschulen,* but there may be a structural effect here); in the Netherlands, a law of 1982 reduced the theoretical duration of university studies from 5 to 4 years and provided for financial aid for students only if their studies did not last for more than 6 years, but in fact only 4 per cent of students complete their studies in 4 years and 18 per cent in 5 years. Although this phenomenon concerns only the Netherlands, we present the data for this country in Table 31 (here again, the position of medicine is rather surprising). For this cohort, entering higher education in 1983/84, the average duration of studies would probably be 6 years, while it was over 7 years before the new law. In Austria, the average duration of university studies is about 8 years. In the United Kingdom on the other hand, the average length of time to obtain a Bachelor Degree is 3.4 years but is becoming progressively longer.

From the standpoint of employment, age is perhaps a more important parameter: the later the diploma is obtained, the more the professional career is reduced. It is of course necessary to distinguish between cases where students have a job that is purely in order to earn money, for example to finance their studies, and those whose work constitutes a first stage in their career, such as young doctors working in a specialist field or research workers. Table 32 shows data relating to Germany, by field of study.

In Norway (Table 33) there was also an extension of the duration of studies between 1970 and 1987, partly due to a higher starting age for higher education. At this level, it is the engineers and doctors who are most "efficient" in their studies. In Germany it is the doctors, but engineering doctorates are not very common. In both cases attention is drawn to the age of graduates in the humanities and social sciences. In Spain, engineering studies require on average 3 years more than the theoretical duration, but for other disciplines the additional duration is in the order of 4 years. These countries were selected because we have more detailed data for them, but the figures show that to obtain a "normal" diploma (that is without accumulating diplomas in different

Table I–31. **Netherlands**

**Proportion of students having obtained
a university diploma in 4 and 5 years**

As a percentage of new entrants

	In 4 years	In 5 years
Agriculture	0	3
Science	2	20
Technology	2	16
Medicine	17	49
Economy	2	14
Law	4	15
Social science	2	13
Humanities	4	13
Total	4	18

Source: I. Coppens, Table I–5.

specialities) the duration of studies and the average age may appear excessive from the standpoint of entry to the labour market.

There is also an increasing propensity to pursue studies at a higher level. In Austria, for example, the proportion of graduates going on to second-cycle studies increased from 32 per cent in 1975/76 to 42 per cent in 1985/86. In Canada, the proportion of Bachelors continuing their studies the following year increased from 37 per cent in 1982 to 51 per cent in 1986 and of Masters from 27 per cent to 35 per cent over the same period. However, there is also an increasing tendency for graduates from short-cycle technical training to change establishment or course and continue with other studies, for example at the university. This is the case in Canada in certain provinces where there is a system of exemptions for moving from the Community Colleges to the universities and also in the United Kingdom where many holders of the Higher National Certificate or Diploma, HNC or HND, go on to obtain a Bachelor degree. It is also the case in France, where in certain specialities between a third and a half of the graduates from University Institutes of Technology go on to further university studies.

There may be very different motivations for this trend. In certain cases it is a matter of adjusting to employment needs: it is estimated that in Canada many jobs that will be created during the present decade will require at least 5 years of post-secondary studies. In certain cases it is a matter of acquiring a higher social status or a diploma giving access to public service jobs. In other cases it is a matter of obtaining a more complete professional profile, for example adding a qualification in accounting or information technology to a management diploma, but it may also, as noted in Chapter 1, be a safety-first strategy with students first setting themselves more easily obtainable objectives, then being ready to undertake studies at a higher level once the first diploma has been obtained (especially if there are exemptions). These are strategies that can be judged positive from the employment standpoint (all the more so because short-cycle training is often more practical and more vocational)

Table I–32. **Germany**

Average age of graduates, by field of study, 1986

	Degree	Doctorat	Fachhochschule
Humanities	28.4	33.2	25.0
Economy, Social science	27.6	33.8	26.4
Mathematics, Science	27.5	30.9	26.1
Medicine	–	30.4	–
Engineering	27.7	34.5	26.6
Arts	27.8	32.7	27.2

Source: M. Tessaring, Table I–9.

Table I-33. **Norway**

Average age of higher education graduates by field of study

	1970	1987
Humanities	29.4	35.1
Social science	27.9	30.4
Law	27.0	28.8
Science	27.9	28.5
Engineering	25.2	25.2
Medicine	27.2	29.6
Total	26.8	28.3

Source: P. Aamodt.

but they call into question the aims of this type of training and reduce the value of the qualification for those who do not continue their studies (the authors of the French report point out however that on the contrary, the tendency to continue studies can cause a shortage of people qualified at this lower level).

The analysis is somewhat different however when it is a matter of studies that are already long. In Italy, almost 90 per cent of the students continuing their studies after the *"laurea"* were following a specialist course in medicine: there can be no question here of excessive prolongation of studies. In several European countries there is development of post-degree training, Master's or other, on which it would appear that employers and recruitment agencies have fairly diverse opinions. The tendency is perhaps now more towards some restriction, with such strategies being more a matter of a race for diplomas and differentiation where the categories concerned have no particular difficulty in finding a job. On the other hand, there is a tendency among the graduates of less favoured categories to continue their studies to avoid unemployment or underemployment. A study carried out in Germany has shown that this is the case with 10 per cent of the graduates in 1979 and over 20 per cent in 1984.

II. PATTERN OF OUTFLOWS

The pattern of outflows from higher education can be analysed by level of training and category of establishment, or by field of study and vocational orientation. In this section we shall consider the first of these two.

Each country has data concerning the diplomas awarded by the various categories of higher education establishments, but this in itself is not enough to determine the structure of outflows. The statistics on diplomas do not generally enable us to know whether we are dealing with gross or net outflows. What is more, the notion of exit (net or gross) is often fairly vague; agreement is required on the statistical criteria adopted. On top of these technical difficulties however there are those concerning the field covered. For example, higher education in Germany now includes the *Fachhochschulen,* which are taken into account by the author of the German contribution,[4] but not by the KMK (Conference of Ministers of Education) which establishes the forecasts, and neither the one nor the other take into account apprenticeship which, as we have seen, constitutes a terminal secondary training for 12 per cent of holders of the *Abitur.* Lastly, in a set of figures serving as an indicator of the functioning of the system we need to take account of the dropouts, often more numerous than the graduates.

The German case is not an isolated one. The situation is similar in almost all countries because the data collected depend on the nature of the authority producing them. In Australia for example, we have information on the outflows from the "unified" higher education system (unified because teacher training colleges were recently integrated with the universities), but very little on outflows from technical and further education (TAFE) which does not come under a federal authority. Not all forms of TAFE are at post-secondary level or taken by young people emerging from secondary education, but some courses are of a level entirely comparable with that of the universities or colleges. In Italy, the authorities collect data on training designated by the Secretariat as "institutional" (which, it must be admitted, also includes regional vocational training at the higher level), but disregard "post-diploma" courses and private courses, the vigorous growth of which has already noted. In the United Kingdom, the discussion is always very rich when it is a matter of universities, polytechnics and colleges, but "sub-degrees" are generally ignored even though they are often awarded by the last two categories of institution, and despite the fact that they represented 36 per cent of gross graduate outflows in 1986 and the average period of study to obtain these sub-degrees is 3.1 years as compared with only 3.4 years for a degree. In Spain, the universities council collects very detailed data on a vast number of establishments but ignores the important higher-level vocational training.

We could go on giving examples of this nature. If we stress such considerations here, it is not just to complain about the inadequacy of the statistical information – there are ways of getting round this obstacle – the main reason is, as suggested in the first two chapters, that in the majority of Member countries a sharp increase in demand pressure for post-secondary education is to be expected at the same time as increasing needs of the economy for qualified and highly qualified personnel, and we need instruments to measure the capacity of existing institutions to meet these requirements. By their very nature, are systems designed to educate 10 to 15 per cent of the generation suitable for receiving a third or a half? We therefore need information covering the whole of the flows from courses of the post-secondary level.

In fact, the information we would like to have on the structure of outflows are concerned not only with the internal balance, for example the relative weights of university and non-university education; for the policy-makers it is also a matter of knowing what is the weight of post-secondary outflows in total outflows. Assuming we know the net outflows, there are several ways of answering this question. *The actual cohort* method is attractive, but since the duration of studies is sometimes very different we would be dealing with different cohorts, both as regards the demographic size and the rate of access to higher education. This is above all of retrospective interest. Austria and a number of other countries have related the number of graduates to the *size of the generation of the corresponding age,* while several countries have adopted the method of *fictive cohorts,* which takes account of the state of a system at a given date, but carries the risk of underestimating the "yield" of the system, through relating the outflows with the entries of the same year and not those recorded 5 or 6 years earlier. The author of the Canadian report points out that this means relating the number of Master or Doctoral degrees obtained between age 27 and 30 to the number of students leaving secondary education at age 13 or 14 (9th Grade), which is not very meaningful; the author also notes that migratory flows need to be taken into account. Given the highly flexible methods of participation in higher education in Canada, which make it difficult to differentiate between net outflows and gross outflows, a more meaningful method would perhaps be to *relate the number of graduates to the average size of the 30-35 age group,* where all the outflows could be considered as net outflows. Lastly, France calculates *higher education outflows as a proportion of all net outflows,* which is of direct interest to the labour market.

One thing that is worth noting is the fact that, in cases where all of these different methods can be applied in the same country, they may produce quite different results. The Secretariat would naturally have liked to be able to present comparable figures on an aspect as important as this. Notwithstanding, it has drawn attention to this question and highlighted the difficulties involved.

Table 34 presents data taken from the country reports. They concern first of all the *internal structure* of outflows (first line, normal print) and then an effort has been made to determine the place of higher education outflows in the total (second line, in bold). In the case of Denmark, Spain, Italy and Norway it has been possible to complete these data by data on the structure of a fictive cohort. In the case of Yugoslavia it is possible that the figures concern gross outflows only. In the case of France, we have seen that it is a matter of the share of the different types of course in total net outflows, and in that of Austria as compared with the size of the generation of corresponding age. It will be noted that data of this type eliminate the problem of the field covered.

1. Internal structure of outflows

It is not necessary to dwell on the *internal structure* and the respective weights of the different types of higher education: this is a question that has been dealt with in the preceding chapters where we pointed out that non-university training has an importance that varies greatly from one country to another. We see it again here, while bearing in mind that the definition of the field is a determining factor – as mentioned earlier, in Italy, the most rapidly expanding sectors of education are not included. It is nevertheless appropriate to consider the concern expressed in some countries. These outflows correspond in fact to very different lengths of study, qualifications and professional profile and it is to be hoped that the structure of these outflows corresponds more or less to labour market requirements. Thus in Belgium (Flemish Community), for example, there is satisfaction about the increase in non-university long-cycle courses, of a more practical and vocational nature, and notably the increase in the number of "industrial" engineers (ESNU), by 90 per cent in eight years, while the increase in university trained "civil" engineers was only 30 per cent. "We thus train three industrial engineers for one civil engineer, which is appropriate for a country with many small and medium enterprises".

In Spain on the other hand there is concern about the fact that the greatest expansion has been in the university faculties, while the growth of the "university schools" has been only very modest: from the employment standpoint an inverse evolution would probably have been preferable.[5] In Austria, there is concern

Table I-34. **Pattern of outflows from higher education**[*]

		D	U	C	T	TT	DO	GT
Germany[a]	1986	7.9	44.8	26.6	20.7	–	–	–
		1.3	**7.4**	**5.4**	**4.2**	**18.3**	**5.6**	**23.9**
Australia[b]	1987	1.2	4.0	61.3	33.4	–	–	–
Austria[c]	1987	–	64.6	35.4	–	–	–	–
			6.2	**3.7**	–	**9.9**	**7.8**	**17.7**
Belgium[d]	1988	–	27.1	12.0	60.9	–	–	–
			7.7	**4.1**	**17.0**	**28.8**	–	–
Canada[e]	1988	1.3	9.0	57.3	32.4	–	–	–
		1.0	**4.0**	**27.0**	**15.0**	**47.0**	–	–
Denmark[f]	1986	–	26.1	33.6	40.2	–	–	–
		–	**6.7**	**8.6**	**10.4**	**25.7**	–	–
Spain[g]	1987	–	63.0	27.0	–	–	–	–
		–	**9.5**	**6.0**	–	**15.5**	**14.5**	**30.0**
United States[h]	1984	8.7	37.7	10.2	4.3	–	39.1	–
France[i]	1989	–	54.1	8.5	37.4	–	–	–
		–	**14.0**	**2.71**	**10.1**	**26.8**	**11.6**	**38.4**
Italy[j]	1987	11.4	58.9	16.9	12.8	–	–	–
		1.3	**6.7**	**2.9**	**2.2**	**13.1**	**16.0**	**29.0**
Japan[k]	1989	–	46.4	25.2	28.4	–	–	–
		–	**22.2**	**13.2**	**11.4**	**46.8**	–	–
Norway[l]	1988	–	24.3	8.3	67.3	–	–	–
		–	**5.6**	**1.8**	**14.2**	**21.6**	–	–
Netherlands[m]	1986	2.9	45.6	51.6	–	–	–	–
United Kingdom[n]	1986	–	16.0	48.0	36.0	–	–	–
Sweden[o]	1989	5.2	37.0	40.1	17.7	–	–	–
		1.2	**8.9**	**9.7**	**4.3**	**24.1**	–	–
Yugoslavia[p]	1988	–	56.2	43.8	–	–	–	–
		–	**4.5**	**3.3**	–	**7.8**	–	–

[*] First line: internal pattern of outflows;
Second line : in bold, place of higher education outflows in the total; definitions in the notes below.
Important note: Due to differences in methods of calculation, the data are not directly comparable. See the text for comments on the methodology and the notes hereunder for details of the classifications used.
a) D = Doctorate, except where it is a first diploma; U = University and teacher training; C = *Fachhochschule;* T = *Fachschule.*
   Proportion of a generation of corresponding age (1960) (considerable variation in the denominator).
b) D = Ph.D; U = Masters; C = Degree; T = Sub-degree. TAFE excluded.
c) U = University; C = Non-university.
   Proportion of a generation of corresponding age. Dropouts: average of two estimates.
d) U = University; C = Non-university long-cycle; T = Non-university short-cycle (Flemish Community).
   Proportion of a generation of corresponding age.
e) D = Ph.D; U = Masters; C = Degree; T = College diploma.
   Percentage of a fictive cohort (number of grade 9 graduates 1988 = 100).
f) U = Long-cycle studies; C = Medium-cycle; T = Short-cycle.
   Percentage of a fictive cohort.
g) U = Faculties and higher technical schools, C = University schools, technical and non-technical.
   Percentage of a fictive cohort.
h) Data from the *1972 National Longitudinal Study*, for 1984. D = Masters and doctorates; U = Bachelor degree; C = Associate degree; T = Vocational certificates.
   Percentage of an actual cohort (1972 high school leavers).
i) U = Universities and *« grandes écoles »;* C = First cycle university; T = University technology diplomas, higher level technicians, junior teachers, health and social work training.
   Percentage of net outflows from initial education.
j) D = Doctorate; U = University diploma; C = Short-cycle "institutional" courses; T = "Non-institutional" courses (see note to Table I-12).
   Percentage of a fictive cohort, base entries into secondary education.
k) U = Universities; C = Junior colleges; T = *Senshu gakko.*
   Proportion of a generation of corresponding age.
l) U = University higher degree; C = First-cycle university qualification; T = Regional colleges.
   Proportion of a generation of corresponding age.
m) D, U = Universities; T = HBO.
n) U = Universities; C = Polytechnics; T = Colleges.
o) Same classification as in Table I-12 (D = Doctorate).
   Proportion of a generation of corresponding age.
p) Percentage of gross exits.

about the weak position of the non-university sector, which admittedly represents 35 per cent of the outflows from higher education, but these are destined above all for public service careers, so that they are scarcely seen in the private sector. The same concern is seen in Italy, where a law has recently established new short-cycle university training with the aim of forming a counterweight to the long courses that represent 70 per cent of outflows, including the "non-insititutional" sector. In the United Kingdom there is concern about the employment of engineers in technician jobs because of the shortage of technicians.[6] On the other hand, we have seen that Norway is giving new priority to long-cycle courses after having favoured the regional colleges for a long period. Many more examples of this type could be found.

There is probably no such thing as an ideal structure. Consultation with employment circles generally makes it possible to determine the orientations to take. Analyses of the evolution of employment structures and professional structures could also provide useful indications. In Chapter 4 we shall see that a considerable increase in the number of medium and higher level jobs is expected. It should also be added that the extension of access to the post-secondary level will go on increasing the field of employment to which training at this level has to prepare young people. In the Secretariat's opinion – if it is permitted to express one – for these combined reasons we must expect a very rapid increase in the need for qualification at this level.

It should be noted that the number of outflows is also connected with the constraints imposed by admission conditions (and possibly subsequent selection) and to the vagaries of demand. A strong increase in outflows from a non-university or first-cycle university course is not necessarily a good sign. These often tend to reflect an absorption of demand rather than preparation for employment, and we shall see in Part Two that some of these graduates have serious difficulties in finding a job and a career. Conversely, there is reason to question the decline of certain short-cycle courses: in certain cases there has been a shift towards long-cycle courses (as in Belgium), but without there being any replacement by new demand. Similarly, we may want to know why the number of graduates from the *Fachschulen* in Germany is falling while this type of training is growing very strongly elsewhere.

2. The weight of higher education in total outflows

Table 34 is not intended to establish a ranking between Member countries on the basis of the number of graduates in each generation (or in the outflows), or the "yield" of higher education, through comparing the ratio of graduates to dropouts. The differences between the initial education systems are too great for such comparisons to have any meaning, unless we embark on a very detailed study and compare fairly similar countries. Among other things, these differences concern the field open and the length of studies (this latter is not an ideal criterion, but it does suggest differences in the level and nature of the requirements between courses lasting 3 to 4 years and those lasting 5 to 6 years).

We would of course like to have more complete and more homogeneous data in Table 34. It can be seen first of all that long courses occupy a fairly variable place depending on the country. These differences are partly due to the length of university studies, which differs from country to country. Not unexpectedly, in countries of a comparable living standard, the social demand for courses lasting five, six or even more years is less than that for university programmes lasting three or four years, which may well seem more accessible.

The data concerning the total output of higher education are no doubt more significant. The figure generally lies between 10 and 25 per cent, with that for Canada, Japan and the United States however being between 40 and 50 per cent. Furthermore, the figures relating to dropouts give cause for concern, all the more so because they

Table I–35. **France**

Trend in the structure of outflows from the education system

Percentages

Levels[a]	1982	1988	2000
1 + 2	10	14	25
3	10	12	20
4	20	19	30
5	45	42	20
6	15	13	5

a) French classification.
Source: F. Pottier and A. Charlot, Figure 18.

often appear to be understated in this table, because they are frequently "concentrated" in certain university courses and are shown here with respect to a bigger denominator.

We have seen that higher education grew very strongly in most countries during the 1980s. It would be very interesting to be able to draw up a table of this type presenting the trend from 1980 to 1990 for example and the existing forecasts and projections for 1995 and 2000. Here we shall simply present the results of a French study on the trend during the 80s and the effort required to meet the needs of the economy in the year 2000. At that date the flow of graduates from higher education will need to amount to 45 per cent of total outflows (Table 35).

III. THE EXTENT OF "VOCATIONALISATION"

The challenges that higher education had to meet during the 1980s were not only of a quantitative nature. It was also necessary to respond to changes in employment needs and make a contribution to the dynamism of the economy. We have seen that one of the biggest challenges was the reduction in recruitment into the public sector and education and a switch to training preparing young people for jobs in the private sector. This shift took place somewhat earlier in certain countries (such as the United Kingdom) while in others it has not yet been completed and *entries* to the disciplines normally leading to public sector employment are continuing to increase; in others again, entries had slowed but outflows are continuing to increase. On the whole however this transition has meant a considerable effort: in Belgium for example public sector jobs represented two-thirds of the graduate destinations at the beginning of the decade, but make up only one-third today. In Germany, teacher training accounted for 55 per cent of university outflows in 1975, but only 19 per cent in 1987. In this context, several countries have spoken of a "vocationalisation" effort to describe the nature of this transition.

The choice of this term is interesting. All higher education has in principle and in fact a vocational aim. We may ask what set of circumstances has inspired the choice of this term. In this respect we may note that the period of "intellectual investment", to take the term used in the 1981 report (see the Preface above), which led to a considerable expansion of recruitment into research, education and the management of public systems, encouraged certain institutions to concentrate above all on teaching the traditional academic disciplines, leaving for others the responsibility of courses of a more "vocational" nature, more practical, more oriented to private sector employment. The "vocationalisation" thus corresponded to an effort to get away from the academic disciplines and more towards training such as that for engineers, which by their nature are not "disciplinary". Thus we see, alongside the traditional arts and humanities, "applied languages" and "preparation for careers in information and communication".

It is on the basis of this distinction that the Norwegian report questions the extent of this vocationalisation. It opposes the "professionals" to the "generalists" (the latter being as it happens the more specialised category). The report points out that between 1979 and 1988 vocationalisation increased only from 83.4 to 85.5 per cent and in the case of the women it even decreased from 87.6 to 86.5 per cent. It concludes that this is a meagre result for a vocationalisation policy. On the other hand, if we consider the university alone, the advance is more significant, from 55.9 to 59.1 per cent. In fact, it would appear this type of measurement, in Norway as elsewhere, does not reflect the true extent of the change if we consider the trend in the proportion of graduates in the humanities and education on the one hand and economics and management on the other (Table 36). Norway has thus been just as effective as many other countries in redistributing the flows between disciplines within the same institutions.

Another interpretation of this vocationalisation is concerned with the distribution of tasks between the different categories of establishment, notably between the university sector and other forms of higher education responsible for implementing the vocationalisation. This is a fairly simplistic idea, but it is often found in more or less explicit form in commentaries on the evolution of higher education. It is tempting to use this interpretation when we see in the United Kingdom virtually zero growth in the university output between 1982 and 1986 (actually down 1 per cent) as against an increase of 56 per cent for the polytechnics and 119 per cent for the colleges (excluding teacher training).[7] Over the period 1979-89, growth in the universities was 8.7 per cent and in the polytechnics 78.4 per cent.[8]

This interpretation however, though certainly not without foundation in the United Kingdom and many other countries, is probably as inexact as unfair. The figures do not reflect the far-reaching changes in attitudes and ideas that have come about in higher education and notably in the university world. On the other hand, they may give a false idea of the scale of this change. Not only do the figures result to a large extent from admission and selection practices, but they also classify as "vocational" types of training that are vocational only in name, as we shall see in Part Two when we examine the unemployment and underemployment figures. In fact the main

Table I-36. **Norway**

Graduates in the humanities and education and in economics and management as a percentage of the total, 1979 and 1988

	Humanities and education		Economics and management	
	1979	1988	1979	1988
University				
Higher degree	14.4	7.6	9.8	16.8
First degree	54.5	32.4	–	–
Colleges	33.1	22.6	7.8	16.0

Source: P. Aamodt.

problem is that higher education (taken in the broad sense adopted in this report) leads to a much wider range of jobs and careers than before. The wave of intellectual investment had partly concealed the extent of this change. The fact is that in the majority of countries, the 1990s will see an even more rapid rate of change.

IV. CONCLUSIONS

Here we are trying to determine the main conclusions that can be drawn from Part One of this report, from the figures we have analysed and also from the comments found in the country reports. As an initial attempt, these conclusions may be summed up as follows:

  i) The demand for higher education is very buoyant. During the 1980s, this cancelled out the effects of the demographic decline in the majority of countries, and higher education as a whole expanded rapidly. In most countries, between one-third and a half of a generation undertake higher studies and several countries have already passed the 50 per cent mark. This trend can but be reinforced during the 90s, in any event during the first half of the decade and we must expect increased demand pressure and further expansion of higher education.

  ii) Demand closely follows, where it does not anticipate, the trend in possibilities and needs. Contrary to the previous period, when the dominant tendency was to consider participation in higher education as a shelter from employment difficulties, during the past decade we have seen a "rationalisation" of behaviours, in the choice of orientations and the efficacy of studies, at least in the courses that lead to good labour market prospects.

  iii) Higher education has in particular been able to deal pretty well with the substantial reduction in recruitment into teaching and the public service, even if certain difficulties do still exist. The 1980s were marked by a transition from this function of preparing young people for the public service to that of training for private sector jobs, notably through the development of economics, commerce and management and sometimes law. However, the quantitative measurements (relating to the evolution in higher education) do not suffice to measure the extent of the "vocationalisation" process, nor of the new dynamism of higher education.

  iv) Demand can express itself only as a function of the choice of institutions open and the selection and admission practices. Although these vary greatly from one country to another, cases can be found everywhere in which higher education (and sometimes that preceding it) has not been able to meet certain demands and certain aspirations. This is probably often the case with scientific and technological training. Often also, through "passive" or "negative" selection mechanisms, demand is channelled into paths in which sometimes neither the content nor the subsequent opportunities are well defined. The result is very great differences between the growth rates of different types of training, with perhaps an excessive development of the "social sciences", which are likely to grow even more in the years to come.

  v) Despite the "rationalisation" of behaviours and of the dynamism of institutions, the yield of higher education remains very inadequate: this economic return however does not take account of all its social and human significance. Dropouts frequently make up between a quarter and a half of net outflows, if not more. These losses are no doubt linked with the quality of the new entrants and their motivation, but they are just as much connected with the range of institutions and selection practices that were designed for a different system and different purposes.

vi) The question is therefore to know how higher education can cope with a considerable increase in demand pressure in the present institutional framework. In many countries, it will be a matter during the coming decade of accepting in half or more of the new generations into higher education and training the majority of skilled personnel within this system.

In Part Two we shall examine the conditions of insertion to the labour market and the destinations of young graduates, and we shall see to what extent the analysis confirms and reinforces these conclusions and this diagnosis.

Notes and References

1. M. Tessaring, Germany, Table 6, Volume I.
2. A. Casanueva, Spain, Table XII, Volume II.
3. F. Bussi, Italy, Table I/3, Volume III.
4. M. Tessaring, Germany, Table A8, Volume I.
5. A. Casanueva, Spain, Table IX, Volume II.
6. R. Pearson, *op. cit.,* p. 3.
7. J. Tarsh, United Kingdom, Table 6, Volume IV.
8. R. Pearson, *op. cit.,* Table 5.1.

STATISTICAL ANNEX

As stated in Chapter 1, this annex contains unpublished data derived from the OECD Education Data Bank on new entrants (Table A1 for ISCED 5, Table A2 for ISCED 6) and graduates (Table A3 for ISCED 5, Table A4 for ISCED 6, Table A5 for ISCED 7), by level and *by field of study*.

The fields of study used are as follows:

1. Education science and teacher training.
2. Humanities, religion and theology.
3. Fine and applied arts.
4. Law.
5. Social and behavioural science.
6. Commercial and business administration.
7. Mass communication and documentation.
8. Home economics.
9. Service trades.
10. Natural science.
11. Mathematics and computer science.
12. Medical science and health-related.
13. Engineering.
14. Architecture and town planning.
15. Trade, craft and industrial programmes.
16. Transport and communications.
17. Agriculture, forestry and fishery.
18. Other and not specified.

For information a table has been included (Table A6) showing the trend for the size of the age group concerned by higher education (the age group 20-24) from 1980 to 2000 in absolute figures (thousands) and indices (1990 = 100).

Table A–1. **New entrants by field of study, ISCED 5**

	(1)	(2)	(3)	(4)	(5)	(6)	(7)	(8)	(9)	(10)	(11)	(12)	(13)	(14)	(15)	(16)	(17)	(18)
AUS88	18 477	6 799	..	1 074	..	5 585	..	..	..	4 455	..	8 641	2 025	412	..	..	1 634	5 101
OST85	2 691	11	..	..	306	899	..	..	463	..	..	468	681	..	..	..	..	46
OST86	2 737	12	..	..	287	450	..	..	486	..	..	433	700	..	..	..	..	91
OST88	2 340	4	6	..	256	684	..	..	481	..	105	423	809	..	109	..	..	90
BEL87[a]	5 259	..	983	..	2 586	10 542	61	..	1 717	744	2 883	6 193	..	106	3 671	83	619	..
DEN86	3 056	685	266	..	..	258	1	..	89	..	..	2 834	1 112	6	664	358	115	494
DEN88	3 450	705	304	..	65	311	..	..	99	..	..	2 791	1 378	7	902	275	71	586
FIN86[a]	1 027	..	483	..	..	491	46	356	339	..	1 763	6 111	5 618	..	..	31	834	123
FIN88[a]	343	36	520	..	..	390	..	354	621	..	1 472	7 703	3 433	..	..	..	667	23
GER86	8 622	630	646	..	..	4 414	..	4 441	492	..	1 133	44 922	19 218	..	4 840	..	8 317	3 566
GER88	294	549	692	..	..	3 525	..	3 814	606	..	406	40 974	23 882	..	5 354	736	7 641	15 546
GRE84	6 554	195	476	..	486	5 164	218	272	1 419	..	243	4 376	6 920	..	185	543	2 443	..
GRE88	..	96	416	..	251	4 845	238	60	1 596	..	894	3 279	5 409	146	834	..	1 633	..
ITA84	658	..	2 826	..	..	..	..	..	..	..	707	..	..	..	..	..	..	4 862
ITA86	414	..	3 018	..	..	..	..	..	..	..	852	..	..	..	..	..	..	4 896
ITA88	381	..	3 191	..	..	..	..	..	..	..	75	..	..	..	..	..	..	4 640
JPN80[b]	43 561	39 631	9 833	..	18 069	..	..	49 358	..	..	156	6 352	16 899	..	..	404	1 655	5 064
JPN86[b]	39 789	51 984	10 665	..	23 647	..	..	56 098	..	..	169	8 590	18 969	..	..	405	1 817	8 574
JPN88[b]	38 519	56 279	10 954	..	28 607	..	..	57 285	..	..	3 212	9 465	20 017	..	..	329	1 672	9 821
SWE88	6 158	8 867	1 384	2 628	4 698	5 650	705	105	180	1 659	1	9 242	12 077	51	446	320	422	7 529
SWI86	464	570	61	2	562	10 112	27	170	..	3	..	523	2 165	..	3 037	..	482	..
SWI88	1 862	554	1 199	6	1 249	8 854	18	1 152	..	2	283	650	5 573	423	2 094	26	746	..
TUR86	7 348	..	365	348	484	4 925	28	..	712	..	485	1 074	7 063	82	300	37	207	..
TUR88	7 880	..	451	391	..	6 563	31	..	1 197	..	..	1 707	10 206	56	500	9	659	..
YUG86	10 465	..	..	525	5 657	931	..	161	347	..	..	1 717	7 452	..	1 494	1 794	1 246	2 320
YUG88	4 836	..	..	428	2 314	434	..	..	323	..	..	1 387	6 650	..	639	727	1 079	1 305

a) Full-time students only.
b) Column 5 is the total of columns 4, 5, 6.
Column 7 is included in column 2.
Column 13 is the total of columns 13, 14 and 15.

70

Table A–2. **New entrants by field of study, ISCED 6**

	(1)	(2)	(3)	(4)	(5)	(6)	(7)	(8)	(9)	(10)	(11)	(12)	(13)	(14)	(15)	(16)	(17)	(18)
AUS88	11 417	30 949	..	1 950	..	24 672	..	..	..	16 736	..	6 636	7 666	2 369	..	..	1 678	..
OST85	602	3 672	571	1 997	1 804	4 283	439	46	..	1 351	924	2 155	1 904	540	..	..	775	719
OST86	639	3 501	1 633	2 135	1 802	4 353	516	59	..	1 563	988	1 928	2 088	707	..	..	826	647
OST88	525	3 331	1 538	2 344	1 793	4 064	498	53	..	1 678	1 543	1 487	2 517	815	..	..	769	2
BEL87[a]	868	3 250	53	3 499	5 111	5 404	207	..	..	3 124	..	2 501	6 460	786	28	..	717	1 235
DEN86[a]	1 978	3 021	443	856	2 391	3 152	356	..	..	1 217	994	1 664	3 459	326	..	..	522	602
DEN88[a]	2 116	3 586	490	1 006	2 670	3 820	439	..	..	1 610	1 187	1 780	3 699	393	..	..	640	679
FIN86[b]	1 990	2 286	253	471	959	1 567	..	21	..	1 252	804	865	1 971	126	..	..	356	26
FIN88[b]	2 933	2 461	279	482	1 080	1 741	..	14	..	1 321	1 631	725	4 663	128	..	..	578	112
GER86[a]	5 160	22 436	4 825	8 351	43 159	6 450	893	1 219	..	16 014	9 788	7 598	37 332	5 085	..	..	4 917	1 534
GER88[a]	6 445	25 238	4 936	10 890	51 049	7 756	1 144	1 347	..	18 040	13 472	8 318	44 249	5 555	..	..	5 000	1 960
GRE84	..	9 002	174	3 468	4 243	2 751	..	..	..	2 646	2 092	2 193	3 567	290	..	..	1 022	..
GRE88	4 060	5 263	173	1 759	3 492	1 575	..	..	..	2 083	1 644	1 671	2 743	474	..	..	1 056	..
ITA84	9 259	37 231	1 446	42 836	63 417	2 774	..	..	..	17 216	10 380	20 673	21 858	12 766	..	..	7 219	144
ITA86	8 117	35 710	1 448	41 814	65 800	3 493	..	..	..	17 382	8 464	17 077	21 834	13 832	..	..	5 857	76
ITA88	8 816	39 864	1 442	46 998	76 262	6 536	..	..	..	19 911	10 644	13 667	27 459	15 574	..	..	5 994	99
JPN80[c]	27 903	58 065	10 670	..	170 909	..	..	8 597	..	9 514	3 202	21 592	..	80 417	..	359	13 210	15 690
JPN86[c]	28 764	66 692	11 292	..	178 124	..	..	9 764	..	10 268	3 698	22 214	86 120	..	..	378	13 526	19 010
JPN88[c]	28 799	74 947	11 499	..	196 475	..	..	9 695	..	11 224	3 726	22 033	92 545	..	..	406	13 908	19 773
SWE88	3 818	898	706	1 358	799	5 293	237	203	13	1 146	1 805	3 309	4 003	202	..	..	302	1 079
SWI86	226	2 359	225	1 399	3 348	..	1	..	..	1 325	433	1 292	1 135	405	..	..	266	..
SWI88	263	2 268	257	1 472	3 789	..	..	..	..	1 395	489	1 219	1 150	455	..	..	250	..
TUR86	10 117	5 915	1 347	2 476	47 610	6 662	1 214	113	562	4 401	2 239	7 837	12 595	1 494	193	..	4 217	..
TUR88	10 663	6 175	1 686	2 513	69 738	7 398	1 224	200	694	5 688	2 738	7 811	11 143	1 505	276	..	4 191	1 827
YUG86[d]	3 924	9 970	1 262	11 169	19 107	984	..	..	814	8 347	..	6 722	38 331	1 163	..	2 620	13 362	..
YUG88[d]	4 319	7 560	1 156	6 107	11 191	868	..	..	1 019	6 005	..	4 513	23 677	750	921	2 976	7 855	..

a) Including ISCED 7.
b) Full-time students only.
c) See Note b, Table A–1.
d) Column 10 is the total of 10 and 11.

Table A-3. **Graduates by field of study, ISCED 5**

	(1)	(2)	(3)	(4)	(5)	(6)	(7)	(8)	(9)	(10)	(11)	(12)	(13)	(14)	(15)	(16)	(17)	(18)
AUS88	13 827	3 158	..	939	..	2 264	..	..	..	1 553	..	3 423	728	196	..	..	697	..
OST86	1 808	38	..	..	312	439	..	..	351	..	..	350	307	..	..	..	..	96
OST87	2 143	43	6	..	215	462	..	..	407	..	43	369	499	..	31	..	..	99
BEL87	7 274	..	515	..	1 955	8 025	80	..	296	206	2 154	4 428	..	45	2 857	15	170	335
CAN86	1 983	21	3 323	..	6 255	14 874	1 807	5	745	..	4 273	10 590	10 005	1 412	..	284	3 473	466
CAN89	2 015	61	3 625	..	6 841	15 420	1 825	1	688	..	3 110	11 520	7 421	1 294	..	240	2 750	811
DEN86	2 773	762	204	..	..	134	22	..	123	..	..	2 235	421	22	597	371	207	..
DEN88	2 450	160	190	..	..	250	26	..	83	..	..	2 356	892	24	700	369	309	412
FIN86	547	100	282	..	..	473	37	..	62	..	947	5 093	4 466	..	..	50	330	..
FIN88	94	21	299	..	..	175	..	..	101	..	672	5 326	2 778	..	..	..	1 170	24
GER88	264	127	232	..	..	2 113	..	3 701	290	..	413	38 351	12 705	..	3 528	..	6 962	15 722
GRE86	6 167	110	233	..	183	956	47	26	335	..	..	942	1 730	31	80	89	360	..
GRE88	2 534	114	210	..	169	1 325	125	39	294	..	14	1 845	1 506	..	186	385	325	..
IRE86	18	136	519	..	36	1 221	61	..	..	869	125	98	1 515	..	..	..	43	..
IRE88	..	125	607	..	22	1 490	46	..	..	1 149	123	114	1 674	..	..	..	36	..
ITA86	155	..	1 479	..	..	..	..	..	..	..	143	..	..	..	..	..	..	2 527
ITA88	147	..	1 606	..	..	..	..	..	..	..	188	..	..	..	..	..	..	3 642
JPN86[a]	36 734	40 563	8 629	..	15 219	..	..	47 917	..	..	138	7 139	15 162	36	..	314	1 638	9 998
JPN89[a]	35 863	54 573	9 402	..	22 211	..	..	54 766	..	..	160	8 129	17 636	87	..	361	1 610	13 939
NET86	12 041	70	2 551	..	5 836	3 870	1 245	374	239	..	..	5 379	..	..	6 909	512	1 270	894
NET88	10 247	47	3 282	..	4 981	4 710	844	433	303	..	..	5 997	..	..	7 143	440	1 444	969
NZL86	1 476	..	17	..	111	90	..	30	..	..	..	1	..	36	15	..	501	23
NZL89	1 764	58	10	3	111	227	..	21	..	..	..	33	..	87	..	..	347	108
NOR86	603	8 535	363	9	2 420	4 542	254	..	36	84	447	2 733	2 492	30	67	342	35	693
NOR88	552	9 601	244	..	2 732	8 854	277	..	97	54	231	118	681	6	32	260	79	1 675
SWE89	4 530	3	87	65	6	759	222	8	65	11	565	5 398	7 996	..	297	222	329	566
SWI86	262	503	1	..	20	28	18	..	354	155	3	135	4 108	29	105	11	41	..
SWI89	359	562	1	4	7	..	20	..	516	128	..	967	5 212	40	253	6	327	..
TUR86	6 484	..	123	129	298	2 656	..	..	..	..	78	39 559	23 258	..	..	..	683	212
TUR89	784	..	230	192	..	3 842	18	..	..	..	210	42 776	20 901	..	..	..	735	338
UKM86[b]	4 560	1 323	2 994	..	33 674	..	..	2 650	..	8 382	..	..	..	..	..	..	..	..
UKM87[b]	5 072	2 550	3 830	..	36 276	..	..	4 004	..	8 867	..	..	..	..	..	..	..	..
USA86	7 391	109 476	4 857	2 259	3 512	117 358	4 110	9 469	12 096	3 105	11 306	66 559	50 242	1 432	22 231	3 649	6 375	10 620
YUG86[c]	6 006	341	49	1 350	3 875	696	2	74	719	139	..	1 380	4 196	26	235	1 210	543	714
YUG89[c]	4 517	91	126	702	3 358	257	..	..	443	67	..	1 323	3 624	40	224	1 142	655	618

a) See Note b, Table A-1.
b) Column 5 is the total of 4, 5 and 6.
   Column 8 is the total of 7, 8 and 9.
   Column 10 is the total of 10 and 11.
   Columns 14 and 16 are included in 8.
   Column 15 is included in 13.
c) See Note d, Table A-2.

Table A-4. Graduates by field of study, ISCED 6

	(1)	(2)	(3)	(4)	(5)	(6)	(7)	(8)	(9)	(10)	(11)	(12)	(13)	(14)	(15)	(16)	(17)	(18)
AUS88	8 413	13 016	..	1 843	..	8 620	..	..	..	7 747	..	3 746	3 590	1 310	..	..	932	..
OST86	322	1 427	819	1 405	520	1 514	62	6	..	429	370	1 699	694	153	..	..	296	92
OST88	355	1 665	874	1 359	533	1 268	82	17	..	441	532	1 726	801	147	..	..	296	29
BEL87[a]	1 148	4 107	29	2 026	4 074	1 293	12	..	..	3 192	..	2 851	3 208	427	72	..	552	528
CAN86	16 356	10 995	3 678	3 386	19 626	17 766	1 773	935	..	6 722	6 187	8 491	8 403	629	..	..	1 291	12 989
CAN89	17 404	13 309	3 921	3 503	22 270	20 554	1 867	1 084	..	7 506	5 229	9 017	7 781	568	..	..	1 231	9 570
DEN86[a]	2 448	639	171	396	594	945	395	..	..	196	141	1 710	1 428	274	..	..	248	624
DEN88[a]	1 291	1 000	153	515	659	1 587	373	..	..	235	175	1 578	2 152	240	..	..	252	512
FIN86	1 205	1 358	82	481	783	1 084	6	16	..	897	476	898	986	151	..	..	332	25
FIN89	2 715	900	142	430	853	1 451	..	17	..	539	492	842	2 595	64	..	..	1 286	44
GER86	23 170	5 899	3 886	7 305	23 251	7 113	635	803	..	6 917	3 477	12 635	23 529	4 886	..	..	4 331	745
GER88	16 539	7 516	4 342	8 641	31 402	7 054	929	787	..	8 807	4 158	13 281	28 418	4 763	..	..	4 288	886
GRE86	..	3 516	58	2 075	1 694	1 750	..	..	..	1 346	1 159	1 549	1 546	231	..	..	445	..
GRE88	1 657	3 272	75	1 285	2 397	1 504	..	..	..	1 457	1 004	1 754	1 385	311	..	..	481	..
IRE86	1 370	2 589	99	234	576	1 087	44	..	..	1 081	260	769	1 200	93	..	..	214	..
IRE88	1 220	2 704	160	228	170	1 485	71	..	..	1 328	259	698	1 181	60	..	..	207	..
ITA86	2 150	11 494	242	9 352	11 104	1 350	..	..	..	5 632	2 339	15 998	5 901	4 394	..	..	3 016	3
ITA88	2 298	12 114	328	10 988	12 795	1 674	..	..	..	5 712	3 008	14 816	6 052	4 417	..	..	2 765	11
JPN86[b]	26 765	54 674	10 311	149 729	..	..	..	7 786	..	9 435	3 379	20 673	..	74 516	..	316	12 318	8 765
JPN89[b]	26 820	55 917	10 079	145 784	..	..	..	7 681	..	9 900	3 395	21 339	..	77 009	..	330	11 555	10 008
NET86[a]	..	2 704	..	2 784	3 407	474	..	..	..	1 401	229	2 279	2 123	..	..	..	695	1 445
NET88[a]	..	5 889	..	3 962	6 345	541	..	..	..	2 471	425	2 303	4 493	..	..	..	1 233	2 177
NZL86	283	1 720	91	337	148	1 394	..	27	..	1 087	..	437	273	188	..	..	275	62
NZL89	250	2 065	119	389	195	1 744	..	29	..	1 172	..	429	450	239	..	..	383	79
NOR86	6 613	408	150	..	350	956	110	1	..	277	237	20	263	..	..	64	13	640
NOR88	7 627	310	268	1	321	1 441	122	..	..	264	202	2 663	1 332	..	2	43	3	975
SPA86	23 127	12 185	1 099	8 947	8 088	3 579	1 858	..	1 391	5 555	1 203	14 428	6 569	1 978	..	..	1 107	4 880
SPA88	23 796	13 542	1 547	12 472	4 024	11 169	2 508	..	1 954	6 041	2 245	14 040	7 497	2 100	..	..	1 515	8 072
SWE89	1 678	264	523	719	429	2 808	198	62	..	530	667	2 917	2 367	88	..	..	215	1 925
SWI86	122	819	69	732	1 435	1 339	..	..	..	683	145	1 233	555	165	..	..	245	..
SWI89	219	1 136	80	1 482	684	5 604	672	116	237	916	311	1 048	667	280	..	..	236	..
TUR86	6 912	3 291	657	1 603	8 077	5 712	660	145	354	1 278	679	4 316	6 870	865	131	..	1 989	1 764
TUR89	13 390	4 245	776	2 285	9 274	..	..	..	..	2 964	1 427	6 232	8 962	1 441	125	..	3 286	7 989
UKM86[c]	7 865	20 713	9 275	..	33 120	..	..	5 026	..	26 969	..	7 416	17 337	..	..	..	1 365	8 072
UKM87[c]	8 959	20 501	9 052	..	36 594	..	..	5 153	..	27 733	..	7 526	18 133	..	..	..	1 385	8 074
USA86	87 221	76 625	36 949	1 197	137 284	238 160	43 248	15 288	12 704	60 255	58 195	64 535	96 209	9 119	..	13 878	21 256	15 700
YUG86[d]	1 395	3 290	557	3 795	5 997	490	44	..	113	1 187	..	3 662	4 907	578	..	378	1 834	..
YUG89[d]	1 184	3 156	775	2 723	4 489	581	..	..	132	1 651	..	3 722	5 856	663	15	385	2 630	79

a) Including ISCED 7.
b) See Note b, Table A-1.
c) See Note b, Table A-3.
d) See Note d, Table A-2.

Table A-5. Graduates by field of study, ISCED 7 total

	(1)	(2)	(3)	(4)	(5)	(6)	(7)	(8)	(9)	(10)	(11)	(12)	(13)	(14)	(15)	(16)	(17)	(18)
AUS88	539	963	..	113	..	945	..	..	..	775	..	267	385	74	..	..	194	..
OST86	19	101	10	33	59	113	..	..	..	90	42	22	167	7	..	..	79	..
OST88	17	105	12	79	60	104	..	..	..	103	48	16	190	6	..	..	106	12
CAN86	3 444	1 848	348	297	2 423	3 571	586	87	..	1 630	617	1 341	1 965	77	..	..	357	1 219
CAN89	3 625	1 919	405	325	2 440	4 105	654	99	..	1 651	721	1 532	1 855	65	..	..	452	1 306
FIN86	16	102	..	22	83	23	..	..	..	159	45	128	104	4	..	..	28	3
FIN89	29	116	..	26	103	23	..	2	..	195	63	592	150	4	..	..	26	3
GER86	313	948	62	647	1 064	..	20	40	..	3 009	278	7 102	1 141	45	..	..	833	28
GER88	331	1 042	67	698	1 150	3	27	44	..	3 619	332	7 666	1 305	69	..	..	934	34
GRE86	..	66	..	65	34	5	..	..	..	185	3	245	33	3	..	..	43	..
GRE88	1	84	..	87	57	4	..	..	..	115	37	675	36	13	..	..	46	..
IRE86	43	169	1	62	109	148	2	..	..	237	25	99	124	11	..	..	43	..
IRE88	63	308	3	72	5	253	5	..	..	231	30	88	173	17	..	..	34	..
ITA86	249	302	..	191	111	..	91	..	..	133	10	12 521	43	25	..	..	225	468
ITA88	59	135	..	225	136	..	26	..	..	91	24	15 344	5	17	..	..	261	247
JPN86[a]	1 481	1 982	602	..	1 813	..	..	141	..	2 063	304	2 399	10 118	..	..	23	2 359	262
JPN89[a]	1 835	2 706	610	..	2 560	..	..	160	..	2 833	440	3 441	12 954	..	..	34	2 893	360
NZL86	138	701	41	83	85	265	71	6	..	527	4	205	332	63	..	..	99	33
NZL89	147	618	30	78	92	249	80	5	..	445	152	159	130	20	..	..	50	25
NOR86	153	480	60	370	434	38	11	..	..	666	152	594	917	76	..	..	254	357
NOR88	178	323	48	403	301	34	9	..	..	390	63	647	817	80	..	..	274	686
SPA86	103	507	47	113	170	68	30	..	..	792	51	806	143	41	..	..	62	..
SPA89	83	334	33	117	85	12	24	..	..	590	45	696	126	35	..	..	71	1 354
SWE89	..	110	..	4	165	..	..	..	..	308	..	397	391	..	..	..	60	..
SWI86	123	358	7	646	252	190	1	..	..	458	56	777	157	4	..	..	100	..
SWI89	24	273	13	155	118	257	25	2	..	546	49	791	146	3	..	..	95	..
TUR86	199	246	72	15	127	476	68	14	..	219	74	891	710	169	..	..	244	..
TUR89	338	370	89	71	240	..	..	..	..	461	162	1 715	818	148	..	..	454	..
UKM86[b]	11 319	2 904	964	..	10 430	..	..	1 989	..	6 408	..	2 356	5 359	..	..	..	719	78
UKM87[b]	12 033	2 980	1 090	..	11 722	..	..	2 476	..	7 060	..	2 566	5 919	..	..	..	619	127
USA86	83 463	25 440	9 138	37 822	25 848	68 106	7 734	2 609	1 095	17 824	12 315	50 648	25 154	3 333	..	16 685	5 493	3 423
YUG86[c]	58	291	70	122	351	40	..	..	..	260	..	736	712	50	..	5	253	74
YUG89[c]	55	306	67	118	390	51	..	..	1	314	..	835	765	62	..	25	279	80

a) See Note b, Table A-1.
b) See Note b, Table A-3.
c) See Note d, Table A-2.

Table A-6. **Population trends in OECD countries**[a]

	20-24 age group (thousands)				20-24 age group (1990 = 100)			
	1980	1985	1990	1995	2000	1980	1985	1990	1995	2000
Australia	1 275	1 342	1 405	1 406	1 307	91	96	100	100	93
Austria	590	658	621	501	431	95	106	100	81	69
Belgium	791	793	711	635	594	111	112	100	89	84
Canada	2 306	2 333	1 949	1 836	1 880	118	120	100	94	96
Denmark	371	397	398	371	318	93	100	100	93	80
Finland	384	378	354	309	331	108	107	100	87	94
France	4 228	4 297	4 249	4 187	3 680	100	101	100	99	87
German Dem. Rep.	1 323	1 418	1 193	947	1 042	111	119	100	79	87
Fed. Rep. of Germany	4 663	5 293	4 990	3 444	2 948	93	106	100	69	59
Greece	697	726	773	713	707	90	94	100	92	91
Iceland	21	22	22	21	20	95	100	100	95	91
Ireland	269	290	330	350	348	82	88	100	106	105
Italy	4 042	4 618	4 727	4 405	3 691	86	98	100	93	78
Japan	7 906	8 190	8 948	9 996	8 484	88	92	100	112	95
Luxembourg	30	30	28	22	21	107	107	100	79	75
Netherlands	1 201	1 271	1 261	1 098	940	95	101	100	87	75
New Zealand	268	281	297	290	253	90	95	100	98	85
Norway	309	313	335	324	275	92	93	100	97	82
Portugal	820	855	851	855	796	96	100	100	100	94
Spain	2 879	3 264	3 278	3 263	3 007	88	100	100	100	92
Sweden	556	587	587	563	496	95	100	100	96	84
Switzerland	465	519	499	415	381	93	104	100	83	76
Turkey	4 031	4 911	5 475	5 883	5 758	74	90	100	107	105
United Kingdom	4 125	4 747	4 595	3 911	3 398	90	103	100	85	74
United States	21 584	21 208	18 761	17 471	17 373	115	113	100	93	93
Yugoslavia	1 886	1 858	1 799	1 814	1 856	105	103	100	101	103

a) The data for 1990 and the projections are based on the medium variant.
Source: United Nations, *The Sex and Age Distribution of Population: The 1991 Revision of the United Nations Global Population Estimates*, New York 1991.

Part Two

ENTRY INTO WORKING LIFE

INTRODUCTION

In Part Two we describe the situation of young graduates from higher education on the labour market. This is not limited to defining the situation of young graduates relative to young people emerging from other levels of training: an effort is made above all to shed light on disparities in the situations of different categories of graduates, according to the level and nature of their studies.

The previous OECD analysis on the "Employment prospects for higher education graduates" concluded that it was necessary to make a certain number of adjustments between supply and demand. In Part One we examined students' reactions to changes in employment structures over the past ten years and the way in which their higher education choices and orientations had changed. It was seen that in most countries shifts in the demand for higher education were a response to changes in employment possibilities, and in particular to the reduction in recruitment for the public sector and education. In some cases this shift in demand was spontaneous, while in others it was strongly encouraged by the authorities or the establishments themselves, but it was no doubt also facilitated by the development of the tertiary sector and of private initiatives. It remains for us now to examine whether the scale of these shifts in demand was adequate or whether other sorts of adjustment were necessary, possibly resulting in deskilling, underemployment and insecure jobs. An examination of the national contributions shows that the flows of young graduates have turned towards new destinations on the labour market, but it remains to be seen whether this shift was a response to the needs of the economy or more in the nature of an absorption phenomenon, young people having used their degree or their level of training to obtain jobs for which they were not really necessary. Various hypotheses may be put forward and it is often difficult to decide between them, because the judgement is not based solely on objective criteria but also on social and cultural norms which may be called into question.

However, the change in destinations, whatever its scale, must not be allowed to obscure other trends that may have appeared during the decade or new ones emerging today. In this connection, we note various preoccupations in the national contributions, whether it is a matter of scientific and technical staff requirements, employment and career prospects for young people emerging from short-cycle higher education or advances in the employment of women. In most countries there is concern about the future for humanities and social science graduates, a group made particularly vulnerable by the reduction of recruitment into education (there is a special project devoted to the situation of these graduates as part of the same Education Committee Activity and we have drawn heavily here on the contributions drafted for this other project). In Part Two therefore we shall endeavour to detect the main trends and salient facts in a more general fashion.

Lastly, without wishing to go beyond the limits of this project, we shall try to bring together the indications in the national reports regarding the evolution of professional structures and the increasing proportion of higher education graduates in the active population. In order to situate this analysis in the broader context we shall try to see what the general pattern of the employment structure is likely to be in the future. In recent decades, higher education policies have tended to oscillate, putting the accent sometimes on the satisfaction of manpower requirements, at others on the response to be made to the social demand for higher education. More or less explicitly, however, care has always been taken to ensure that the gap between supply and demand does not become too great. For the coming decade it can be expected that on the one hand qualified staff will become both qualitatively and quantitatively a resource of even greater strategic importance for OECD countries, and on the other hand that the pressure of demand for higher education from young people emerging from secondary education will considerably increase, as noted in several national reports (see, for example, the Austrian report). It is therefore necessary to start thinking in terms of a situation where the flows of graduates from post-secondary education will no longer occupy a statistically marginal place, as is still the case in certain OECD countries, notably in Europe, and will no longer be oriented towards certain professions or distinct sectors of employment, but will form the majority of recruits in most sectors of activity.

In the introduction to this report we pointed out the reasons why attention has tended to be concentrated on the flows of young graduates rather than on the stocks. The main changes that have taken place in the course of the past decade were outlined, but to measure their scale and significance and to identify new trends and highlight the differences in the situations of different countries, we need a more detailed analysis, centred on entries to working life and based on surveys of graduate insertion and early career paths.

This is a choice that entails a certain number of technical and methodological difficulties. It can be noted first of all that while the analysis of supply and, more generally, the higher education "output" enables us without too much difficulty to maintain an overall view of the flows and the various transformations they go through before appearing on the labour market, it quickly becomes impossible to maintain such a unified view when it comes to taking into account the multiple parameters necessary to a description of their entry to the labour market. Longitudinal studies are always simple in the beginning but rapidly become so complex that it is necessary to envisage the combined use of several approaches to interpret the results.

This difficulty is compounded by the diversity of the sources and survey techniques. There are few countries that have a permanent or regular monitoring system covering all exits from higher education at the same time. Generally we have to use surveys carried out at different times and using different methods. What is more, these surveys are not carried out for the same purpose. The users of information on entry to working life are the authorities, higher education establishments, information and orientation services, students, and possibly analysts and researchers. Their interests, needs and criteria are not the same. It is therefore difficult to arrive at a satisfactory synthesis at the national level. Furthermore, depending on the type of survey generally used in a country, the style of this synthesis is different, as is the type of information collected. This is clearly seen in the national contributions.

In fact there is a great diversity in the approaches adopted in Member countries to the analysis of graduate employment. Certain approaches derive from work on the economics of education and put the accent on costs and benefits; others are more concerned with educational planning and future manpower requirements. Some are interested above all in the situation of graduates on the labour market, while others again put the accent on the employment sector and type of job obtained. It goes without saying that these different approaches correspond to implicit assumptions that do not always coincide.

As might be expected, the main difference between the approaches adopted in the national contributions is between those that concentrate on the usual variables of labour market studies and those that are more interested in the structural changes that underlie the variations in employment conditions. This is why the Secretariat, in its orientation note trying to define an analytical framework acceptable by all, had proposed that data relating to graduates' destinations should be kept separate from those relating to the transition conditions (in this study the term "destination" refers to the sector of employment, the nature of the job, the functions exercised, etc.; in certain countries, and notably in the United Kingdom, in the "*first destinations surveys*" the term also covers certain data relating to the status of young graduates on the labour market).

The authors of the national contributions on the whole fully appreciated the value and complementarity of the two approaches, but data on the modalities of entry to working life are much more frequently available than those concerning destinations. Wherever possible the latter have been completed by data concerning stocks. In practice, the authors, just as they had enriched the part of their report concerning trends in the demand for education by adding data on new enrolments and progress in studies, completed their analysis of the entry of young graduates to working life by adding data on overall employment, the proportion of graduates in the active population and in the different branches of economic activity. These stock data were no doubt added in many cases to make up for the lack of statistical sources concerning flows and their destinations, but this enlargement of the problem makes it possible to better situate the analysis in its context and the enrichment is sufficiently great for us to adopt the same approach in this synthesis report.

Part Two therefore contains three chapters:
i) Chapter 4 describes the general evolution of employment and unemployment over the past ten years, thus defining the employment context for higher education graduates;
ii) Chapter 5 analyses the conditions of entry to working life for different categories of graduates, based on a fairly large set of parameters;
iii) Chapter 6 discusses the destinations, *i.e.* the sector of employment and the nature of the jobs occupied by young graduates.

Chapter 4

THE GENERAL TREND

I. THE GENERAL LABOUR MARKET SITUATION

At the beginning of this report it was noted that in the late 1970s and early 1980s the employment situation was bad and there was considerable concern about graduate unemployment, whereas now the climate is fairly optimistic and the accent is on the strong demand for very highly qualified people, even if this optimism has been somewhat cooled by the recent slowdown in economic growth. The aim of this chapter is to give a very brief outline of the evolution of the general labour market situation over the past ten years in order to define the context for the discussion.

Table 1 shows the trend in unemployment rates in the OECD countries during the 1980s. It will be noted that unemployment increased in the early years to reach a maximum about the middle of the decade, but did not begin to decline until towards the end of the 1980s and even then this reduction was generally not great enough for unemployment rates to return to their initial level. Only Australia, the United States, Finland, Portugal and Sweden succeeded in bringing unemployment back below the 1980 level. In Canada the present level is close to that of 1980. In Japan the unemployment rate remained very low throughout the decade. Unemployment was generally higher in Europe than in the other countries, and above all it started to diminish later and at a slower rate. In fact it is still growing in Denmark, Italy and Norway.

Table II–1. **Unemployment rates, 1980-1989**
Percentages

	1980	1981	1982	1983	1984	1985	1986	1987	1988	1989
Canada	7.4	7.5	10.9	11.8	11.2	10.4	9.5	8.8	7.7	7.5
United States	7.0	7.5	9.5	9.4	7.4	7.1	6.9	6.1	5.4	5.2
Japan	2.0	2.2	2.4	2.6	2.7	2.6	2.8	2.8	2.5	2.3
Australia	5.9	5.6	6.7	9.8	8.5	7.8	7.9	7.8	6.8	5.7
New Zealand	2.2	3.6	3.5	5.6	5.7	4.1	4.0	4.1	5.6	7.1
Austria	1.9	2.5	3.5	4.1	3.8	3.6	3.1	3.8	3.6	3.1
Belgium	7.9	10.2	11.9	13.2	13.2	12.3	11.6	11.3	10.3	9.3
Luxemburg	0.7	1.0	1.2	1.6	1.7	1.6	1.4	1.6	1.4	1.2
Denmark	6.9	10.3	11.0	11.4	8.5	7.3	5.5	6.9	7.2	
Finland	4.6	4.8	5.3	5.4	5.2	5.0	5.3	5.0	4.5	3.4
France	6.3	7.4	8.1	8.3	9.7	10.2	10.4	10.5	10.0	9.4
Germany	3.2	4.5	6.4	7.9	7.9	8.0	7.6	7.6	7.6	6.8
Greece	2.8	4.0	5.8	7.9	8.1	7.8	7.4	7.4	7.7	
Ireland	7.3	9.9	11.4	14.0	15.6	17.4	17.4	17.6	16.7	
Italy	7.5	7.8	8.4	9.3	9.9	10.1	10.9	11.8	11.8	
Netherlands	6.0	8.5	11.3	11.8	11.9	10.9	10.3	9.6	9.2	8.3
Norway	1.6	2.0	2.6	3.4	3.1	2.6	2.0	2.1	3.2	4.9
Portugal	7.7	7.4	7.3	7.8	8.4	8.5	8.5	7.0	5.7	5.0
Spain	11.1	13.7	15.6	17.0	19.7	21.1	20.8	20.1	19.1	16.9
Sweden	2.0	2.5	3.1	3.5	3.1	2.8	2.7	1.9	1.6	1.3
Switzerland	0.2	0.2	0.4	0.9	1.1	0.9	0.8	0.7	0.6	0.5
United Kingdom	5.6	9.0	10.4	11.2	11.1	11.5	11.6	10.4	8.3	6.1

Source: OECD Databank.

Table II-2. **Unemployment rates, by sex, 1980-1989**

	Men										Women									
	1980	1981	1982	1983	1984	1985	1986	1987	1988	1989	1980	1981	1982	1983	1984	1985	1986	1987	1988	1989
Canada	6.8	6.9	10.9	11.9	11.0	10.2	9.3	8.4	7.3	7.2	8.4	8.3	10.8	11.6	11.3	10.6	9.8	9.3	8.3	7.9
United States	6.7	7.2	9.6	9.6	7.2	6.8	6.7	6.0	5.3	5.0	7.4	7.9	9.4	9.2	7.6	7.4	7.0	6.2	5.5	5.3
Japan	2.0	2.3	2.4	2.7	2.7	2.6	2.7	2.8	2.5	2.2	2.0	2.1	2.3	2.6	2.8	2.7	2.8	2.8	2.6	2.3
Australia	4.9	4.6	6.2	9.8	8.5	7.7	7.6	7.4	6.4	5.3	7.4	7.1	7.5	9.9	8.3	8.0	8.4	8.3	7.3	6.2
N.-Zealand	2.0	3.2	3.0	5.2	5.3	3.8	3.5	4.0	5.6	7.1	2.7	4.3	4.6	6.4	6.4	4.8	4.6	4.2	5.6	7.2
Austria	1.3	1.9	2.8	3.5	3.9	3.6	3.2	3.6	3.2	2.8	2.8	3.6	4.8	5.1	3.6	3.5	3.1	4.1	4.0	3.6
Belgium	4.6	7.0	8.7	10.0	9.9	8.8	8.1	7.8	7.0	6.1	13.5	15.4	17.0	18.3	18.3	17.7	16.9	16.4	15.0	13.7
Luxembourg	0.5	0.8	1.0	1.3	1.3	1.3	1.1	1.3	1.3	1.1	1.2	1.3	1.7	2.1	2.4	2.2	1.9	2.0	1.6	1.6
Denmark		10.0	10.7	10.7	7.6	5.9	4.1	5.9	6.3		10.7	11.2	12.3	9.6	8.9	7.1	8.1	8.2		
Finland	4.6	5.0	5.4	5.6	5.3	5.3	6.0	5.7	5.0	3.5	4.6	4.6	5.2	5.2	5.0	4.6	4.6	4.3	4.0	3.4
France	4.2	5.3	6.0	6.3	7.7	8.3	8.4	8.3	7.7	7.0	9.4	10.6	11.2	11.2	12.6	12.9	13.1	13.6	13.1	12.6
Germany	2.5	3.7	5.8	7.2	7.3	7.3	6.7	6.8	6.7	5.9	4.4	5.7	7.4	9.0	8.9	9.1	9.0	8.8	8.9	8.2
Greece	2.2	3.3	4.7	5.8	6.0	5.7	5.1	5.1	4.8		4.1	5.7	8.0	11.8	12.2	11.7	11.6	11.3	12.5	
Ireland	7.4	10.3	12.1	15.3	17.0	18.9	19.0	19.4	18.7		7.0	8.9	9.7	11.1	12.2	13.8	13.7	13.5	12.3	
Italy	4.7	5.0	5.6	6.2	6.5	6.7	7.3	8.0	8.0		13.0	13.4	13.9	15.3	16.3	16.6	17.6	18.5	18.6	
Netherlands	5.6	8.2	11.4	10.6	10.9	9.7	9.0	7.2	7.1	6.3	7.1	9.0	11.3	14.0	14.0	13.1	12.8	13.6	12.5	11.5
Norway	1.2	1.6	2.3	3.2	3.1	2.1	1.5	1.7	3.0	5.1	2.3	2.7	3.0	3.8	3.2	3.1	2.6	2.6	3.4	4.7
Portugal	4.0	4.0	4.0	4.7	5.8	6.3	6.4	5.2	4.0	3.3	13.3	12.3	12.1	12.2	12.2	11.7	11.4	9.4	8.0	7.2
Spain	10.4	12.9	14.4	15.6	18.4	19.5	18.9	16.7	14.8	12.6	12.7	15.8	18.5	20.3	22.8	24.8	25.0	27.2	27.4	25.2
Sweden	1.7	2.3	2.9	3.4	3.0	2.8	2.7	1.9	1.6	1.3	2.3	2.6	3.4	3.5	3.3	2.9	2.7	1.9	1.6	1.4
Switzerland	0.1	0.2	0.4	0.9	0.8	0.7	0.6	0.6	0.5	0.4	0.3	0.3	0.5	0.9	1.4	1.1	0.9	0.9	0.8	0.6
United Kingdom	6.6	10.9	12.6	13.3	13.0	13.3	13.5	12.4	10.0	7.7	4.2	6.0	7.0	8.0	8.3	8.7	8.9	7.6	6.0	4.0

Source: OECD Databank.

Table II–3. **Unemployment rates, by age group and by sex**

	1980	1981	1982	1983	1984	1985	1986	1987	1988	1989
Canada										
Men 20-24	..	..	..	..	..	..	..	..	..	..
Men 25-29	6.9	7.2	12.1	13.7	12.8	11.5	11.1	9.4	8.3	8.3
Women 20-24	..	..	..	..	..	..	..	..	..	..
Women 25-29	8.1	9.0	10.9	11.5	12.3	11.5	10.4	9.9	9.2	8.9
Finland										
Men 20-24	4.9	6.3	7.5	8.2	7.5	7.5	8.8	8.3	7.2	5.3
Men 25-29	5.7	6.3	6.3	5.9	4.9	5.5	5.6	5.6	4.5	3.4
Women 20-24	7.0	7.0	7.7	8.3	8.3	6.8	6.8	7.0	6.5	5.7
Women 25-29	5.1	4.3	5.0	5.1	4.5	5.1	4.5	4.5	3.9	3.3
France										
Men 20-24	7.8	9.8	12.0	13.5	18.1	20.7	19.4	18.0	17.5	15.0
Men 25-29	3.9	5.5	6.3	6.3	8.2	9.4	9.8	9.8	9.3	8.4
Women 20-24	17.1	18.8	20.5	21.9	26.5	27.3	25.4	27.1	26.0	24.1
Women 25-29	8.4	9.5	11.0	11.1	12.2	13.5	14.1	15.5	14.6	16.0
Germany										
Men 20-24	3.0	5.6	9.2	10.4	9.8	8.8	7.8	7.8	..	..
Men 25-29	2.4	4.4	7.2	8.3	8.0	7.4	6.7	6.9	..	..
Women 20-24	5.6	8.2	10.7	12.8	12.2	11.7	10.5	9.3	..	..
Women 25-29	5.9	8.4	10.7	12.8	12.9	12.9	12.0	11.3	..	..
Italy										
Men 20.24	18.0	18.5	20.0	21.3	22.5	23.9	24.5	25.9	25.7	25.1
Men 25-29	6.2	5.9	7.0	8.3	8.7	9.0	10.3	11.9	12.5	12.8
Women 20-24	24.8	25.7	27.5	30.1	33.8	35.1	37.0	38.1	37.5	36.9
Women 25-29	13.3	14.0	14.6	17.0	18.3	19.0	21.3	23.6	24.4	24.6
Japan										
Men 20-24	3.6	3.6	3.6	3.8	3.8	3.8	4.4	4.3	4.2	3.8
Men 25-29	2.0	2.4	2.5	2.6	2.3	2.4	2.4	2.6	2.4	2.1
Women 20-24	3.3	3.7	4.4	4.3	4.9	4.5	4.7	4.3	4.2	3.8
Women 25-29	3.6	3.7	3.3	3.8	4.2	4.8	4.8	4.6	4.4	3.9
Portugal										
Men 20-24	6.7	6.4	6.8	12.3	13.2	14.2	13.1	8.9	7.2	8.5
Men 25-29	3.8	4.4	3.4	4.0	7.0	7.7	7.6	6.6	3.8	4.1
Women 20-24	25.6	22.0	23.2	24.5	26.2	23.2	22.6	17.3	15.5	14.3
Women 25-29	11.5	14.3	14.8	12.3	13.3	14.7	16.0	14.4	9.5	10.4
Spain										
Men 20-24	18.4	22.3	25.9	27.9	32.4	35.3	36.0	31.6	28.7	24.2
Men 25-29	13.1	16.5	17.9	19.3	22.4	25.6	23.4	21.7	19.7	17.1
Women 20-24	23.6	29.8	33.6	38.4	43.6	47.3	46.8	46.8	45.3	41.2
Women 25-29	11.3	15.7	22.0	23.8	25.7	29.6	29.9	31.6	33.9	32.1
Sweden										
Men 20-24	3.5	4.9	6.2	6.7	6.2	6.4	6.3	4.5	3.3	3.0
Men 25-29	1.9	2.9	3.5	4.0	3.7	3.7	3.5	2.6	2.3	2.0
Women 20-24	3.9	4.6	5.8	6.9	7.0	6.3	6.1	4.3	3.5	2.9
Women 25-29	2.7	3.2	3.9	4.0	3.5	2.8	2.9	2.0	2.0	1.7
Switzerland										
Men 20-24	0.29	0.24	0.52	1.27	1.59	1.30	0.94	0.84	0.68	0.47
Men 25-29	0.24	0.21	0.43	1.01	1.33	1.12	0.88	0.84	0.76	0.57
Women 20-24	0.37	0.30	0.59	1.26	1.70	1.58	1.34	1.21	1.00	0.69
Women 24-29	0.34	0.30	0.62	1.27	1.47	1.41	1.30	1.32	1.18	0.97
United States										
Men 20-24	11.5	12.2	15.0	14.6	10.9	10.4	10.1	9.1	8.2	8.1
Men 25-29	7.7	7.7	11.3	11.0	7.6	6.9	6.9	6.0	5.4	5.2
Women 20-24	10.3	11.1	13.0	12.7	10.8	10.6	10.2	9.3	8.4	8.2
Women 25-29	8.0	8.4	9.9	9.7	8.0	7.9	7.7	6.6	6.0	5.9

Source: OECD databank, except for Switzerland (OFIAMT) and Canada (LFS).

Table 2 shows that, except in Finland, Ireland and the United Kingdom, women have been worse affected by unemployment than men. In certain countries, such as Belgium, France, Greece, Italy, the Netherlands, Portugal and Spain, the female unemployment rate is almost twice that of the male. On the other hand, the gap remained very small in Japan and Sweden over the whole period, while it was significantly reduced in New Zealand.

The youth unemployment rate has remained higher than the total unemployment rate everywhere, and the youngest cohorts are always those with the highest rate of all. It would appear that the relative position of young people did not noticeably improve during the period. Using the OECD database we have traced the unemployment trend for the 20-24 and 25-29 age groups, corresponding to the arrival on the labour market of young people from post-secondary education in the nine countries for which these data are available (Table 3). In its broad lines, this trend corresponds to that of overall unemployment, with a maximum towards the middle of the decade. It can be seen that, with respect to 1980, the situation has deteriorated in France, Germany, Italy, Portugal and Spain, while the unemployment rate remains low in Japan. The relative situation of the two age groups remained substantially the same, though the situation of the 25-29 age group deteriorated in Germany and Italy. Except in Sweden, unemployment among women was significantly higher than among men. While there was a relative improvement in Portugal, especially among the youngest age group, unemployment rates reached very high levels in France, Italy and above all Spain.

These data show that, contrary to what the present optimistic climate may lead us to believe, even though it has been tempered by the duration of the current recession, the general labour market situation has not improved, except in a few countries, and on the contrary unemployment is now higher than in 1980. In the present situation it is difficult to forecast the evolution of the employment situation or even to construct scenarios beyond the short-term future. A plausible hypothesis, though perhaps on the optimistic side, taking into account both the demographic trend and the recent trend towards slower growth, is that the trend observed in the late 1980s will be maintained. This constitutes a first major component of the context for the entry of young graduates to the labour market.

II. EMPLOYMENT GROWTH

A. Overall employment growth

What might explain the present climate is the fact that during the past ten years the economic situation has gradually but constantly improved. The growth experienced by the OECD countries has led to a considerable expansion of employment and in certain countries activity rates have reached unprecedented levels. While at the beginning of the 1980s, when the economies of Member countries were still suffering from the effects of the second oil shock, employment remained stable or even fell in certain countries (mainly European countries), there was accelerated growth from 1983/84 until at least 1989.[1] The countries that experienced the greatest growth in employment were Australia, Canada and the United States. Growth was more modest in Europe, with substantial differences between countries. Thus while employment has grown strongly in Portugal, Spain and the United Kingdom during the past three years, it has slowed considerably in Denmark and Norway.

In all countries, female employment has grown more rapidly than male, and even in the early years of the decade female employment grew more, or fell less quickly, than that of men. This trend, already a long-term one, further reduced the gap between male and female participation rates, but the female rate is still below the male.[2] Another trend worth pointing out is the increase in part-time employment which, except in the United States, Canada and the Nordic countries, grew more rapidly than total employment. Part-time work is "traditionally" frequent among women, but during the 1980s the proportion of women in part-time work remained stable, while that of men increased.[3] It is likely that both these trends concern mainly the lower skill levels – the female participation rate increases rapidly with educational level – but they also constitute an element of the social and economic context which reflects, but may also determine, their behaviours.

B. Sectoral contributions to employment growth

It was the service sector that made the biggest contribution to employment growth during the period, this being a continuation of the long-term trend. Similarly, agricultural employment continued to fall, except in Turkey and the Netherlands. A new feature was industrial employment, which was still falling at the beginning of the 1980s, except in Turkey, but began to grow again after 1983. Table 4 shows that the trend appeared first in the non-European countries, in Australia, Canada, the United States and Japan, but also in the Netherlands. Elsewhere in Europe the trend only appeared later and here again there are substantial differences between countries,

Table II–4a. **Civilian labour force by sector of economic activity**
Mean annual growth rates in percentages
Agriculture

	1973-75	1975-79	1979-83	1983-88	1989	1990
Australia	−3.3	0.1	0.8	0.4	−5.1	2.6
Austria	−13.1	−3.1	−1.0	−3.0	−1.1	1.1
Belgium	−2.8	−3.2	−2.3	−1.7	−1.0	−
Canada	−0.8	1.1	0.0	−1.2	−3.4	−0.9
Denmark	0.2	−2.7	0.1	−2.9	−3.3	−
Finland	−5.6	−5.6	−0.6	−4.7	−8.4	−5.0
France	−4.1	−3.0	−3.2	−3.2	−3.2	−3.6
Germany	−4.0	−4.4	−3.6	−2.7	−6.1	−5.1
Greece	−2.0	−2.5	1.0	−1.7	−4.3	−
Iceland	0.0	−1.2	−0.2	0.4	−	−
Ireland	−3.4	−1.8	−3.8	−2.6	−1.8	−
Italy	−3.2	−2.2	−4.1	−4.1	−5.2	−2.6
Japan	−3.2	−1.9	−3.5	−2.2	−2.3	−2.6
Luxembourg	−5.6	−3.7	−5.0	−2.9	−3.1	−
Netherlands	−1.7	−0.6	−1.0	2.8	0.7	−
New Zealand	0.8	1.9	0.4	2.1	−3.8	−
Norway	−8.3	0.3	−2.1	−2.0	−1.5	−2.3
Portugal	−1.9	−1.8	−5.0	−1.6	−6.2	−4.1
Spain	−5.4	−3.7	−3.3	−3.6	−5.7	−7.0
Sweden	−2.8	−1.9	−1.4	−4.5	−5.4	−6.3
Switzerland	−2.0	−1.6	−1.6	−0.9	−1.0	0.5
Turkey	−0.1	−3.1	0.6	1.3	0.3	−
United Kingdom	−3.3	−0.8	−1.6	−1.3	−2.4	0.4
United States	−0.9	0.0	0.2	−1.2	1.6	0.7
North America	−0.9	0.2	0.2	−1.2	0.9	0.7
OECD Europe	−1.8	−2.9	−1.6	−1.2	−2.4	−
Total OECD	−2.0	−2.3	−1.7	−1.4	−2.0	−

Table II–4b. **Civilian labour force by sector of economic activity**
Mean annual growth rates in percentages
Industry

	1973-75	1975-79	1979-83	1983-88	1989	1990
Australia	−2.3	−0.8	−2.0	2.1	5.8	−2.6
Austria	−0.7	0.6	−0.1	0.2	1.6	−
Belgium	−1.9	−2.7	−4.1	−1.5	2.3	−
Canada	0.6	2.5	−2.5	2.9	2.0	−3.4
Denmark	−4.5	0.9	−3.8	1.3	−1.1	−
Finland	1.9	−0.5	0.3	−1.2	2.7	−0.3
France	−1.1	−1.0	−1.9	−2.1	0.5	0.8
Germany	−4.4	−0.4	−1.3	0.1	1.1	2.5
Greece	0.7	2.7	0.5	−0.3	1.5	−
Iceland	2.8	1.9	2.2	1.8	−	−
Ireland	0.3	2.0	−2.5	−1.9	2.0	−
Italy	1.2	−0.2	−0.8	−1.7	0.0	1.3
Japan	−2.2	0.5	1.0	0.6	2.3	1.4
Luxembourg	1.1	−3.1	−2.0	0.0	1.8	−
Netherlands	−2.6	−0.8	−3.0	2.4	2.6	−
New Zealand	2.8	−0.6	−1.0	2.7	−4.9	−
Norway	2.4	−1.0	−1.9	0.9	−6.9	−3.3
Portugal	1.0	1.7	2.0	0.6	2.8	0.9
Spain	1.5	−1.7	−3.7	0.4	3.4	2.8
Sweden	1.9	−2.1	−1.8	0.9	1.4	−0.1
Switzerland	−5.4	−1.7	−1.2	0.8	1.1	0.9
Turkey	3.8	4.7	1.8	3.6	1.6	−
United Kingdom	−1.9	−0.7	−5.4	−1.0	2.2	−0.5
United States	−3.5	4.1	−2.2	1.8	1.1	−1.2
North America	−3.1	4.0	−2.2	1.9	1.1	−1.4
OECD Europe	−1.2	−0.5	−2.0	−0.2	1.4	−
Total OECD	−1.9	1.0	−1.6	0.6	1.5	−

Table II–4c. **Civilian labour force by sector of economic activity**
Mean annual growth rates in percentages
Services

	1973-75	1975-79	1979-83	1983-88	1989	1990
Australia	2.7	2.1	1.9	4.3	5.6	3.2
Austria	2.7	2.2	2.1	2.2	1.9	2.5
Belgium	1.7	2.0	0.6	1.7	1.5	–
Canada	4.4	3.2	2.0	3.0	2.3	2.3
Denmark	0.7	3.1	1.1	3.1	–2.0	–
Finland	3.3	1.4	2.7	2.3	2.7	0.7
France	1.8	2.3	1.4	1.6	2.2	2.0
Germany	0.4	1.5	2.1	1.6	2.1	3.4
Greece	1.8	2.4	3.1	2.9	2.4	–
Iceland	3.2	3.0	4.1	4.7	–	–
Ireland	2.0	2.8	2.1	0.8	–0.8	–
Italy	3.2	2.5	2.5	2.8	1.0	2.1
Japan	1.8	2.4	2.1	1.7	2.4	2.9
Luxembourg	4.0	2.9	2.0	3.6	5.5	–
Netherlands	1.2	2.1	2.5	4.3	2.2	–
New Zealand	3.7	1.9	0.6	2.4	–1.6	–
Norway	3.0	4.5	2.2	2.4	–1.7	–0.1
Portugal	3.7	2.6	6.6	2.0	5.8	5.7
Spain	0.3	0.6	0.4	3.7	5.9	4.0
Sweden	3.3	2.7	1.5	1.2	2.0	1.8
Switzerland	0.1	1.3	3.3	1.9	1.3	1.6
Turkey	5.5	5.2	2.4	3.9	2.2	–
United Kingdom	2.0	1.3	0.2	2.9	4.0	1.6
United States	2.6	3.5	1.8	3.2	2.5	1.2
North America	2.8	3.5	1.8	3.2	2.5	1.3
OECD Europe	1.7	2.0	1.7	2.5	2.4	–
Total OECD	2.2	2.6	1.8	2.7	2.5	–

Source: OECD Databank.

with strong growth in Spain and Portugal but a rapid decline in Norway. Industrial employment is generally more sensitive to the economic situation than service sector employment. It was hit by the two recessions resulting from the oil shocks and more recently, as can be seen from the table, it has been affected by the slowdown in economic growth. But, insofar as no major difficulties are foreseen for the medium term, more vigorous growth can be expected in this sector over the next few years.[4]

The service sector grew strongly throughout the OECD area for the whole of the period. Growth was greatest in North America, Australia and in European countries like the Netherlands, the United Kingdom, Spain, Greece and Turkey. It fell only in Norway and also in New Zealand just over the past two years. A more detailed analysis of service sector employment shows that the greatest growth was in "Banking, insurance, real estate and business services" (Table 5). This strong growth may partly explain the more moderate growth of the industrial sector. In industrial enterprises, many service activities are increasingly tending to be contracted out and are therefore classified as "business services". Many of these activities, such as recruitment, auditing, computer services, require high skill levels. Another branch that significantly increased its share of total employment, though at a slower rate during the second half of the 1980s, is "Community, social and personal services". Lastly, "Wholesale and retail trade and restaurants and hotels" experienced moderate growth (Table 6).

In a study of higher education graduate employment, it is particularly interesting to follow the evolution in public sector employment and its share of total employment, notwithstanding the differences in definitions from one country to another. Table 7 shows that in the United States and Japan, the public sector share of total employment fell throughout the decade. While it was possible to slow its growth in the second half of the 1980s in certain other countries such as Australia, Denmark, the Netherlands, Sweden, Switzerland (where it dropped from 16 per cent in 1980 to 11.2 per cent in 1986) and the United Kingdom, growth continued everywhere else, though at a significantly slower rate: in Norway for example, growth was halted at central government level, but local authority employment took over from it. It turned out to be very difficult for governments to control this

Table II-5. **Change in sectoral shares of total employment**

Percentage points

	1980-1984									1984-1989								
	1	2	3	4	5	6	7	8	9	1	2	3	4	5	6	7	8	9
Canada	-0.3	-3.0	-2.4	-3.2	-3.0	0.6	-2.2	1.2	2.3	-4.4	-2.4	-1.0	-1.1	3.5	0.3	-0.2	2.3	-0.2
United States	-1.8	-1.9	-2.5	0.6	0.4	0.8	-1.3	4.1	0.3	-2.7	-7.6	-1.6	-2.7	0.6	-0.1	0.1	2.7	0.6
Japan	-3.9	-8.6	0.2	2.9	-2.0	0.4	-1.7	3.8	1.4	-3.2	-3.8	-0.6	-4.2	0.6	-0.0	0.3	3.4	0.5
Australia	-1.2	1.6	-2.7	2.7	-4.1	-0.7	0.8	4.0	2.4	-3.2	-0.9	-2.0	-8.6	3.5	0.8	-1.2	3.4	0.0
New Zealand	0.6	-0.3	-1.6	3.0	-0.9	0.2	-1.5	2.6	1.0	-1.7	-2.6	-5.6	-8.0	-0.7	2.8	-3.6	4.8	3.3
Austria	-2.8	-2.7	-0.9	-1.3	-2.7	1.5	0.3	1.2	1.9	-3.3	-5.8	-0.9	-0.2	0.6	0.1	0.1	3.1	1.4
Belgium	-0.2	-0.7	-1.9	0.3	-7.1	1.2	-0.2	3.0	1.9	-2.6	-16.6	-1.9	-2.2	1.0	0.5	-1.6	4.3	0.7
Denmark	-2.9		-2.7					4.3	1.0	-3.8	-0.1	0.8	1.7	-0.8	0.6	6.6	-1.3	
Finland	-2.5		-3.5		0.1	0.2	-1.4	3.0	3.4	-6.2	-11.8	-1.7	0.3	1.2	1.0	-0.6	5.1	2.0
France	-2.8	-2.2	-1.9	3.1	-3.5	0.9	1.5	1.6	2.4	-3.7	-6.4	-2.2	-1.0	-0.4	0.8	-0.2	3.8	1.3
Germany	-2.5		-1.5					1.5		-5.0		-5.2			0.6	-0.0	-31.9	0.9
Greece	-0.7	8.0	-10.8	-0.2	-3.7	1.0	-1.8	-45.0	4.7	-2.5	-3.8	0.3	3.2	-2.9	1.6	-2.6	5.0	3.4
Iceland	-3.8		-1.2	2.6	-0.4	2.0	-1.7	4.9	1.3	-2.5	-1.9	-4.0	-2.1	2.9	-1.2	4.5	1.6	
Ireland	-2.3	-1.2	-2.7	2.9	-3.6	1.1	0.8	5.5	3.4	-2.0	-6.7	0.2	-1.4	-3.8	1.1	-1.6	2.5	
Italy	-4.5	-1.8	-2.8	-1.2	3.0	-1.6	5.8	3.6	-4.6	1.7	-1.4	-2.2	0.7	1.5	5.5	2.4		1.8
Netherlands	0.3	6.4	-2.3	1.6	-4.1	-0.0	1.5	2.3	1.5	-1.0	1.8	-0.6	-4.3	-2.9	-0.3	-0.8	-0.1	1.3
Norway	-3.4	14.1	-3.4	1.7	0.2	-0.1	-0.4	2.9	2.1	-2.3	1.1	-2.4	0.2	-0.9	1.5	-1.8	4.9	0.5
Portugal	-3.4		6.9					113.5		-4.4		-5.8	3.3	-0.6	1.1	-0.8	-39.1	1.4
Spain	-1.0	1.8	-2.1	2.1	-4.1	1.0	-0.4	3.4	4.0	-6.8	-6.0	-0.9	-2.1	3.9	2.0	0.4	5.8	1.8
Sweden	-2.2	-0.1	-2.0	1.8	-2.5	0.1	-0.2	2.7	1.6	-7.0	-6.9	-0.4	-3.0	1.2	1.2	0.2	2.3	0.0
Switzerland	-0.8	-5.2	-1.6	0.2	0.1	0.3	1.3	2.3	1.1	-3.6	-7.7	-3.5	-2.2	6.1	1.9	-0.4	2.9	0.4
Turkey	-0.8	-0.9	1.8	1.3	-1.3	1.5	0.1	0.5	1.3	-1.2	0.2	0.9	1.1	2.1	1.6	0.8	0.7	1.6
United Kingdom	-0.4	-3.4	-4.7	-1.9	-0.6	1.3	-0.9	5.5	2.0	-3.6	-12.2	-2.2	-3.6	1.4	-0.5	-1.1	4.9	0.5

1. Agriculture.
2. Mining and quarrying.
3. Manufacturing.
4. Electricity, gas and water.
5. Construction.
6. Wholesale and retail trade and restaurants and hotels.
7. Transport, communications.
8. Banking, insurance, real estate and business services.
9. Community, social and personal services.

Source: OECD Databank.

Table II-6. Sectoral share of total employment

	1 1980	1 1989	2 1980	2 1989	3 1980	3 1989	4 1980	4 1989	5 1980	5 1989	6 1980	6 1989	7 1980	7 1989	8 1980	8 1989	9 1980	9 1989
Canada	5.4	4.3	1.8	1.4	19.7	17.0	1.2	0.9	5.8	6.1	22.5	23.4	7.3	6.6	9.5	11.2	26.7	28.9
United States	3.6	2.9	1.0	0.6	22.1	18.5	1.2	1.1	6.3	6.5	21.5	22.1	5.7	5.4	8.4	11.3	30.4	31.6
Japan	10.4	7.6	0.2	0.1	24.7	24.2	0.5	0.5	9.9	9.4	22.5	22.8	6.3	6.0	5.7	7.8	19.4	21.0
Australia	6.5	5.3	1.3	1.4	19.7	16.0	2.1	1.7	7.7	7.8	23.7	24.0	7.3	7.1	8.2	11.3	23.4	25.8
New Zealand	10.9	10.3	0.4	0.3	25.2	17.7	1.1	1.1	7.1	6.6	17.1	19.8	8.5	6.7	7.0	9.8	22.7	27.8
Austria	10.5	8.0	0.6	0.4	29.5	27.2	1.3	1.2	8.8	8.2	17.1	18.3	6.3	6.4	5.0	6.2	20.8	24.0
Belgium	3.2	2.8	0.8	0.3	25.2	21.2	0.9	0.9	7.8	6.1	15.9	17.1	7.5	6.9	6.2	8.6	31.2	34.9
Denmark	7.3	5.8	0.1	0.1	0.0	19.5	0.0	0.7	0.0	6.8	14.2	14.5	6.9	7.4	6.6	9.7	34.8	34.4
Finland	13.5	8.9	0.0	0.2	27.0	21.5	0.0	1.2	7.6	8.1	14.2	15.0	7.9	7.3	5.5	7.9	23.8	30.0
France	8.7	6.4	0.6	0.4	25.8	21.3	0.9	1.0	8.6	7.3	16.0	17.2	6.2	6.5	7.5	9.6	25.7	30.2
Germany	5.3	3.7	0.0	0.7	43.7	31.6	0.0	0.9	0.0	6.6		16.3	0.0	5.9	51.0	7.9	0.0	26.5
Greece	30.3	26.6	0.0	0.6	30.2	19.3	0.0	1.0	0.0	6.3	16.4	7.8	6.6	39.5	4.4	14.3	17.7	
Iceland	13.2	10.5	0.0	..	24.5	21.6	0.8	0.8	10.1	9.3	13.4	15.8	7.3	6.5	5.4	7.4	25.3	27.9
Ireland	18.3	15.4	1.0	0.6	21.3	19.2	1.2	1.3	9.0	6.7	16.4	17.9	6.1	5.9	5.7	7.8	20.2	24.9
Italy	14.3	9.8	1.1	1.1	26.8	22.6	0.0	0.0	10.0	8.8	18.7	21.6	5.6	5.6	2.6	4.0	21.0	26.6
Netherlands	4.9	4.7	0.1	0.2	21.5	19.0	0.9	0.8	9.0	6.5	17.4	17.1	6.2	6.3	9.2	10.0	30.9	34.9
Norway	8.5	6.6	0.6	1.1	20.4	15.8	1.0	1.1	7.6	7.3	17.1	18.3	9.2	8.3	5.4	7.6	30.1	33.5
Portugal	27.3	19.0	0.6	0.8	26.0	25.3	0.5	0.9	9.5	8.3	11.8	15.2	4.1	4.2	2.0	3.5	18.2	22.8
Spain	19.3	13.0	0.8	0.6	25.5	22.3	0.7	0.7	9.0	9.3	17.5	20.1	5.8	5.8	3.4	5.2	17.9	22.9
Sweden	5.6	3.6	0.4	0.2	24.2	21.9	0.9	0.8	6.8	6.5	13.7	14.6	7.0	7.0	6.7	8.3	34.8	37.0
Switzerland	6.9	5.6	0.2	0.1	31.7	24.8	0.7	0.6	7.1	9.6	18.5	20.6	5.9	6.1	8.3	10.5	20.6	22.1
Turkey	54.9	50.6	1.3	1.3	11.8	13.1	0.7	0.8	5.1	5.2	9.0	10.2	3.7	3.9	2.2	2.3	11.2	12.6
United Kingdom	2.6	2.1	1.4	0.7	28.3	20.8	1.4	1.1	6.5	6.8	19.3	19.8	6.3	5.8	7.3	11.5	26.8	29.7

1. Agriculture.
2. Mining and quarrying.
3. Manufacturing.
4. Electricity, gas and water.
5. Construction.
6. Wholesale and retail trade and restaurants and hotels.
7. Transport, communications.
8. Banking, insurance, real estate and business services.
9. Community, social and personal services.

Source: OECD Databank.

Table II-7. **Employment in the public sector as a percentage of total employment**

	1975	1976	1977	1978	1979	1980	1981	1982	1983	1984	1985	1986	1987	1988	1989	1975-1984	1980-1984	1984-1989
Australia	4.8	4.7	4.7	4.7	4.4	4.5	4.6	4.7	5.0	4.9	4.8	4.8	4.8	4.3	..	-1.7	2.0	-3.6
Belgium	15.7	16.4	16.7	17.5	18.2	18.9	19.4	19.9	19.9	20.2	20.5	20.8	20.1	20.2	20.0	3.8	1.6	-0.7
Denmark	22.5	22.5	23.1	23.7	25.3	26.3	26.8	27.5	27.5	27.6	27.5	27.6	27.6	27.7	27.6	3.0	1.2	0.1
Finland	14.3	15.2	15.7	16.2	16.6	16.9	17.5	17.8	18.3	18.6	19.2	19.5	20.1	20.6	21.1	3.8	2.4	2.4
France	..	..	20.0	20.3	20.4	20.5	20.7	21.0	21.5	21.7	22.4	22.7	22.8	22.9	23.0	1.1	1.4	0.7
Germany	13.2	13.5	13.6	13.9	14.1	14.1	14.1	14.2	14.2	14.2	14.3	14.4	15.6	15.5	15.4	1.6	0.2	1.9
Italy	13.8	14.0	14.4	14.5	14.6	14.5	14.8	14.9	14.9	15.1	15.2	15.2	15.5	15.6	15.7	1.5	1.1	0.7
Japan	6.5	6.5	6.5	6.6	6.6	6.7	6.7	6.7	6.6	6.6	6.4	6.4	6.4	6.3	..	0.4	-0.4	-0.9
Luxembourg	9.7	9.9	10.2	10.4	10.6	10.8	10.8	11.0	11.1	11.3	11.4	11.4	11.3	11.4	11.4	2.3	1.1	-0.2
Netherlands	13.6	14.1	14.4	14.6	14.7	14.9	15.4	15.9	16.2	16.1	16.0	15.8	15.7	15.4	15.1	1.9	2.1	-1.5
Norway	19.9	20.8	21.3	22.1	22.7	23.2	23.9	24.4	25.1	25.2	25.2	24.8	25.1	25.7	26.9	3.3	2.0	1.7
Portugal	..	..	8.6	9.2	9.6	10.0	10.4	10.9	11.5	11.9	11.1	11.4	..	..	..	5.7	4.4	2.0
Spain	..	..	..	..	..	10.6	11.4	11.7	12.1	12.8	13.5	13.6	13.5	..	..	..	4.8	0.1
Sweden	..	..	..	..	..	30.4	31.2	31.7	32.1	32.7	32.6	32.3	31.7	31.7	31.9	..	1.8	-0.6
United Kingdom	20.8	21.4	21.2	21.2	21.2	21.1	21.8	22.0	22.4	22.0	21.8	21.8	21.6	..	..	0.4	1.1	-0.4
United States	14.8	14.5	14.1	13.8	13.5	13.6	13.5	13.5	13.4	13.0	13.0	13.0	12.9	12.7	..	-2.3	-1.1	-0.7

Source: OECD Databank.

growth during the 1980s but it is nevertheless possible, in view of these figures and taking account of the good employment opportunities in the private sector, that there will be a reduction in public sector employment within the next few years.

III. STRUCTURAL TRENDS

A. The structure of employment

When the employment situation becomes difficult and the extension of education has led to an increase in the number of young graduates, the first question that comes to mind is whether the absorption capacity of the economy will be sufficient to enable all these new graduates to find jobs.[5] It is probably evading the question to point out that graduates still have a privileged position on the labour market or that higher education represents a long-term investment for the economy and society, or that forecasts of manpower requirements have constantly underestimated the need for qualified people and the absorption capacity of the economy. The reason is that the question has an implicit component and in order to find the answer it is necessary to decide what is considered a "satisfactory" job for a graduate and define the notion we have of the correspondence between training and employment. This is not the place to discuss this notion, which will be taken up again later in the report, but it is important to bear in mind that the idea of "satisfactory" jobs for graduates adds a further dimension to the discussion of adjustments between supply and demand. The authors of the national contributions have taken account of this dimension implicitly or explicitly in their discussion of higher education admission policies or of disparities of situation on the labour market.

In order to define the context for the insertion of young graduates into working life it is therefore necessary to give some indication of the trends in employment structures and in particular of the relative weight of "high level jobs" in total employment. For the moment we shall simply say that the relative trend of these higher level jobs, the definition of which may vary from one author and one country to another, gives an adequate idea of the trend of employment opportunities for graduates.

There are of course very different views on the general orientation of employment trends. Certain commentators talk of a tendency towards "deskilling", *i.e.* a constant lowering of the level of qualifications really required in economic activity. This argument has actually lost a good deal of its force, but authors like Levin and Rumberger consider that new technologies are not bringing any perceptible increase in the level of skills required and that the majority of new jobs created are at a low level,[6] while others consider that the rate of increase in skill levels will slow during the 1990s.[7]

Another hypothesis frequently mentioned is that of the "polarisation" of employment: increases in the number of very high and very low-skill jobs, diminution in the number of intermediate level jobs.[8] The author of the Canadian contribution fears that this tendency will affect graduates' employment prospects.

Neither of these two hypotheses can be dismissed, for mechanisms of this type are at work and the trend may become dominant, at least at certain times and in certain sectors. However, the great majority of analysts agree on a global increase in the skill level, and the debate is mainly concentrated on the rate and extent of this trend. Bishop and Carter,[9] for example, consider that the forecasts by the Bureau of Labor Statistics have

Table II–8. **United States**

Contribution of high level jobs to total employment growth

Percentages

	Observed		Forecast 1988-2000		
	1978-89	1986-88	1988-90	BLS	B&C
Managerial	25	29	21	18	35
Professional	22	20	22	20	27
Technical	5	3	10	6	8
Sub-total	52	52	53	44	70

Source: US Bureau of Labor Statistics (BLS) and Bishop and Carter, *op. cit.*

Table II–9. **France**

Managers and professionals as a proportion of total employment

Observed and forecast, 1982-2000

	% total employment 1982	% total employment 2000	% average annual change
Liberal professions	1.1	1.4	2.0
Public service managers	1.1	1.3	1.7
Teachers, scientists	1.6	2.2	2.5
Information, art, entertainment	0.5	0.7	3.0
Private administrative and commercial managers	2.6	4.4	3.9
Engineers	1.7	3.0	1.9
Sub-total	8.6	13.0	–
(in thousands)	1 857	3 226	3.1
Total employment	21 466	24 623	0.8

Source: "Éducation et économie : une autre approche de l'avenir", Haut Comité Éducation-Économie, Paris, 1987.

constantly turned out to be underestimated and that this is the case in particular with the forecasts for the 90s. The authors of the national contributions consider on the whole that this third hypothesis reflects the dominant trend today. A recent study conducted in Germany (western Germany) shows that requirements for highly skilled workers will increase substantially over the next 20 years. This increase will be due to the spread of new technologies, changes in the organisation of work and the expansion of both the service sector and number of service jobs.

In order to shed light on this trend, we present here some figures showing the increasing number of "high level jobs" in the active population and their share in overall employment growth. For this latter parameter we can use United States Bureau of Labor Statistics data relating to "managerial, professional and technical"

Table II–10. **United States**

Managers, executives and professionals as a proportion of total employment

Observed and forecast, 1982-2000

	% total employment 1982	% total employment 2000	% av. annual change
Executives	9.5	10.2	1.8
Managers	2.1	2.2	1.6
Accountants, auditors	0.8	1.0	2.4
Marketing	0.2	0.3	2.0
Professional	12.1	12.9	1.7
Electrical engineers	0.4	0.4	2.8
Computer professionals	0.3	0.4	4.1
Primary teachers	1.4	1.4	1.3
Lawyers	0.5	0.5	2.2
Doctors	0.4	0.5	2.3
Sub-total	21.6	23.1	–
(in thousands)	24 121	30 808	1.8
Total employment	111 623	133 030	1.3

Source: Bureau of Labor Statistics.

Table II-11. **United Kingdom**

High level jobs as a proportion of total employment

Observed and forecast, 1971-1995

	% total employment		% av. annual change		
	1971	1995	1971-81	1981-86	1986-95
Managers	2.4	3.6	2.3	1.4	2.0
Education	3.3	4.5	2.2	0.6	1.4
Health	3.0	5.3	3.2	2.7	1.8
Other professionals	3.5	5.8	2.4	3.2	1.8
Arts, humanities	0.6	1.3	2.3	4.6	3.1
Engineers, scientists	1.9	3.6	2.8	3.0	2.1
Sub-total	14.7	24.1	–	–	–
(in thousands)	3 580	6 099	←	3.9[a]	→
Total employment	24 143	25 677	–0.06	0.24	0.63

a) 1971-95.
Source: Institute of Employment Research, University of Warwick, 1987.

(Table 8). This table shows that the total for these three categories explains over half of employment growth since 1978. The BLS forecasts that for the period to the year 2000 the figure will be about 45 per cent, already a considerable proportion, but Bishop and Carter put it as high as 70 per cent. Even though this grouping does not necessarily correspond to what we might define as "high level jobs", it does already give an idea of the rate of change in professional structures.

The proportion of high level jobs in total employment growth is a useful parameter for our purposes because it puts the accent on the need for renewal in the active population and thus on employment opportunities for young graduates. A simpler parameter, which perhaps makes it easier to "visualise" the trend is the proportion of these jobs in total employment, which can be completed by the annual average percentage variation. Tables 9, 10, 11, 12 and 13 show the rates of growth in the number of such jobs and certain sub-categories in France, the United States, the United Kingdom, Germany and Japan respectively. It will be noted that the share of these categories in total employment, the extent of growth over the longer term and the annual variations are fairly different from one country to another; this depends both on the jobs selected to represent these categories and, as we have seen, the hypotheses adopted for the forecasts. What emerges clearly from these tables on the other hand

Table II-12. **Germany**[a]

Trend in the proportion of high level jobs in total employment

Observed and forecast, 1976-2010

	% total employment			% annual variation	
	1976	1987	2010	1976-1987	1987-2010
Research & development, planning	4.6	4.7	7.0	0.7	2.0
Management, organisation, coordination	4.3	5.5	9.3	2.8	2.6
Applying laws and rules	4.8	4.2	5.3	–0.9	1.4
Caring, teaching, consulting, information	9.0	10.4	15.9	1.8	2.2
Sub-total	22.6	24.8	37.5	–	–
(in thousands)	5 826	6 699	10 886	1.3	2.1
Total employment	25 738	27 035	29 032	0.4	0.3

a) The former territory of the GDR being excluded.
Source: Institut für Arbeits- und Berufsforschung, 1989/1991.

Table II–13. **Japan**

Managers and professionals as a proportion of total employment, 1975-1988

	% total employment				% av. annual change		
	1975	1980	1985	1988	1975-80	1980-85	1985-88
Professionals	7.0	7.9	9.3	10.6	12.8	17.7	14.0
Managers and executives	3.9	3.9	3.6	3.8	0	–7.7	5.5
Sub-total	10.9	11.8	12.9	14.4			
(in thousands)	5 700	6 580	7 490	8 610	15.4	13.8	14.9
Total employment	52 330	55 440	57 840	59 830	5.9	4.3	3.4

Source: Statistical Yearbooks.

is that the average annual variations for higher level jobs are, but for certain exceptions such as lawyers in the United States, much higher than those for total employment. It can be seen that in the United States the number of high level jobs increased 1.4 times as fast as total employment, but taking account of differences in definition, it increased 4 times as fast in Japan and 6 times in the United Kingdom.

It can thus be concluded that the number of jobs of the type normally sought by young graduates is increasing significantly faster than total employment. It is of course necessary to study the balance between supply and demand, *i.e.* compare this trend with the higher education "output". It is also necessary to analyse in greater detail the future of the different employment categories and the proportion of graduates in each. The national contributions show that this is the subject of in-depth study in certain countries. Examination of the tables gives a good idea of the general trend however.

B. The structure of the labour force by educational attainment

Without going into a detailed study of supply and demand, it is nevertheless useful to the description of the employment context for graduates to have information on the breakdown of the labour force by educational attainment. We first present some general information, then the data on the proportion of graduates in different sectors of economic activity and their distribution between sectors.

1. *General trends*

The expansion of education systems over a long period has had the effect of significantly changing the breakdown of the population by educational attainment. This evolution is the subject of a recent OECD study,[10] which concentrated on following the trends in the percentage of the labour force that had not completed upper secondary education (level A) and the percentage of those with a university degree (level E), and shows a significant reduction in the former and a significant increase in the latter. These trends are clearly much more marked if we consider the youngest age groups. It is in Belgium, Canada, Japan, Norway, Spain, Sweden, Switzerland and the United States that the pace of change has been most rapid.

This general improvement in the educational level has been particularly striking in the case of women. In the countries covered by this study, women in the 20-24 age group are often less numerous at level A (the exceptions being Austria, Germany, Sweden, Switzerland and the United Kingdom) and more numerous at level E (except in Japan). As regards level E, it should be noted that women often enrol for short-cycle post-secondary studies, which could explain in particular the exception of Japan, and also that they often terminate their university studies earlier than men, which could explain their relative advantage in the age group considered.

As the groups with the highest level of education or qualification are also those with the highest activity rates,[11] the improvement in the breakdown of the population by educational attainment will be reflected and even amplified in the labour force. The authors of the national contributions stress the pace of this transformation. The relevant data are given in Table 14.

This change in the structure of the labour force has again been more rapid among the women. Table 15 presents data on the increase in the number of graduate working women compared with that of men. it shows that in the countries considered (with the exception of Japan) the number of women graduates in employment

Table II-14. **Proportion of (university) graduates[a] in the labour force**

Percentages

	%	Year	%	Year
Germany[b]	7.0	1976	10.2	1987
Australia	3.0	1970	10.3	1988
Canada	11.1	1981	15.0	1988
Denmark	15.3	1983	17.0	1988
Spain	6.9	1980	11.4	1989
United States[c]	16.2	1980	17.0	1987
France[d]	12.2	1983	14.5	1988
Japan	9.0	1980	13.0	1987
Norway	12.0	1975	22.0	1989
Netherlands	13.2	1979	16.6	1985
Sweden	7.0	1976	12.0	1991
Switzerland	5.7	1980	6.1	1989
Yugoslavia	11.0	1978	13.3	1988

a) See national contributions for definitions of the categories of graduates covered.
b) Universities plus FHS (universities only: 5.9 per cent in 1976; 7.2 per cent in 1989).
c) 1980: population aged 25 and over; 1987: population aged 18 and over. Graduates: first or higher degree.
d) Levels ISCED 5 + 6 (level 6 only: 6.2 % in 1983, 7.3 % in 1988).
Source: Digest of Education Statistics 1991, Tables 10 and 12.

increased much more quickly, but despite the clear progress women are still in the minority among the graduates in employment. There are fairly substantial differences between countries, those with the highest proportion of female graduates in employment being Denmark, Spain and Japan (with 48.7, 45.7 and 45.3 per cent respectively) and those where it is lowest being Austria, Italy and Australia (30, 38.1 and 35 per cent). In Germany in 1987, graduates represented 7.6 per cent of the female labour force and 12 per cent of the male.

A number of conclusions can be drawn from these data. The first is that the output of the initial training systems has become a vital element for the dynamics of employment structures. Not so long ago, graduates were still fairly marginal on the labour market and, taking account of other structural factors, graduate employment could still be considered to be for the most part a separate problem. Today they make up a considerable proportion of the labour force, especially in view of the fact that the figures generally used in the national studies refer to university graduates only. The second conclusion is that the expansion of training systems is historically fairly recent, so that there are still considerable structural differences between age groups, which already gives an idea of the recruitment problem for enterprises. The third is the improvement in the situation of women: through the effects of participation rates, the structure of the female labour force could rapidly become more ''skilled'' than the male.

Table II-15. **Increase in the number of female (university) graduates[a] in employment**

Percentages

	Women	Men	Year
Austria	57.0	26.8	1981-88
Canada	79.0	..	1981-88
Denmark	21.8	18.8	1983-88
Germany	35.4	30.1	1982-89
Japan	28.3	41.2	1980-89
Spain	8.6	12.3	1987-89
Sweden	29.6	16.7	1981-91

a) See Table 14, note a.

2. *Educational attainment by sector*

The 1981 report stressed the importance of the public sector for graduate employment, showing that in the European countries this sector employed between half and two-thirds of the graduates from higher education, the proportion being even higher among those with higher degrees. It also pointed out the importance of the public sector as an employer of female graduates. As regards the stock data, the situation has not changed very much, and for the countries where such data are available, it can be seen that over half the graduates are working in the public sector (Table 16).

While in some countries there has been a slight dilution of the concentration of graduates in the public sector, the proportion of graduates in total employment in this sector has continued to increase. In Germany for example, where the concentration of (university) graduates in the public sector fell from 74 to 68 per cent between 1976 and 1985, the proportion of graduates in public sector employment increased from 21 to 26 per cent over the same period. In Norway, where the concentration scarcely fell at all between 1975 and 1989, the proportion of graduates increased from 26 to 37 per cent. Thus, while the overall growth of public sector employment slowed (see Table 7 in this chapter), it is still very important as an employer of young graduates since its internal structure is evolving and the proportion of graduate staff is increasing.

The recent study by the Secretariat mentioned above gives information on the structure of employment by educational attainment in the different sectors of activity. Agriculture remains the sector where the percentage of people who have not completed secondary education is the highest and the percentage of university graduates the lowest. There is a similar situation with a low proportion of graduates in the industrial sector, and notably in construction. These differences are obviously less marked in the countries where the number of graduates in the labour force is very high, such as the United States, Canada and Japan. However it can be seen that in the countries considered, the proportion of graduates in manufacturing is generally growing faster than in the service sector; the exceptions being Austria, where this proportion is growing fastest in "other services" (which include the public service) and Japan, where it is the financial services that are evolving most rapidly. The service sector is the one where the proportion of graduates is highest, even higher in some countries like the United States, Canada and Japan, than the proportion of people who have not completed secondary education.[12]

The data in the national contributions agree on what certain authors call the "degree of academisation" (Tables 17 to 25). The proportion of graduates in agriculture remains very low, even though it is rapidly increasing in Germany. The proportion also remains low in the secondary sector, but is increasing significantly and, in countries like Germany and Italy, more rapidly than in the service sector. The service sector is by far the most "academised" and the branch where the proportion of graduates is highest is that of "education, research and culture". In the countries for which we have separate data (and taking account of the differences in classification) this proportion amounts to over half of total employment: 60 per cent in Germany, 52 per cent in Spain and Yugoslavia, with the proportion still increasing in these last two countries while it is tending to diminish in Germany. This could indicate approaching saturation. Another branch where the proportion of graduates is high is "financial services", to which "business services" are sometimes added. In most cases the percentage of graduates in these branches is increasing, though in Germany and Austria, where "financial services" are presented separately, the number of graduates is relatively modest (6 or 7 per cent of total employment), while in Spain it is over 20 per cent. In Norway the proportion of graduates in these two branches together increased from 23 per cent in 1975 to 41 per cent in 1989, thus even passing the public sector (37 per cent). It would be interesting to be able to identify better the phenomena within these two branches, notably to see

Table II–16. **Concentration of (university) graduates in the public sector**

As a percentage of total graduates employed

Austria	65	1981	69	1987
Belgium	–	–	60	1985
Canada	54	1984	48	1988
Denmark	66	1984	58	1987
Finland	–	–	54	1985
Germany	74	1976	66	1989[a]
Italy	–	–	50	1985
Norway	58	1975	57	1989
Sweden	63	1981	58	1991
Switzerland	59	1981	52	1989

a) Universities only (U + FHS: 1976, 62%; 1989, 56%).
Source: National studies.

Table II-17. **Germany**

Graduates[a] as a proportion of total employment, by sector in 1976, 1982 and 1989

Percentages

	1976	1982	1989	% variation 1976-1982	% variation 1982-1989
Agriculture	0.6	1.0	2.4	38.9	95.2
Manufacturing	3.2	4.2	6.5	30.2	60.6
Commerce	2.6	3.2	4.2	28.5	38.8
Banking and insurance	4.5	6.7	8.5	67.2	41.2
Research, education & sports	65.2	67.4	62.0	20.4	13.3
Health	19.4	18.4	19.6	16.1	26.2
Business consultancy	28.2	31.0	34.9	36.7	68.8
Public sector, social security	10.8	13.8	17.3	42.7	27.7
Total	7.3	9.1	11.6	27.6	31.7

a) *Fachhochschulen* and universities.
Source: M. Tessaring, German report and update.

Table II-18. **Australia**

Graduates as a proportion of total employment, by sector

Percentages, selected branches

	Distribution	Proportion
Agriculture	2.7	1.7
Manufacturing	5.1	8.5
Wholesale and retail trade	3.8	7.9
Financial and business services	17.1	18.0
Public adm. & defense	15.2	7.6
Community services[a]	25.7	45.2
Personal and other services	4.4	3.1

a) Mainly education and health.
Source: Bruce Williams, Australian contribution to the humanities and social sciences project.

Table II-19. **Austria**

Graduates as a proportion of employment in certain branches of the private sector, 1985-90

Percentages

	1985	1990[a]	% change 1985-1990
Energy, water	3.1	3.4	9.7
Chemicals	2.6	2.7	3.8
Timber and paper	1.9	2.3	21.1
Wholesale and retail trade	2.8	3.1	10.7
Banking and insurance	5.9	5.6	−5.1
Transport & communications	1.3	1.5	15.4

a) Projection.
Source: K. Schedler, Austrian report, Part II.

Table II-20. **Spain**

Graduates as a proportion of total employment by sector, 1987 and 1989

Percentages

	1987	1989	% change 1987-1989
Agriculture	1.1	1.1	0.0
Industry	4.8	5.3	10.4
Commerce	4.5	4.9	8.9
Transport	5.6	5.7	1.8
Communications	13.3	14.5	9.0
Banking and insurance	21.8	23.9	9.6
Business services	28.1	34.4	22.4
Education, research, culture and health	50.3	52.0	3.4

Source: A. Casanueva, Spanish report.

Table II-21. **France**

Graduates (ISCED levels 5 et 6) as a proportion of total employment in 1989 and change between 1983 and 1989

Percentages

	ISCED 5 %	ISCED 5 Change	ISCED 6 %	ISCED 6 Change
Agriculture	1.2	+39.8	0.8	-12.2
Industry	5.2	+26.0	4.9	+6.3
Construction and public works	2.1	+27.0	1.7	-9.9
Services	10.3	+18.5	10.6	+19.4
Business services	4.4	+27.2	4.2	+11.0
Trade services	13.0	+25.5	11.8	+30.2

Source: Formation-emploi, No. 33, Table 7.

Table II-22. **Italy**

Graduates as a proportion of total employment by sector, 1984-1988

Percentages

	1984	1988	% change 1984-1988
Agriculture	0.7	0.7	0.0
Industry	1.5	1.9	26.7
Services	10.0	10.8	8.0

Source: F. Bussi, Italian report.

Table II–23. **Norway**

Graduates as a proportion of total employment by sector, 1975-1989

Percentages

	1975	1989	% change 1975-1989
Primary & secondary sectors	6	11	83
Commerce & communication	7	12	71
Finance & business services	23	41	78
Public administration	26	37	42

Source: P. Aamodt, Norwegian report.

whether the increase in the proportion of graduates is due to the needs of consultancy and contracting services in management, engineering, computers, architecture, etc. (as suggested by the German and Austrian examples), or recruitments in banking and insurance (as in Spain). It would still not always be clear however whether this was a response to the requirements of the economy or rather the absorption of excess graduates.

In order to describe the context for graduate employment we have gathered in this section some data on the structural trends: first the employment structure, then the structure of the labour force by educational attainment. The data presented, necessarily limited in volume, show some major trends and the most marked differences. It would be desirable to push this analysis further, even though the reliability of the data available on each of these topics is limited. Several questions merit in-depth study:

  i) *Types of graduate recruitment*

  When we observe an increase in the number of graduates in a branch of activity (and it is not sure that the number of "high level jobs" is a very different measure) we would like to know the nature of this increase. In Germany, Austria and the Netherlands, for example, it is often asked whether the predecessor in the same job had a university degree, *i.e.* whether it is a case of replacement. It is possible to go further, as in Japan[13] and Austria[14] and determine whether it is a case of replacement, the increased demands of the job, or a supply effect. The aim is to make every effort, using objective data, to determine whether it is a case of demand or absorption.

  ii) *Relative position of graduates and segmentation*

  There is an impression that during the past ten or fifteen years, despite or because of the employment crisis, the situation of post-secondary education graduates has remained very favourable, but that on the contrary it has significantly deteriorated for the lower levels of educational attainment, more particularly

Table II–24. **Sweden**

University (U) and all post-secondary education graduates (T) as a proportion of total employment by sector

	1971 U	1971 T	1981 U	1981 T	1991 U	1991 T
Private sector						
Industry	1.8	2.9	4.2	7.4	6.4	13.8
Other private	2.8	5.0	7.3	11.5	8.8	18.6
Public sector						
Health	4.9	13.1	9.6	22.3	10.6	31.2
Public services	19.8	29.7	33.1	45.8	35.4	57.4
Education & research	44.5	57.6	44.0	58.8	47.1	64.6

Source: National Board of Universities and Colleges, Dan Andersson.

Table II–25. **Yugoslavia**

Graduates as a proproportion of total employment, 1978-1988

Percentages

	1978	1988	% change 1978-1988
Education & culture	46.7	51.7	10.7
Health & social services	23.1	27.1	17.3
Social & political organisations	31.5	36.4	15.5
Financial & other services	25.0	28.9	15.6

Source: H. Hanic.

in the case of women and in the service sector. If this is correct and if this situation persists – which is likely – there will be a considerable impact on education policies. Another question that needs analysing is the relative position of higher education graduates according to the level of the qualification (for example ISCED 5 and 6), in terms of recruitment and also subsequent career. It would be interesting to know whether the position of graduates of ISCED 5 level is not threatened by the overall trend.

iii) Disparities between branches of activity

The structural disparities between branches of activity (in terms of employment or educational level) are an accepted fact. Even if these disparities are diminished with the increase in supply, they remain considerable and, to a certain extent, surprising. One hypothesis[15] is that graduates head for certain types of jobs (and not simply to a certain level) and that there are regulations that make it possible to preserve these correspondences even if the penetration of graduates in the financial and business services branch may be interpreted as the substitution of graduates for people with secondary education diplomas, for whom this branch was formerly a usual destination. There are probably certain social or cultural constraints that dissuade graduates from heading for new sectors.

iv) Educational attainment gaps between generations

We have just mentioned social constraints whose origins lie on the supply side and which explain why graduates head for certain types of job where they are already well represented. Conversely, in certain branches of activity there are clearly difficulties in accepting flows of young people whose educational level is very much higher than that of the average employee, and even that of the executives and managers. Such an influx is in fact a threat not only to professional hierarchies, but also to cohesion and communication within the enterprise. There is thus reason to ask whether the generation gap is not a factor helping to maintain the existence of disparities between branches. It would be desirable to be able to examine at the micro level if necessary which jobs or services graduates are recruited into in branches where the percentage of graduates remains low. It is of course in industry that this question is particularly important.

IV. THE PRESENT CONTEXT

As the OECD had already carried out an analysis of employment prospects for higher education graduates in 1980, it was thought useful in this chapter to trace the main trends in the employment situation over the past ten years and contrast the pessimism that was prevalent at the beginning of the 1980s with the rather optimistic climate that characterises the present situation. In 1970, the problem was not always perceived in terms of an excess of graduates, but there was an awareness of the need for substantial reorientations in the flows of young graduates. Today, this concern has not disappeared,[16] but the accent is more frequently on the need to increase the supply of young graduates.[17] In this introductory chapter to Part Two we have tried to explain the change in the climate and the attitude. Part One showed that the reorientation of higher education demand, spontaneous or otherwise, could be a first explanatory factor – the data presented above reveals others.

Let us note first of all a certain number of what might be called "negative factors". The first is no doubt that in the majority of countries it has not really been possible to control the growth of public sector employment: thus the scale of the adjustments and reorientations thought necessary in the late 1970s was reduced accordingly. The excessive growth of the public sector has often been attributed, at least partly, to the excess supply of graduates;[18] but other factors are also at work, such as the difficulty of rationalising and modernising these services, less subject than private enterprises to profitability requirements, and also the simple logic of growth. A certain number of services included in the private sector should probably be added to the public sector because they tend to have behaviours close to those of the public service.

A second factor is the persistence of unemployment. To the extent that the selectivity of school systems means that higher education graduates are considered the most capable and, conversely, doubt is cast on the abilities of those who have not reached this level of education, and to the extent that employers may raise their requirements in view of the abundance of supply, graduates as a group will retain their advantage on the labour market. Globally, their unemployment rates will be lower than the average and they will maintain an advantage in terms of wages, even if these advantages will be reduced as the graduate supply increases. In many countries, concern with employment prospects is not concentrated only on the most disadvantaged, but also on those "who have only secondary education", whether general or vocational.

A third factor, which will be discussed in more detail below, concerns the nature of the adjustment between supply and demand. It would probably be wrong to qualify some of these adjustments as "negative", but the fact that young graduates are accepting insecure and deskilled jobs in traditional employment sectors rather than turning towards new activities can scarcely be qualified as "positive" either. There is at least a certain passivity in the face of changes in employment opportunities.

This chapter has also shed light on a certain number of positive factors. The growth of employment first of all, which was accompanied, at least towards the end of the 1980s, by a fall in unemployment rates. While the unemployment rate remains high, and even very high among young people in certain countries, it is this trend that seems to be responsible for the current optimistic climate, even if this optimism implies resignation on the part of some people. Some thirty years ago, when the period of "intellectual investment" in teaching, research and the management of public systems began, there was a similar optimism. This period has come to an end, but at the same time as the relative closing of public service openings – fairly slow, and cushioned by time – there has been a revival of growth in the private sector that has brought a new dynamism and released new energies.

It can be seen that employment growth in the private sector is to a large extent due to branches of activity that require high skill levels, such as banking, insurance and above all business services. We have also seen, subject perhaps to some errors of appreciation due to differences in classifications, that the average level of qualifications required has grown rapidly and that in particular the proportion of "high level jobs" aspired to by post-secondary education graduates has grown very quickly. According to some commentators this growth is often under-estimated. This is admittedly a very global view that needs to be discussed branch by branch, but it is a constant that the development of information technologies together with new forms of management and work organisation and the very fact that jobs are held by people with a much higher educational level than before all contribute to the increasing complexity of tasks and the growing need for qualified staff.

There nevertheless remain a certain number of uncertainties that need to be borne in mind in the following chapters:

i) the difficulty of determining the nature, positive or negative, of the adjustments between supply and demand and whether they are responses to the needs of the economy or simply constitute an absorption phenomenon, and of judging whether they reflect mainly dynamism, passivity or resignation;

ii) uncertainty about the evolution of professional structures, it being generally accepted that there has been an increase in the average level of qualifications demanded, and hence an increase in the number of high level jobs, but its impact at the "upper middle" level remains to be determined;

iii) another uncertainty is connected with the distribution of graduates between sectors: some sectors are virtually saturated, while in others the proportion of graduates remains marginal. Depending on whether the social constraints discussed in the 1981 report can be overcome, these other sectors, and in particular industry, may become major openings for graduates.

Notes and References

1. *OECD Economic Outlook,* 1989, Table R 16.
2. *OECD Employment Outlook,* 1990.
3. *OECD Employment Outlook,* 1990, Table 1.5.
4. *OECD Employment Outlook,* 1989.
5. Y. Coppens, Netherlands, Volume III.
6. H. Levin and R. Rumberger, "Educational Requirements for New Technologies" in *Educational Policy,* Vol. 1, No. 3, 1987.
7. L. Mischel and R. Teixeira, *The Myth of the Coming Labor Shortage,* Economic Policy Institute, Washington D.C., 1990.
8. J. Myles, "The Expanding Middle: Some Canadian Evidence on the Deskilling Debate" in *Canadian Review of Sociology and Anthropology,* 1988, XXV.
9. J. Bishop and S. Carter, *The Worsening Shortage of College Graduate Workers,* Center for Advanced Human Resources Studies, Cornell University, Ithaca, N. Y., 1990.
10. *OECD Employment Outlook,* 1989, Chapter 2.
11. *Ibid.*
12. *Ibid.,* Table 5.17.
13. Mr. Kaneko, Japan, Table 17, Volume III.
14. K. Schedler, Austria II, Table 15, Volume I.
15. F. Pottier and A. Charlot, France, Volume III.
16. K. Schedler, *op. cit.*
17. S. Fornäng, p. 16; Bishop and Carter, *The Worsening Shortage of College Graduate Workers, op. cit.*
18. M. Barbagli, *Disoccupazione intellettuale,* UPM, Bologna, 1974.

Chapter 5

THE TRANSITION CONDITIONS

I. THE RISK OF UNEMPLOYMENT

In analysing the situation of graduates on the labour market, there is often a tendency to concentrate firstly on unemployment. For the political leaders, unemployment constitutes a simple and striking indicator. For public opinion, notably in countries where the university degree has retained all its prestige, graduate unemployment has something shocking and unacceptable about it, since it calls into question the idea that higher education guarantees a good job. Graduate unemployment is nothing new however, though it is true that in the majority of OECD countries graduate unemployment was unusual between the end of the Second World War and the late 1970s or early 1980s, and has never been on such a scale as to call into question the received ideas of public opinion. It is for this reason that the first part of this chapter deals with the question of graduate unemployment although, in the opinion of the Secretariat, this is not a good indicator of the state of the relationship between higher education and employment, as will be seen later. Graduate unemployment is usually compared with total unemployment, or where the data permit, unemployment rates are presented by educational attainment level.

We shall first compare graduate unemployment with total unemployment among the active population. Table 26 presents some figures taken from the national contributions on the evolution of unemployment among university graduates compared with total unemployment. No international comparisons will be made because the definitions and survey methods vary greatly from one country to another. These data are simply intended to give an idea of the relative position of graduates on the labour market. It will be noted that the graduate unemployment rate is less than half that of total unemployment in Finland (17 per cent), Canada, France, Norway and Italy (32, 38, 40 and 44 per cent respectively). It is between half and three-quarters in Yugoslavia, Australia, Denmark, Germany and Sweden (50, 56, 57, 63 and 77 per cent respectively). It is as much as 82 per cent in Spain and seems to be even higher in the Netherlands, but these two measurements are no doubt not comparable. We shall go on later to examine the situation in more detail for those countries where data by educational attainment are available.

A first observation that emerges from an examination of the country reports is that the graduate unemployment rate tends to vary in the same way as unemployment in general. Thus in most countries, graduate unemployment, which was already a subject of concern in the late 1970s, continued to increase in the early 1980s to reach a maximum about the middle of the decade before starting to decline again. In Australia, both total and graduate unemployment rates fell, while both increased in Yugoslavia. In Denmark and Norway, total unemployment began to grow again towards the end of the 1980s and graduate unemployment moved in parallel with it. In Italy on the other hand, total unemployment is still growing, while graduate unemployment is falling slightly. The reverse is true in the Netherlands, where total unemployment is falling, but graduate unemployment is clearly rising. All this suggests that there are other factors at work in addition to the general labour market situation.

A second observation is that the female graduate unemployment rate is significantly higher than that of the male, though the difference varies greatly from one country to another. In Italy, the female graduate unemployment rate is about one and a half times that of the male; in France, the Netherlands and Switzerland it is almost double. Several authors attribute this difference to the fact that women tend to choose disciplines that are less directly vocational than those chosen by men.[1] In Spain, where we have seen that total unemployment remains very high (16.9 per cent in 1989, 25.2 per cent for the women) the gap between the male and female graduate unemployment rates is even greater: 7.6 per cent for the men and as high as 24.3 per cent for the women, so high that the author of the Spanish contribution[2] considers that unemployment in Spain is first and foremost female unemployment. In Finland and the United Kingdom on the other hand, female graduate unemployment rates are much the same as, or even lower than, the male rates. Since the unemployment rate in Finland is close to 1 per cent, this is understandable, but in the United Kingdom there is some surprise at this situation and the author of the UK contribution[3] suggests that women are perhaps more inclined than men to accept jobs of a lower level and a lower wage.

Table II-26. **Trend in total (T) and university graduate (D) unemployment rates during the 1980s***

Germany[a]	D	2.2	(1980)	4.2	(1990)
	T	3.6		6.9	
Australia	D	8.0	(1984)	4.5	(1988)
	T	9.4		8.0	
Canada	D	3.2	(1981)	2.5	(1989)
	T	7.5		7.8	
Denmark	D	–		4.6	(1988)
	T	–		8.0	
Spain	D	14.9	(1987)	13.8	(1989)
	T	20.6		16.9	
United States	D	6.2	(1980)	4.2	(1986)
	T	7.0[b]		6.9[b]	
Finland	D	1.1	(1985)	–	
	T	6.3		–	
France	D	3.8	(1980)	3.6	(1989)
	T	6.3		9.4[b]	
Italy	D	5.8	(1984)	5.3	(1988)
	T	10.4		12.0	
Norway	D	0.7	(1980)	2.0	(1989)
	T	1.8		4.9	
Netherlands	D	3.5	(1980)	8.4	(1989)
	T	6.0[b]		8.3[b]	
Sweden	D	0.6	(1980)	1.0	(1989)
	T	2.0[b]		1.3[b]	
Yugoslavia	D	4.5	(1980)	7.5	(1988)
	T	12.0		14.9	

* Because of differences in the definitions used, the actual figures are not comparable across countries.
a) Universities and *Fachhochschulen*.
b) OECD Databank.
Sources: Country reports and supplementary data.

A third observation is that unemployment affects above all young graduates. Tables 27 and 28 below show the magnitude of this difference for Italy and Spain, admittedly countries where the overall unemployment rates are high. Table 3 above (Chapter 4) shows that unemployment rates among young graduates of 25 to 29 may be higher than those of non-graduates of the same age, who entered the labour market earlier. The fact is that in all countries graduate unemployment, despite the impact of present restructuring on the employment of executives and managers, remains above all a phenomenon associated with entry to the labour market and the initial years of the career. On the other hand, the French and Spanish reports stress that in the case of women, unemployment does not only affect the 25-29 age group; in Spain female graduates of 30 to 44 still have an unemployment rate of 10 or 11 per cent, which shows that their employment difficulties continue for a good part of their working lives.

There is nothing specially new nor surprising about these three observations. It is perfectly understandable that because of their education or the selection processes associated with it, graduates have a relative advantage on the labour market. It was even suggested above that this advantage may increase when the employment situation deteriorates, because employers are able to raise their requirements. In other words graduates are recruited at a lower level and lower pay than previously, a process known as "substitution". This reasoning remains fairly theoretical however, because in fact the possibilities for substitution are not infinite, for reasons associated either with the employers or the graduates themselves (otherwise graduate unemployment would theoretically be zero). Other factors have to be taken into consideration to explain the graduate unemployment level.

Table II–27. **Spain**

Unemployment among university graduates by age group, 1989

Percentages

	M + F	F
20-24 years	53.02	60.31
25-29 years	30.77	38.45
30-44 years	6.82	11.16
Total	13.77	24.34

Source: A. Casanueva, Spanish report.

Several rapporteurs point out that in order for graduates to maintain their position on the labour market, even measured solely in terms of unemployment rates, it has been necessary for a certain equilibrium between supply and demand to be re-established. In Yugoslavia, the economy has simply not been able to absorb the considerably increased number of graduates. The Norwegian report links the level of graduate unemployment with the reduction in public sector recruitment. Several other rapporteurs point out that this reduction in public recruitment has combined with the increase in the number of graduates to maintain or even increase their unemployment rate. Thus the Austrian report states that 70 per cent of the unemployed graduates are teachers or doctors, while in Spain primary school teachers, arts graduates and doctors make up 60 per cent of the unemployed graduates. In Germany and the Netherlands, graduate unemployment has increased significantly in recent years and this is due to the fact that they normally head for the public sector. Denmark and the United Kingdom distinguish between two phases. The UK report states that the increase in the number of graduates, the reduction in public recruitment and the weakness of the economy caused graduate unemployment to increase until 1982 but that various adjustments and an improvement in the economic situation has since made it possible to improve the absorption of young graduates. The Danish report points out that until 1985, the Danish economy was not able to absorb all new graduates, but there has since been a greater flexibility and graduate unemployment has been falling, even though total unemployment began to rise again towards the end of the 1980s.

The graduate unemployment rate is thus an indicator that does not reflect only the general labour market situation. It is naturally connected with variations in supply, which have often been very rapid, notably during the 1970s; on the other hand, measures restricting admission to higher education, for example in the Nordic countries and later in Yugoslavia, have an effect on the unemployment level after some lapse of time. Several rapporteurs point out that graduate employment is less exposed to conjunctural fluctuations, because there are relatively few of them in industry and a far greater concentration in the service sector, notably public services. However, by virtue of this very fact graduate employment is very sensitive to structural trends, such as the reduction of recruitment in education and the public service. The danger announced in the 1981 report seems to have been avoided only thanks to the economic upturn and notably the growth of financial and business services. Various authors also suggest that the adjustment has been perhaps more apparent than real: public sector recruitment has

Table II–28. **Italy**

Unemployment among university graduates by age group, 1988

Percentages

	M + F	F
25-29 years	24.7	28.4
30-39 years	4.4	6.2
Total	5.3	8.5

Source: F. Bussi, Italian report.

Table II–29. **Canada**

Unemployment rate by educational level and age group, 1989

Percentages

	A	B	C	D	E	F
15-24 years	21.5	14.0	9.6	6.9	4.3	12.2
25 +	13.5	8.7	7.8	5.7	3.5	7.8

A) 9 years schooling.
B) Secondary.
C) Some post-secondary.
D) Post-secondary certificate or diploma.
E) University degree.
F) Total.
Source: R. McDowell, Canadian report.

continued under other forms, at the local level in Norway, under the pressure of graduates in difficulty, as in Austria, through job creation programmes as in Norway and Belgium. It is also noted that unemployment affects above all graduates from disciplines that normally lead to teaching and public sector jobs. This will be discussed in greater detail below when we examine the disparities between graduates from different disciplines.

Certain countries collect information on unemployment according to educational attainment or skill level. This makes it possible to better define the relative position of graduates on the labour market, and above all the disparities between graduates from the different levels of post-secondary education itself. A common belief is that the higher the level of educational training the lower the risk of unemployment. This is perfectly illustrated with the case of Canada in Table 29, and except for the primary level, that of the United States in Table 30.

This simple relationship corresponds to the intuitive notion of the value of training in society and in the world of work, which has been given various theoretical labels. It applies equally well in countries like Canada and the United States, where participation is very high, including at post-secondary level and where training leading to a first degree is mostly general so that substitution mechanisms work more easily. It was pointed out above, in the comments to Table 26, that graduate unemployment is lower than total unemployment everywhere.

We have seen that the labour market does not necessarily function in such a simple way and that structural factors may alter this relationship. For example, in Tables 31 and 32, for Italy and Spain, we can see that it is young people from secondary education that have the highest unemployment risk. The author of the Spanish report even points out that the graduate unemployment rate is the same as for those with primary education. This is due to the fact that these categories, at their very different levels, are often more or less strongly vocation-oriented, whereas young people from secondary school have often only a general education, and also to the fact that young people head towards different sectors of employment according to their educational level. In this respect, the phenomenon of substitution which leads to the recruitment, notably in the private service sector, of higher education graduates instead of young people with only a secondary education, shifts the risk of unemploy-

Table II–30. **United States**

Unemployment rate by educational level and age group, 1990[a]

Level completed	Total	16-19	20-24	25-34	35-44	45-54	55-64	65 +
Primary school	9.9	30.6	13.8	10.3	9.0	7.8	5.4	3.7
1 to 3 years secondary	12.2	18.0	19.3	12.7	8.6	6.2	4.3	4.0
Secondary diploma	5.8	12.7	9.4	6.3	4.8	3.4	3.2	2.7
1 to 3 years tertiary	4.2	8.4	5.9	4.2	3.6	3.3	2.8	3.7
4 years or more tertiary	2.4	7.7	5.0	2.5	2.1	1.9	2.3	2.0
All levels	5.5	15.7	8.8	5.5	4.1	3.5	3.3	3.0

a) For the definition of ''unemployment rate'', see E.S. Hunt, Table I-22.
Source: *Digest of Education Statistics 1991*, Table 355.

Table II-31. **Italy**

Employment rate by educational level, 1988

Stock data; percentages

Primary	8.3
Lower secondary	13.9
Upper secondary	15.6
University	5.3
Total	12.0

Source: F. Bussi, Italian report.

---

ment, notably in the case of women. Situations similar to those observed in Spain and Italy can also be seen elsewhere.

It can also be seen in the case of Spain that people with post-secondary diplomas have an unemployment rate lower than that of university graduates. This is often the case. In Sweden in 1989, unemployment among university graduates (at most three years of study) was in the order of 1 per cent and that of holders of post-secondary diplomas (at most two years of post-secondary study) about 0.7 per cent. In Denmark, where there is a distinction between three levels of higher or post-secondary education, the unemployment rate in 1988 was about 4.6 per cent for holders of short- and long-cycle diplomas and 2.9 per cent for those with training of medium duration. In Germany, since 1979 the relationship between the level of post-secondary training and unemployment risk has reversed: in 1987 unemployment rates were 3.4 per cent for those with technical school diplomas, 4.0 per cent for graduates of the *Fachhochschulen* and 5.7 per cent (and clearly rising) for university graduates (Table 33). In the Netherlands, unemployment among post-secondary diploma-holders remains stable, while that among degree holders is clearly rising. One of the reasons may be that the short-cycle post-secondary courses are usually very much of a vocational nature, frequently closely linked with the world of work, especially at local level. Access to employment, notably for young people, is thus facilitated. Most authors however point out the structural nature of these disparities, and in particular the impact of public sector recruitment. This is no doubt true for short-cycle post-secondary courses, which often lead to primary school teaching or to jobs in the paramedical field. We saw in Part One however that teacher training flows had considerably diminished. The determining factor is thus connected with a lack of employment opportunities for university graduates from disciplines that normally lead to teaching or other public service employment, notably the humanities and social sciences.

Unemployment rates can therefore provide useful information on the situation of graduates on the labour market. In this section we have considered only stock data (to which age group data can be attached), but we know that unemployment mainly affects young people and variations in stock data do give an idea of the situation for young graduates. Conversely, as pointed out by the Australian contribution to the humanities and social sciences project, in the absence of stock data, indications concerning the situation of young graduates give an idea of that of all graduates.

Table II-32. **Spain**

Employment rate by educational level, 1989

Stock data; percentages

No education	16.42
Primary	13.75
Secondary	21.38
Post-secondary	12.28
University	13.77
Total	16.89

Source: A. Casanueva, Spanish report.

Table II–33. **Germany**

Unemployment rate by level of qualification, 1976, 1985, 1990

Stock data; percentages

	1976	1985	1990
No qualification	6.4	17.1	15.0
Apprenticeship	3.1	6.7	4.9
Technical schools	2.7	3.7	3.0
Fachhochschulen	3.4	4.5	3.4
Universities	1.9	5.4	4.7
Total	4.2	9.1	6.9

Source: M. Tessaring.

However, the Secretariat considers that unemployment data are not enough to give a clear idea of the conditions of entry into working life for young graduates. In order to interpret them it is necessary to introduce considerations of a structural nature, which do not always have a direct relationship with the overall situation of the labour market. It is also necessary to take account of the modalities of insertion, which vary according to the level of the qualification and the discipline. However, one may question the value of creating categories by diploma level when disparities are often greater within categories than between them. We have seen above for example that the differences between unemployment rates by age or between men and women are often greater than the difference between the average graduate unemployment rate and the total unemployment rate. We have also seen that the unemployment rate depends on the propensity of graduates to accept lower level and lower paid jobs (and that of employers to hire them), a factor reducing the comparability of male and female unemployment rates, for example. It is thus necessary to take a whole set of parameters into account.

II. THE TRANSITION PARAMETERS

In order to describe the conditions for the entry into working life of young graduates, their initial experience of the world of work (and of their destinations, which will be analysed in Chapter 6), the usual sources of information are rarely adequate: censuses, employment surveys and questionnaires to enterprises all generally concern the whole of the active population and therefore cannot provide the more detailed information we would like to have on the employment of highly qualified staff and in particular of young graduates. Complementary sources of information are obviously necessary.

Examination of the national contributions shows that most countries have very rich information available. There are many longitudinal studies, studies of cohorts and samples, follow-up studies, retrospective studies, insertion and career path studies. Certain surveys cover the whole of the country, others a region or province, others again combine regional studies to obtain results close to the national reality. Certain studies concern all diploma-holders of a given level, others are concentrated on a discipline or professional field. Surveys are sometimes carried out by public bodies at national level, sometimes by associations or private foundations, sometimes by a university interested in what becomes of its own graduates.

This is not the place to analyse the information resources and techniques now available in OECD countries, and in any event most of the national contributions give a brief indication of the statistical sources. It must nevertheless be said that there are fairly big disparities between countries. For example, a certain number of countries where the statistical information is otherwise excellent, do not yet have anything other than stock data. It is a fact that in the present economic situation it is above all the young graduates who experience employment difficulties, and with these data it is possible to arrive at interesting conclusions regarding their labour market situation and even the disparities between categories, but several rapporteurs regret not being able to use other sources. In other cases, there are many surveys and abundant information, but the statistical studies are carried out by different organisations using different methods and variables, so that the results are often not comparable when they are not downright contradictory. Few countries in fact have a regular and permanent monitoring system for flows of labour market entrants, notably for those from higher education.

It should also be pointed out that there are sometimes still considerable gaps in the information, most of which concerns university graduates only. For various reasons depending on the country, short-cycle post-secondary education, especially courses provided by the private sector, are often very inadequately covered by the statistical apparatus. It would perhaps be fairer however to emphasize the progress that has been made rather than what still remains to be done.

The biggest problem encountered by the rapporteurs is nevertheless the lack of coherence in and coordination of statistical sources. It is desirable that the various research studies should fit into an overall plan, obeying certain technical rules and using the same parameters. It will be a good thing if this project stimulates reflection in Member countries and leads to a "minimum-standard catalogue of transition and flow surveys".[4] It could perhaps at the same time stimulate some ideas on the nature of the entities that could conduct or coordinate this research and present comprehensive and coherent results to policy-makers.

We have said that unemployment rates are certainly a valuable indicator, but insufficient in themselves to provide information about the insertion of young graduates and their early careers. It is striking that most of the national contributions, at least those from countries where the necessary information was available, resorted more or less explicitly to the combination of parameters. This ranged from the simple juxtaposition of unemployment rates and proportions of graduates having obtained only short-term jobs, to much more complex combinations of variables making it possible to establish a ranking of the different types of training. Table 34, taken from the German contribution, is an interesting example.

Among the variables or parameters used, we find first the "traditional" variables used in labour market analysis: unemployment rate, duration of first job search, activity rates, stability of employment, part-time work, full-time work. It would be tempting to add the wage or relative wage to this initial list, but this variable is subject to interpretation and we prefer here to put it with the following group. This second group could include a whole series of variables which, while they refer to a particular graduate, do not enable us to say whether his situation is satisfactory or not, for the simple reason that low pay, a subordinate level, a temporary job may be the result of personal choice or particular circumstances, or alternatively they may be characteristic of the initial period of a normal transition towards stable employment. In certain professions, such as medicine, or for access to the public service in certain countries, it is even a compulsory phase, difficult but holding promise for the future. On the other hand, when a high proportion of graduates from a particular discipline or group of disciplines is in such a situation, it may be thought that their relative situation on the labour market has significantly deteriorated. Several authors add less traditional data to this group of variables, such as participation in job creation programmes, notably in the public sector, or an increased propensity to continue studies beyond the first degree. Again we also find data relating to more subjective aspects, based on the views of the graduates themselves or their employers. It may be considered that in this type of survey, the questions asking whether the predecessor in the job had a

Table II–34. **Germany**

Entry conditions for higher education graduates by field of study, 1983

Percentages

Field of study	Classification by group*							
	1	2	3	4	5	6	7	8
Teacher training	57	4	2	4	13	1	10	9
Humanities, social sciences	36	10	12	7	17	4	11	3
Law	67	4	6	2	7	–	13	–
Economics	65	5	17	11	–	1	1	–
Mathematics, science	53	6	12	4	16	4	3	2
Medicine	47	4	5	2	39	–	4	–
Engineering	79	–	11	1	5	–	2	1
Total	59	4	9	4	14	1	6	3

* Group definitions:
1. Short job search, highly satisfactory job, stable job prospects.
2. Long job search, highly satisfactory job, stable job prospects.
3. Short job search, unsatisfactory job, stable job prospects.
4. Long job search, unsatisfactory job, stable job prospects.
5. Short job search, highly satisfactory job, poor job prospects.
6. Long job search, highly satisfactory job, poor job prospects.
7. Short job search, unsatisfactory job, poor job prospects.
8. Long job search, unsatisfactory job, poor job prospects.

Source: Minks, Reissert (1985), quoted in M. Tessaring, German report.

degree or not and whether this degree was the same are fairly objective, but those that concern job satisfaction are obviously much less so. In this group we can also include questions on the correspondence between training and the job in terms of level or use of knowledge, on the possibility of the same job being open to someone with a degree in a different discipline, of a lower level, or without a degree at all. Such data are more difficult to use. All of this demonstrates the wide variety of parameters or groups of parameters that can be used to describe the situation of young graduates, based not only on the authors' perception or the data available, but also on the characteristics of national labour markets.

While these groupings of parameters are sometimes necessarily of a somewhat *ad hoc* nature, we can see that there is concern in some countries on the one hand not to simply give a snapshot of the situation of young people and in particular their first job, but to cover a period of some years and show their progress towards a steady job, and on the other to use only a limited number of types of data, as objective as possible, to give a brief and synthetic view of the entire process, such as the total duration of job search periods or the time taken to obtain a steady job. In most cases however this requires improvement in the basic data and the harmonization of sources.

A. Overview

The first section of this chapter was devoted to an examination of the relative position of graduates on the labour market, as measured by unemployment rates. Although we deliberately used stock data only, we already managed to draw some conclusions regarding the employment of young graduates. We intend to add more detail to these conclusions, using the results of the longitudinal studies described in the national contributions. Once again we shall avoid making international comparisons, for these surveys use very different methods and, above all, cover periods ranging from less than six months to three years and more. The aim here is to shed light on the disparities in the situations of graduates from different disciplines and see whether there are similar trends in different countries.

We already know that graduates from disciplines that normally lead to public sector employment, and notably teaching, are very exposed to unemployment, to the extent that the unemployment among these particular categories has an impact on the relative position of all graduates of a given level. Such types of training exist at both post-secondary (ISCED 5) and university level (ISCED 6): it would appear that in general the risk is greater at university level, perhaps because the post-secondary establishments are subject to tighter control, or because the effects of the demographic trend on the employment of primary school teachers are more direct and of longer standing. However, what throws a somewhat different light on this is the fact that in a number of countries, like France, we are seeing an upturn in teacher recruitment, at least for some subject matters.

In order to refine this first conclusion we can begin by comparing the unemployment risk of different graduate categories, using the different relevant variables found in the surveys. In *Germany*, the highest rates of unemployment are those for teachers and for graduates in languages, psychology, sociology and medicine.[5] In *Australia*, it is the graduates in the humanities and psychology who have by far the greatest difficulty in finding a full-time job,[6] with graduates in education and social work also experiencing difficulty. In *Austria*, it is graduates in psychology and the social sciences followed by young doctors, arts graduates and newly qualified teachers.[7] In *Belgium*, it is graduates is psychology and educational science, philosophy and the arts, physical education, sciences and social sciences who have the biggest unemployment risk, the risk being least for lawyers, economists and engineers.[8] In *Canada*, where unemployment is low, it is young graduates in technology and biology who have the greatest difficulty, while those with training in the field of health are very well placed. Among the university graduates, doctors have very easy access to employment as do young teachers, mathematicians and physicists, while graduates in the humanities, social sciences, the fine arts and biology are worst placed.[9] In *Denmark*, the risk of unemployment is high for graduates in the humanities and psychology.[10] In the *United States*, where participation rates in higher education are higher and where consequently fluctuations in the recruitment for the public services or the teaching profession have far less impact on young graduates' access to employment (at least at the Bachelor Degree level), graduates in the more ''general'' fields (liberal arts) are those with the highest unemployment rates.[11] In *Finland*, where unemployment is low, those most at risk at Bachelor level are graduates in the humanities and sciences and for the women graduates in law; at Master level it is again humanities and sciences but also this time psychology and law for both sexes.[12] In *France*, those most exposed to unemployment are graduates in the social sciences and psychology and, among those with short-cycle university training (IUT), those seeking careers in the social services and information; higher level ''*techniciens*'' (BTS) find a stable job more easily.[13] In *Italy*, where we have seen that the situation of young graduates is generally very unfavourable, young engineers and economics and commerce graduates nevertheless find stable jobs fairly easily, while the worst placed are young doctors, almost a third of whom are still unemployed three years after qualifying.[14] In *Norway,* it was the graduates in the humanities and sciences who were the most exposed until 1987, but since then the deterioration in the economic situation has been very unfavourable to young engineers and those with diplomas from the regional colleges.[15] In the *Netherlands,* where reference is made to the "absorption capacity" of the economy, young graduates in the humanities, psychology and social sciences, whether they are from higher technical education (HBO) or the universities are in a very unfavourable situation, as are those with education diplomas from the HBO and graduates in agricultural science.[16] In *Sweden,* where unemployment is low, graduates in the humanities and social sciences are those who find the greatest difficulty in obtaining employment, all the more so because access to teacher training is strictly planned.[17] In the *United Kingdom,* as in *France,* the risk of unemployment is very much connected with the type of educational establishment, but it is the university graduates for whom it is lowest, followed by those from polytechnics and colleges; whatever the establishment, young engineers and graduates in mathematics, physics and management always have a lower risk of unemployment that those from other disciplines.[18] In *Switzerland,* the unemployment rate is below average for lawyers (1.0 per cent) and engineers (1.7 per cent); by contrast, for social science and humanities graduates, despite a substantial fall, it is still well above the average (5.6 and 5.5 per cent respectively). What is more, 13 per cent of social science graduates and 11 per cent of humanities graduates stated that they had taken jobs that bore little or no relationship to their training.[19] In *Yugoslavia,* where an "absorption" indicator that can be compared with that in the Netherlands is used, it is doctors and graduates in the humanities and social sciences, followed by young scientists and mathematicians, who are the most disadvantaged; at post-secondary level, it is above all those with qualifications in the social sciences and biological technologies.

This rapid survey already leads to some more precise conclusions. First, at the end of the 1980s employment in education always had a decisive influence on the position of graduates on the labour market. Several factors are at work here. Most important is the organisation of teacher training: where this is associated with certain university disciplines, for example the humanities and sciences, these graduates generally have difficulty in finding a job; where teacher training is distinct – which is often the case with primary teachers – it is subject to tighter planning and those who qualify have hardly any risk of unemployment. On the other hand, the labour market for *other* graduates, notably in the humanities, is much narrower, as shown by the example of Sweden.[20]

Second, certain disciplines such as psychology, the social sciences (but excluding economics and management, which are sometimes attached to them) and also medicine and biology, mainly lead to the public sector in the broad sense (we include here the health professions, where private practice is generally financed by a public system of social security contributions). Graduates in psychology and the social sciences are in a very unfavourable situation virtually everywhere, and this is also frequently the case with graduates in biology (and more generally the "life sciences", to adopt the expression in the French contribution, which includes here agrofood, agricultural engineering, etc.). On the other hand, the situation of young doctors varies greatly from one country to another: excellent in Canada, very bad in Italy and a good many other countries. Since it is a sector that is neither completely public nor completely private, planning is not very strict and the authorities are not always able to directly regulate admissions.

Third and last, technology and engineering, economics and management graduates generally have good prospects, though there are certain exceptions: Norway, where openings for engineers and technicians have been hard hit by the recent slowing of growth; Denmark, where admission to higher education has been planned for some time, access to training leading to the public sector having been greatly restricted and orientation towards technical training strongly encouraged, so that the relative position of engineers is now less favourable than it was. It is pointed out in the Swedish contribution that the employment prospects for graduates in this group are very sensitive to changes in the economic situation.

We now intend to add detail to this overview, using the other transition parameters and examining in turn the situations of the different categories of graduates. It is not a matter in this report of studying in detail the employment prospects in each profession or branch of activity – this is more the theme for monographs that could be produced by the professional associations – our aim is to identify the broad trends and if possible to explain them. To this end we have grouped the disciplines into four categories: science and technology; humanities and social sciences; economics and law; and finally medicine and paramedical disciplines. This choice is largely dictated by the information we already have on the employment situation. It does not appear to correspond to any national or international classification and is simply intended to facilitate discussion.

B. Scientific and technical disciplines

This first group includes first of all the training of engineers and technologists and also the paths leading to agricultural engineering and the agrofood sector: then come mathematics and the sciences. This can give rise to certain difficulties of classification, such as putting information science with biology, but these are not of great significance in our discussion.

1. *Engineers and technologists*

In most countries engineering graduates are still among the most advantaged for access to employment; minimal initial unemployment, short job search periods, direct access to a steady job, initial wage among the highest. It is considered in many countries that the number of engineers is insufficient, when there is not talk of an actual shortage. in France, the *Haut Comité Education-Economie* expressed the wish in 1988 that the number should be rapidly doubled through an annual increase of 7 to 8 per cent in graduate flows. Table 35 shows the estimates drawn up by Egor, an international recruitment agency.

According to these estimates there is a substantial deficit in several countries. In *France* it is considered that every graduate receives several job offers as soon as he qualifies. This situation may be explained either by the stagnation of supply or the increase in demand. However the situation appears quite different in certain countries. We have already spoken of *Norway*, where engineers and graduates from the regional colleges have suffered from the recent recession. The authors of the German and Danish reports put forward a comparable argument to explain their particular situations. The author of the *German* contribution explains the rise in unemployment among engineers by the fact that the employers had complained of shortages in the beginning of the 1980s, which gave rise to a big public debate and resulted in an increase in the number of young people studying engineering, who are now qualified and entering working life. In *Denmark,* the very rapid rise in the wages of young engineers at the beginning of the 1980s had a similar effect. However the wages of young graduates in *Germany* remain among the best, notably in computer sciences, industrial engineering, mechanical and electrical engineering (in third place after doctors, physicists and chemists according to a 1987 study and in top place in private industry according to a 1989 study). In *Denmark,* the wages of young engineers (25 to 29) are the highest in the categories, regardless of whether they have completed long university courses or other shorter courses (*akademie* or *teknikum*); middle-level engineers even have a wage higher than that of university graduates in other disciplines. In *Australia,* if we look at the relative position of young engineers, we see that they are in the leading group: from the standpoint of access to full-time employment they are behind those with medical or accounting training (this is a first degree so that doctors are excluded); as regards wages, they come behind the health professions and earth sciences, who overtook them in 1987.[21] The author considers that this trend is not marked enough to indicate a shortage, but nevertheless recognises that the supply of engineers in Australia depends as much on immigration as on flows of young graduates. He also points out that there has been concern about recent developments in subject choices at secondary level: the number of young people qualifying for entry to science and technology courses could become insufficient. In the *Netherlands,* the data in the national contribution, which speaks of average or good employment prospects for engineers from both the universities and the HBO, are not incompatible with the Egor estimate. The wages of engineering graduates nevertheless come in third place, after the doctors and economists; those with HBO qualifications in second place after the economists.[22] In any event the engineers occupy a sound position on the labour market and perhaps both the forecasts of coming shortages and those of a deterioration in these graduates' positions will prove true only for certain disciplines and certain places. In *Switzerland,* Federal Polytechnic school engineers find employment quite readily and their situation in

Table II–35. **Supply and demand for engineers in 1990**
Thousands per year

	Supply	Demand
Germany	31.0	31.0
Belgium	4.7	8.7
Denmark	4.0	3.2
Spain	8.7	14.0
France	14.0	25.0
Italy	8.5	23.0
Netherlands	11.0	9.0
Portugal	2.0	3.5
United Kingdom	18.0	26.0
Sweden	2.6	2.9

Source: Egor, Paris, 1990.

this respect even improved between 1983 and 1989, taking into account all of the parameters used in the *Association suisse pour l'orientation universitaire* ASOU surveys.

Among the engineers there are differences according to the branch. These differences are obviously fairly closely linked with the particularities of each national situation and variations in supply and demand in the different branches. Very often electronics and computer sciences are the best placed, but in *Austria*, for example, it is the metallurgists who are most sought after. But there is no doubt some general validity in the ranking established by the authors of the *French* report, with general engineers at the top, and chemical engineers, agricultural engineers and other life sciences specialists at the bottom. After one or two years at work, in 1987, the chemical engineers earned only 85-90 per cent as much as the others and the agricultural engineers 75 per cent. In *Belgium,* the unemployment rate for engineers in general was 1.9 per cent, that of chemical and agricultural engineers 6.2 per cent; the proportion of insecure jobs was respectively 1.9 and 12.5 per cent. The civil engineers also often find themselves in a rather unfavourable position. In *Germany* the starting wage for civil engineers is even lower than the average for university graduates,[23] but this is not true everywhere: in *Austria* they are better placed than the electrical engineers,[24] while in the *United Kingdom* they are the ones who find it easiest to get a job.[25] The same is true for *Switzerland* where civil engineers are much in demand.

The employment opportunities for graduates in agricultural engineering and disciplines leading to associated industries do not follow the same logic as those of the other technical disciplines. The situation of agriculture and the agrofood industries may be excellent in certain countries and certain branches and very bad in others. Returning to the French classification, it would appear that the prospects are less favourable than for other engineers, but are about the average for training of the same level. The disparities are fairly large. In *Norway* they were among those graduates who found jobs most easily in 1989, without there being any apparent deskilling.[26] In *Australia* the situation has been deteriorating since 1977: the starting wage has fallen from seventh to fifteenth rank over the period and the increase in wages over five years seems to be below the average.[27] It can be said that in *Italy* and *Austria* their situation is a little more favourable than for the average graduate. This is also the case in *Belgium* for graduates from Ghent, but in Louvain the agricultural engineers are classified among the graduates "at risk". In neither case however does there seem to be any deskilling. In *Canada, France, Switzerland* and the *Netherlands,* the employment prospects are less favourable. In *France,* the situation of graduates of ISCED 6 level is not so good as that of people with short-cycle post-secondary training in computers or electronics. In *Canada* too this discipline is one of the more disadvantaged, but here the biological sciences are included. We can thus see a general trend but with very marked disparities, connected with both the national situation in this sector and the specialities within it.

Young people from non-university training (this term, often used in the description of higher education systems, is scarcely satisfactory here, insofar as in several countries engineers are trained in establishments separate from the university and, conversely, short-cycle technical training may be given in universities or establishments belonging to them) are benefiting in most countries from the strong demand for skilled personnel. In countries where the economic situation is less favourable, their relative position has deteriorated more than that of the engineers. When a particular speciality is affected, people qualified at this level suffer most. By and large however, like the engineers, they are in a privileged position. In *Denmark* and *Germany,* their wages are higher than those of university graduates in non-scientific disciplines.

Naturally their position relative to engineers varies according to the country, depending on the specific place occupied by this type of training in higher education and on the speciality. In *Denmark,* the gap between their initial wage and that of engineering graduates is about 10 per cent.[28] A study carried out in the chemical industry in the *United Kingdom* indicates a gap of 10 per cent for holders of the HND-HNC with respect to graduates with a first degree and about 25 per cent to those with a doctorate; broadly speaking, from the point of view of access to employment, the position of HND holders is a little less favourable than that of graduates, with unemployment/temporary job rates of 13 and 10 per cent respectively and slight deskilling.[29] In the *Netherlands* the initial wage gap is in the order of 20 per cent.[30] In *Germany* the gap is also in the order of 20 per cent. It has been shown that during the recession at the beginning of the 1980s, 30 per cent of those with *Fachhochschule* qualifications were performing functions similar to those of graduate engineers, and no deskilling was noted (at skilled worker level).[31] In *Norway,* the economic situation has not affected the employment level of engineers, on the contrary, but the situation of those with regional college qualifications has deteriorated. The respective rates of correspondence between the level of the job and the level of training, which were respectively 84 and 85 per cent in 1985, are now 94 and 72 per cent. On the other hand, the wage gap remained at 15 per cent throughout the 1980s.[32] In *Belgium,* where the employment prospects remain good, there is competition with engineers, which brings a certain upgrading. In *France,* almost half the young people at this level have direct access to a steady job, as against 80 per cent for engineers.[33] The wage gap is also greater, in the order of 40 to 45 per cent. The difference varies greatly with the speciality however: in terms of access to employment, computer and electronics specialists approach the level of engineers, while chemists and biologists remain very far behind.[34] Chemical laboratory technicians from the Community Colleges in *Canada* are also in an unfavourable position.[35] The question that arises at this level, therefore, is not that of access to employment, but rather that of subsequent progress in a career.

2. *Scientific disciplines*

It is only to be expected that there will be certain differences between the situation of young scientists and that of young engineers on the labour market and big disparities in the employment opportunities for different scientific disciplines. The first reason is that in many countries the main function of scientific training has been to prepare people for jobs in education and research. Recruitment into public sector research has fallen sharply, while in education there are still shortages of teachers in the scientific disciplines, so here young scientists are better off than the arts graduates. However, the development of post-compulsory schooling has not always sufficed to compensate either for the demographic trend or the increased supply: the problem is therefore to find new openings outside these traditional sectors. Here the scientists are in competition with the engineers and technologists.

In certain countries the "cultural gap" between engineers and scientists is fairly narrow and both can be found in private sector enterprises. In other countries this gap, and the difference in prestige that may go with it, is much greater and young scientists may have difficulty in switching. In *France,* the recruitment of science graduates from the universities (as opposed to the engineers trained in separate schools) into the private sector, and notably into industry, is considered to be one of the significant features of the 1980s.

It is thus relevant to ask what is the relative position of science graduates with respect to the average graduate and the engineers. It is in *Germany* that the position of scientists seems to be the most favourable. We have seen that a 1987 study placed the physicists and chemists ahead of the engineers, with an average wage 6 per cent higher than the engineers and 17 per cent higher than the average; a 1989 study of private industry puts them after the industrial engineers and computer specialists, but still in the leading group. It is interesting to note also that it is the chemists who have the most favourable situation, contrary to other countries.[36] The scientists are also well placed in *Denmark,* behind the engineers and economists, the wage gap with the engineers being about 20 per cent.[37] In the *Netherlands,* where the employment prospects for young scientists are considered satisfactory, their wages are only 3 per cent lower than the engineers, but the latter are only 7 per cent above the average and it is the economists and doctors who are far in the lead with wages 25 per cent above the average.[38] In *France* the situation is probably more favourable, notably for the increasing number of young scientists who obtain a higher degree (DEA-DESS). From the standpoint of access to employment, they are situated between the engineers and those from short-cycle technical training (with the exception of chemical engineers and chemists). The wage for holders of a *licence* or *maîtrise* is 10 per cent lower than the average for engineers, 5 per cent for those who have obtained the DEA-DESS. It should be pointed out that half of the first group and three-quarters of the second enter the private sector.

In other countries however, young scientists are a long way behind the engineers, or about the average for university graduates. This is the case in *Finland,* where holders of a Bachelor's degree have a wage about the average and the holders of a Master's are somewhat worse off with a salary about 10 per cent below the average, both groups being among those who have the greatest difficulty in finding a job.[39] In *Belgium* and *Italy* the scientists are about the average for graduates from the standpoint of access to employment, perhaps in a slightly more difficult position in *Belgium.* This is also the case in *Canada,* where, other things being equal, from the standpoint of access to employment the scientists are in a situation comparable to that of the engineers two years after qualifying, *i.e.* about the average, but five years after qualifying, the engineers have gained a certain advantage.[40] In *Sweden,* after five years the scientists' wages are 25 per cent below those of the engineers.[41] In *Austria,* the initial wage is about the average: 98 per cent for mathematicians and physicists, 83 per cent for chemists. Three years later, they are respectively 90 and 74 per cent of the average, as compared with the mechanical engineers who earn 31 per cent above the average initially and 19 per cent above after three years.[42] In *Norway,* the scientists too are suffering from the economic difficulties and their unemployment rate rose above the average for graduates in 1989. Since 1987 they have been relying on the public sector. Wages, which had risen above the average towards the mid-1980s have fallen back slightly below it, while the wages of arts graduates have improved.[43] In *Switzerland,* the situation of scientists as regards employment one year after graduating is scarcely better than that of arts and humanities graduates, and way behind that of graduates in technical sciences. However, there are fairly wide disparities between specialities: whereas the employment situation of mathematicians is similar to that of engineers, chemists are the worst off of all: only 3 out of 4 of them were in gainful employment one year after graduating, compared with a figure of 90 per cent for mathematics graduates who had a job.

Table II–36. **France**

First jobs for science graduates by discipline, 1978-1984

Percentages

First jobs	SEF[a] 1978	SEF[a] 1984	SES[b] 1978	SES[b] 1984	SN[c] 1978	SN[c] 1984	SVC[d] 1978	SVC[d] 1984
Engineers and managers	14	7	50	51	6	7	20	10
Technicians and supervisors	5	4	35	32	16	13	33	31
Teachers with tenure	36	50	4	6	14	36	3	14
Teachers without tenure	44	35	8	9	58	34	24	30
Lower level jobs	1	4	3	2	6	10	20	15

a) SEF: exact sciences.
b) SES: applied sciences.
c) SN : natural sciences.
d) SVC: life sciences, chemistry.
Source: F. Pottier and A. Charlot, French report, Table III-8.

Two conclusions can thus be drawn from our examination of the national contributions. First, the situation of young scientists, at least mathematicians and physicists, is comparable with the average for university graduates, and more favourable in some countries. Second, despite the diversity of the criteria used, there is little deskilling to be seen even in those countries where their situation is not very favourable. Can it be concluded then that in certain cases the position of scientists is close to that of engineers, while in others it is closer to that of teachers? To answer this question we would need to know the differences in wages between the education sector and the private sector, and account would have to be taken of the destinations of graduates by speciality and by level. The Norwegian report, indicating wage by level and function (p. 315) already suggests that any shift towards the public sector (as is the case) implies a reduction in the *average* wage of scientists, teaching being the least well paid function. The French report shows that the destinations of holders of the *licence* or *maîtrise* depend very much on the speciality: Table 36, taken from this contribution, shows the extent of these differences. The exact sciences lead mainly to teaching, applied sciences to jobs as engineers or managers, but also in some cases to jobs as technicians and supervisors; the natural sciences lead mainly to teaching, usually without tenure, and also to the private sector but here in middle-level jobs; chemistry and the life sciences seem to have no clear destinations, but often lead to jobs of a lower level. This example shows the extent of the disparities within this graduate group and at the same time the necessity to study the transition conditions in connection with the destinations, which are the subject of Chapter 6.[44]

C. The humanities and social sciences

Many countries have a very broad interpretation of this category, notably including the economic sciences, management and even accounting. In this report, as indicated above, we adopt a more restrictive definition, examining separately the cases of economics and law, which constitute a more homogenous category from the standpoint of employment.

Examination of the national contributions shows that this definition still covers a very broad field, including literature, languages and the arts, philosophy, history and geography, psychology and sociology and the political sciences. In many countries, the educational sciences and teacher training also constitute an important component. Lastly, applied social sciences such as preparation for careers in social work, may also be included and may have a certain numerical importance, notably at ISCED 5 level, though in view of the content perhaps some of this training should come under the heading of management.

This category not only covers a very broad field, it also represents a substantial proportion of the graduate flow, as was shown in Part One, notably for women. We also know that with the cuts in public service recruitment, especially in education, it is often difficult for graduates in this category to find jobs. This is one of the reasons why a special project has been devoted to this particularly vulnerable sector.

In view of the wide variety of disciplines it is difficult to know what groupings and sub-categories would be useful for studying the conditions of labour market entry and destinations. A practical difficulty is that the groupings used in different countries, notably for the collection of statistics, are not the same and are not necessarily superimposable. There is sometimes a tendency to make a distinction between the more academic disciplines and those with a more vocational orientation, but here we have preferred to distinguish between a first group of disciplines that lead mainly to research and teaching at different levels in the system, and a second group comprising sociology, psychology and the political sciences. The employment of graduates in the first group depends to a large extent on the resources the authorities are able to devote to the education sector (and possibly to research) and on the combined effects of demographic factors and enrolment rates. What is more, access to this type of training is regulated as a function of anticipated employment opportunities in several countries. These are two arguments in favour of attaching training for social service careers to this first group, but this is not always possible for practical reasons.

1. Disciplines leading mainly to teaching

There is an implicit assumption in this heading: that the type of training received by graduates in this first group does for the most part lead to jobs in the education sector. In fact we do observe (see also Chapter 6) that for "arts graduates" (we shall use this term for convenience) the main opening still remains teaching. There are also great disparities when it comes to entry into working life. The data do not always enable us to make a distinction, but whether a graduate has access to a job in education or not seems to be a determining factor everywhere.

In certain countries, where teacher training constitutes a separate discipline, it is to be expected that this will facilitate access to employment for the young people emerging from it. In *Canada* for example, it is considered that their situation is very good in this respect, access to the teaching profession and admission to the training colleges being regulated. In the two years following qualification, teachers are the least exposed to unemployment apart from the health professions and five years after qualifying they are still in this position, whereas graduates in arts and the fine arts are among the least advantaged: after two years the unemployment rates are 13 and 16 per cent, as against 5 per cent for education graduates. These differences tend to disappear after a few years.[45] In terms of correspondence between the level of training and the level of employment, the gap still diminishes over time, but remains significant: after two years, 31 per cent of the education graduates, 52 per cent of the arts graduates and 61 per cent of the fine arts graduates consider themselves underemployed; after five years the figures are 34, 43 and 44 per cent respectively. The last two categories of graduates are in fact the most disadvantaged. A similar situation is found in *Finland:* minimum unemployment in education at both Bachelor and Master level, while it is the arts graduates who are in the worst situation, particularly for the men. Similarly in terms of the job level, education graduates for the most part have satisfactory jobs, while among the Bachelors of Arts there is considerable deskilling.[46] In terms of wages, Bachelors of Education are about the average, Bachelors of Arts slightly below; Masters of Education have no wage advantage from the level of their degree, while Masters of Arts have a slightly higher wage, though still 10 to 12 per cent below the average.[47] In *Switzerland,* although arts graduates are in a better position than social science graduates, they often have jobs for which a university degree is not required, which implies a certain degree of deskilling.

Although *France* does not make the same distinction at university level, it is possible to study the differences in situations according to the orientation of disciplines. On the whole the conditions of access to employment are a little above the average – though a higher degree is necessary (DEA-DESS) for the entry conditions to be as good as those of holders of an ISCED 5 level diploma (BTS, IUT) in a sought-after discipline.[48] On the other hand, in terms of deskilling the figures put forward are 8 per cent for arts, 14 per cent for languages and as much as 51 per cent for applied languages that do not lead to teaching.[49] The interesting thing about this example is that the relatively favourable situation of graduates from the "pedagogic" disciplines is not due to the planning of admissions, but to a revival of recruitment into secondary teaching, which is expected to continue during the 90s. In *Norway,* while the *relative* situation of arts graduates is favourable in terms of unemployment risk and wages, this is due mainly to the restrictions imposed during the late 191970s to avoid a surplus of graduates in these fields.

We have given a few examples of countries where the situation of arts graduates, at least those going in for teaching, is relatively favourable. In many other countries, these graduates are among the most disadvantaged whether it be in terms of access to employment, wages or job level. In *Germany,* young teachers are having difficulty in finding jobs; among holders of the *Abitur* (final secondary certificate), whether they have continued their studies or not, the unemployment rate among teachers is by far the highest, 16 per cent as against an average of 7 per cent.[50] There is also a high proportion of jobs of a high level, but only temporary. The wages for graduates are 20 per cent below the average. The *Australian* report on humanities and the social sciences points out that wages in the public sector, and notably in teaching, have increased much less rapidly than in the private sector, so that the starting wages for teachers fell from sixth to thirteenth place between 1977 and 1988. In *Austria,* young teachers and arts graduates are among the most exposed to unemployment: after two years 38.5 per cent of the teachers and 40.9 per cent of the arts graduates had still not found a job. Initial wages are the lowest among university graduates; two years later, their absolute and relative position has improved, but is still about 12 per cent below the average.[51] In *Belgium,* graduates in philosophy and the arts are among those most exposed to unemployment (11.7 per cent as against an average of 6.5 per cent), the most exposed being graduates in "educational and psychological sciences", grouped as a single category (14.2 per cent); after the scientists these are the categories most likely to occupy temporary jobs (half of them). One-third consider themselves to be underemployed and underpaid. The results are similar for both Ghent and Louvain.[52] In *Denmark,* while the entry conditions are more satisfactory, the wages are the lowest, both for arts graduates and people from teacher training colleges.[53] In *Italy,* arts graduates are the category most often found in temporary jobs (40.3 per cent as against an average of 28.1 per cent), but unemployment is lower than the average.[54] In the *Netherlands,* employment prospects in this sector are bad and wages 20 per cent below the average.[55] In *Sweden,* there is a deskilling rate very much higher than the average (65 as against 45 per cent) and wages are slightly lower. In the *United Kingdom,* the "unemployment/temporary employment" rate is 28 per cent for English graduates as against an average of 12 per cent[56] (see also Tables 40 and 41 below). With the exception of graduates with a diploma in education, the arts graduates are also those with the greatest proportion of deskilled jobs.

What conclusions can we draw from this rapid survey? The average wages of young arts graduates are below the average, but teaching jobs (notably for this category, which includes primary teachers, which is not the case with science graduates) are often not so well paid as jobs in the private sector, so that in this category the wage does not have the same value as an indicator as it does with other graduates. On the other hand, the proportion of temporary, insecure and lower level jobs is very high. This has a different significance according to whether we are considering the situation of young people entering the teaching profession or those seeking a job in some other sector.

In the case of young teachers (on the arts side, but also in the sciences) this generally has a significance somewhat different from that normally found in employment surveys. Admittedly, it is in certain cases a preparatory stage for access to the public service,[57] but very often it is associated with the very insecure status of being without tenure or an "auxiliary" teacher or, more recently, with the creation of temporary jobs in the public sector under programmes to combat unemployment. The public services are increasingly using these programmes (financed by the employment services) to maintain their staff levels or to perform tasks that would otherwise no longer be done at all. Over half of the graduates going into the public sector in Germany have only fixed-term contracts or have been taken on as part of job creation schemes. The same trend is to be seen in Belgium.

In both cases, young graduates performing the same tasks as their colleagues with tenure, but for very much lower pay, first worry about whether their contract is likely to be renewed, then whether they have any hope of being given a permanent job. This is probably the way in which the figures referring to deskilling and poor pay, which refer more to their status than to the use of their skills, should be interpreted. Accepting this insecure status, which can be obtained rapidly, is a gamble, the result of which depends on the eventual recruitment prospects and possibly the political weight these people represent.

As for the young arts graduates who do not enter the teaching profession, their situation is even more insecure. In both *Germany* and *Belgium,* many of them have to resort to "created jobs" in the public sector, no doubt in comparable material conditions, but with much less chance of renewal of the contract or achieving tenure. If they have not found a training job in the private sector, they stand a considerable risk of being marginalised. If the indicator of deskilling adopted is the proportion of graduates classified as white- or blue-collar workers or secretaries, these rates, often high enough already, must be considered to underestimate the phenomenon: the proportion should be calculated not with respect to total flows, the greater part of which enter teaching, but with respect to those who do not enter this profession. Women are no doubt more willing to accept deskilling, which may explain why in several cases their unemployment rate is lower than that of men.

2. *The social sciences*

In the other disciplines in this first category, *i.e.* psychology, sociology, and also certain arts disciplines that have no direct link with teaching (we have cited the case of applied foreign languages in France), artistic training and that preparing people for careers in social work and cultural activities, the employment prospects depend less on the characteristics of a particular sector and its evolution. They do however depend to a large extent on the employment possibilities in the public sector, so that in present circumstances this means that the conditions of entry are generally worse than those of candidates for the teaching profession.

In *Germany,* the proportion obtaining a satisfactory and steady job (in 1983) was only 46 per cent, as against 61 per cent for teachers and an average of 63 per cent; the deskilling rate was 33 per cent as against 25 and 22 per cent respectively; some good jobs but with no future were no doubt the result of job creation in the public sector. The wages for university graduates and those from the *Fachhochschule* were the lowest for this category,

20-23 per cent below the average. In the *Austrian* survey, the proportion of graduates who had not yet found a job after two years was the highest of all categories (60 per cent). In *Belgium,* psychology (grouped as we have seen with the educational sciences) had the highest unemployment rate (14.2 per cent), while the political and social sciences were in a more or less average situation for all the factors considered, the position being similar in Ghent and Louvain. In *Canada,* social science graduates from both the Community Colleges and the universities were also situated close to the average. In *Finland,* both Bachelors and Masters were well below the average, though this affected mainly the women. In terms of deskilling (see Table 39 below), there is a very substantial difference between the position of Bachelors and Masters in the social sciences and above all in psychology, where the ratio of the indicator used is 26:3 overall and 36:3 for men. In *France,* holders of a *licence* or *maîtrise* or higher degree (DEA-DESS) in sociology or psychology and holders of IUT certificates aspiring to careers in social work are among those most exposed to long-term unemployment (15 to 20 per cent have a total duration of unemployment of over a year) and only 40 per cent find access to a steady job; they have in fact very little advantage over young people from secondary education. Among the psychologists, while half the holders of a higher degree obtain managerial jobs, this proportion is only one-quarter for those with a first degree. In *Italy* on the other hand, graduates in social science and politics are among those who obtain a steady job most quickly, after the engineers and economists, and they have a lower than average unemployment rate.[58] Together with the lawyers they are the group who most often obtain employment through competitive examinations. In fact, when they obtain a steady job in this way, they are the least satisfied as regards the use of their skills and, with the arts graduates, their wages. In *Norway,* social science graduates, 90 per cent of whom enter the public sector, consider they have a job that suits their level. In the *Netherlands,* where the employment prospects in this sector are bad, whatever the level of the degree, wages are also among the lowest (ahead of languages and culture). The situation is similar in *Sweden.* In the *United Kingdom,* social science graduates have greater difficulty in access to employment than arts graduates, and as in their case the difficulties are greater for graduates of polytechnics and especially the colleges than for university graduates. On the other hand, women seem to find work more easily, suggesting that they are more willing to accept lower level jobs (see Table 40). In *Switzerland,* the situation of social science graduates has improved since 1985, particularly in the case of education graduates; however, in 1989 46 per cent of them were in a job for which no university degree was required.

The picture is not equally gloomy everywhere. It is possible to make some observations, which we shall discuss in more detail below. The first is that the more "vocational" disciplines, such as psychology, can give access for some to high-level jobs, but the most striking feature, as pointed out by the Finnish report, is that there are very great disparities. These graduates are found at the highest levels, but also at the lowest. A second observation is that the level of the degree – the type of training perhaps being only secondary – plays an important role, whether it is required for entry to the public service examinations (like the *Masters* in Finland or the *Laurea* in Italy) or whether it indicates a certain level of aptitude and a certain capacity for work, which can also be measured as a function of the prestige of the establishment (as in the United Kingdom). Those who have a higher degree or are from a prestigious establishment can gain access to high-level jobs, possibly in their speciality; the others present themselves on a different market, where their general level of education is appreciated but where they are not considered to have any special skills. The situation of young people from short-cycle courses fits into this twofold logic of the level of the qualification and the vocational nature of the training, one being able to partly compensate for the other: in France, training leading to careers in social work or information are in a similar situation to university graduates in psychology or sociology, but in fact have only a slight advantage over those from secondary education.

D. Economics and law

This category includes a fairly large range of disciplines, mostly with a vocational orientation. They lead to both the public and private sectors. In all countries, legal studies constitute a separate group and the conditions of access to employment have a specific character. The economics group covers a great variety of subjects and includes macroeconomics, enterprise management, accounting and commerce. The national statistics include subgroups that do not necessarily correspond, distinctions sometimes being made between what is theoretical and what is more vocational, or between macroeconomic and microeconomic, or again between accounting and economics. By and large, no doubt thanks to the expansion of employment in the private tertiary sector, these graduates have favourable employment prospects, though here again there are big disparities.

1. Economics

Young economics graduates are among the best placed for access to employment, immediately following the engineers. In the *Netherlands* for example, employment opportunities are excellent and wages for both university graduates and for those from the HBO are even better than those of engineers.[59] In *Italy,* like the engineers, they have ready access to steady jobs and the least risk of unemployment. Wages are satisfactory and there is little deskilling.[60] In *Belgium,* despite a certain proportion of temporary jobs – comparable with that of the engineers – their situation is extremely favourable: the risk of unemployment is minimal and there is little underemployment.[61] More generally, however, their situation is less clear-cut.

In *Germany,* access to employment in 1983 was comparable with that of engineers: 70 per cent of economics graduates (as against 79 per cent of the engineers) found steady and satisfactory jobs. On the other hand, there was a substantial amount of deskilling, essentially in the steady jobs: 29 per cent as compared with an average of 12 per cent (33 per cent for the social sciences). Wages (1984) for both university and *Fachhochschule* graduates were a little lower than those of engineers. In private industry (1989) management graduates were in an average situation, with a slight advantage over the economists. In *Australia,* this group was about average; "accountants" (probably management) having an advantage over the economists in terms of wages and access to employment and coming immediately after the scientists and the health professions. In *Austria,* wages initially and two years after qualifying come immediately after those of engineers. The Austrian report points out however that graduates in economics and management were the most numerous to occupy "new jobs" (29.8 per cent) and a considerable proportion occupied jobs that were not previously held by graduates (32 per cent as compared with 41 per cent for arts graduates and psychologists). The report concludes that, while on the whole economics graduates lie about the average as regards wages and job level, a good number are forced to accept jobs of a lower level. In *Canada,* the conditions of access to employment are about average, a little above for university graduates, a little below for those from colleges. As regards the correspondence between level of training and job level university graduates are about the average, but college graduates are much more exposed to deskilling.[62] In *Denmark,* the salaries of young people with qualifications in economics (long cycle) and commerce (medium cycle) come immediately after the engineers, those with management qualifications at both levels being slightly less advantaged.[63] In *Norway,* the situation was excellent in the mid-1980s, but has since deteriorated with the increase in supply and the recent economic crisis; young economists have had to seek less well paid jobs in the public sector and half of them consider they do not use their training. The risk of unemployment has increased above all for people from the regional colleges, who normally find jobs in the private sector.[64] In *Switzerland,* we find far more economists than lawyers, engineers and scientists and, of course, doctors in jobs for which the employer has not insisted on a degree in the subject concerned, or in jobs for which no university degree was required. This could be considered as deskilling; however, although in this respect the situation of these economists is similar to that of arts or social science graduates, unlike the latter they do not consider that their professional activity does not match up to their education and training.

The case of *Finland* warrants particular attention. Unemployment rates here are very low, approximately 2 per cent. It is not very significant to point out that unemployment rates among young economists are lower than average, though it is perhaps worth mentioning that for Bachelors the rate is 4.4 per cent for the men and 0.6 per cent for the women, while for Masters it is 1.2 for the men and 1.5 for the women. This suggests that women are aware that a Bachelor's degree is not enough to enter a management job and are more inclined than men to accept lower level jobs. On this subject, the author of the report points out that many graduates, notably in economics and management, have to accept lower level jobs in the private sector. The proportion of Bachelors in blue- or white-collar jobs is 29 per cent, 47 per cent for the women; the proportion of Masters in these jobs is still 15 per cent and 22 per cent respectively (studies at this level last six or seven years). Table 39 below shows that these rates of deskilling are even higher than those of arts and social science graduates.

The well documented case of *France* is interesting to examine. Access to employment is good for all three levels of higher education diploma (ISCED 5: IUT, BTS; ISCED 6; *licence-maîtrise;* ISCED 7; DEA-DESS). Certain highly vocation-oriented people at "*technicien*" level find jobs as easily as those at the highest level. Certain specialities, marketing techniques at ISCED 5 level and economic and social administration at ISCED 6 level have a higher risk of unemployment. The authors note that with the considerable expansion of this type of training, notably in the private sector, a reversal of situation could occur during the 90s, notably at ISCED 5 level. As regards the risk of deskilling, there is a marked hierarchy by qualification level and also by speciality. At ISCED 5 level, 38 per cent of the IUT holders are underemployed and 57 per cent of the BTS holders. At ISCED 6 level (the criteria used cannot be the same), only 48 per cent of the graduates in law and economic sciences (here grouped as a single category) obtain management jobs, as against 61 per cent for holders of a higher degree and 78 per cent for those from the *grandes écoles*.[65] On top of these disparities there is an internal differentiation: for example 42 per cent of those with economics at level 5 and 40 per cent of those with management obtain higher level jobs, but only 33 per cent of those with "economic and social administration".

There is also a double hierarchy in the *United Kingdom.* There is only a small amount of deskilling (in terms of the proportion of young graduates occupying blue- or white-collar jobs) but an advantage for accounting pathways over management and economics is emerging (see Table 40 below). This advantage is much greater if we consider employment/temporary job rates; four times higher for economists than for accountants (perhaps partly explained by the greater facility of access to trainee accountant jobs). The hierarchy of institutions also has a marked effect: in the case of the economists for example, the rate is 10 per cent for university graduates, 27 per cent for those from polytechnics and 42 per cent for those from the colleges (Table 40).

Economics and management graduates at present enjoy a privileged situation, though there are considerable disparities. These may be even more marked than in the case of the social sciences, for among the latter the proportion obtaining higher level jobs is generally low and deskilling more frequent. To explain these differences, there is first of all the equilibrium between supply and demand: the expansion of employment in the service sector has perhaps been overtaken by the expansion of training (notably in the private sector). But the ease of entry into working life is also the resultant of the combination of three factors: the more or less vocational nature of the training, the level of the qualification, and the prestige of the educational establishment.

2. Law

Legal training, given mainly in the universities, has not experienced expansion or proliferation comparable to that in management training. Access to employment has been facilitated by the development of the service sector and on the whole good conditions for entry to active life can therefore be expected. In several countries, access to the legal professions requires an additional period of apprenticeship or further training, as does access to the higher echelons of the public service. This partly explains fairly modest initial wages and a proportion of temporary jobs, but does not explain certain difficulties in finding employment. There are also some disparities.

From the information available, it can be said that for a number of countries law graduates are in a roughly average situation with regard to access to employment, wages and the use of skills. This is the case in *Denmark* and *Sweden.* In some countries their position is even very favourable. In *Belgium,* with the exception of criminologists, lawyers have a position comparable with that of engineers and economists as regards access to employment, while they are among the best placed, behind the health professions, from the standpoint of the use of their skills. In the *Netherlands,* it is considered that employment prospects for lawyers will be more favourable in the future, but at present salaries are not far behind those of engineers. In *Norway,* while the situation has deteriorated somewhat in recent years, wages remain slightly below average. In *Italy* on the other hand, while the proportion of law graduates obtaining a steady job is comparable with the average, the unemployment rate after three years is very high (27 per cent as against an average of 18 per cent).

In *Germany,* law graduates had good conditions of access to stable employment in 1983, but (unlike the economists) there was still a relatively high proportion of temporary and lower level jobs (13 per cent, the average being 9 per cent), which may partly correspond to training periods. The importance of these initial training periods is highlighted by the data for Australia and Austria. In *Australia,* the initial wage for lawyers was in 20th (and last) place in 1979, but five years later these same lawyers were in 3rd place, behind the medical professions and ahead of the engineers. In *Austria,* the initial wage was in 15th place; after two years, while the lawyers had gained only three places, they had received an increase of 30 per cent, like the economists. In *France,* the mobility study shows that in three years there is a significant increase in the proportion of graduates occupying higher level jobs, from 36 to 47 per cent, but not such a great increase as for economists, up from 27 to 45 per cent. There is also a deskilling rate of approximately 15 per cent, but on the whole employment opportunities are satisfactory. In *Switzerland,* the employment situation of law graduates improved between 1983 and 1989, by which time it had become relatively good. Lawyers' income, however, at the start of their career is less enviable, due to the amount of training they have to undergo.

It is interesting to consider the cases of Finland and the United Kingdom. In *Finland,* the unemployment rate among young Bachelors of Law are higher than the average: 3.4 as against 1.8 per cent, but this time it is the women who have the higher unemployment rate: 4.3 per cent as against 2.4 per cent for men. At Masters level, the rates are among the highest, but equivalent for men and women. If we consider the number of blue- and white-collar workers, we find very high rates for Bachelors (25 per cent for the men, 33 per cent for the women), while for Masters the figures are in the order of 6 per cent. We find here a phenomenon comparable with but even more marked than that of psychology: there is also a very high proportion of deskilling among people with Masters degrees in management, again with considerable differences between men and women (see Table 40). In the *United Kingdom,* law graduates who do not pursue their training beyond degree level are very disadvantaged as compared with graduates in economics, management and above all accountancy as regards access to employment (see Table 41). Here again there is a considerable difference between the universities and the polytechnics; the rates of unemployment/temporary employment are twice as high for the latter: 30 per cent as against 12 or 13 per cent. Graduates from the colleges have an unemployment rate of 25 per cent, but as compared with the economics pathways worse might have been expected.

Legal training leads on the whole to more homogeneous destinations. Access to employment is satisfactory, as is the use of skills. Wages are about average, but this can hide certain internal disparities: young lawyers, automatically classified among those with high level jobs, do not earn high wages for all that. There is everywhere still a minority of lawyers who have difficulties in entry to working life and can only obtain temporary jobs. It can also be seen that in some countries, studies leading to a first degree (insufficient perhaps to enter the regulated professions or to sit the public service examinations) are in a situation comparable to that of economics and social science disciplines and the deskilling rate can be considerable.

E. Medicine and paramedical disciplines

Berganza: De cinco mil estudiantes que cursaban aquel año en la universidad, los dos mil oían medicina.
Cipio: Pues, que vienes a inferir de eso?
Berganza: Infiero, o que estos dos mil médicos han de tener enfermos que curar (que sería harta plaga y mala ventura), o que ellos han de morir de hambre.

M. de Cervantes, Coloquio de los perros (ca. 1613)

The health professions to a large extent form a totally separate sector of employment (it would nevertheless be interesting to study, as in the case of teaching, the extent of the "hiving-off" effect, to use the expression coined by the author of the Belgian contribution). The national contributions give little information about what happens to people with qualifications in this field and it would appear that this sector is not covered by the survey system in certain countries, as it was in *France*. The data available nevertheless enable us to highlight some big differences between countries, demonstrating the efficiency or otherwise of regulation systems. There are also differences between the higher qualifications and the short-course paramedical sector.

First, there are countries where the situation for those qualified in the health field is extremely favourable. In *Norway*, the initial unemployment rate is the lowest of all and initial salaries, despite the recession, remain 30 per cent higher than the average.[66] In *Finland*, unemployment is minimal, especially for the men (a little higher in dentistry) and the wages are highest (for medicine and dentistry, pharmacy being slightly lower).[67] We would also mention Canada and Sweden. In *Canada*, at both college and university level, graduates are in first place in terms of access to employment as well as wages (Table 37). In *Sweden*, wages are by far the highest: after five years, doctors are 60 per cent above the average and after ten years 86 per cent; dentists and pharmacists are 12 per cent above the average after five years and respectively 10 and 25 per cent above the average after ten years. However, we have no data on entry into these professions. Conversely, the situation is very bad in Austria and Italy. In *Austria*, two years after qualifying, 58 per cent of the doctors had still not found a job (as compared with 41 per cent of arts graduates and 60 per cent of social science graduates). Together with the teachers they account for 71 per cent of graduate unemployment.[68] On the other hand, the initial wages of doctors are the highest (18 per

Table II-37. **Canada**

Median annual earnings for university graduates employed full-time, by sex, five years after graduation for 1982 graduates, and 2 years after graduation for 1986 graduates

Thousands C$

	1986 graduates in 1988			1982 graduates in 1987		
	Men	Women	Total	Men	Women	Total
Health professions	37	30	32	50	32	34
Engineering/applied sciences	30	30	30	36	32	35
Business/commerce	30	26	28	36	31	35
Math./physical sciences	30	29	29	35	32	35
Education	30	28	29	33	29	30
Social sciences	27	25	25	30	27	28
Humanities	26	24	25	28	25	26
Agriculture/biological sc.	24	23	24	29	26	27
Fine/applied arts	24	24	24	24	18	22
Total	30	26	28	34	28	30

Source: Statistics Canada.

cent above the average), but only 7 per cent above after two years. Pharmacists' wages, among the lowest initially (17 per cent below average) catch up with the average after two years. In *Italy,* after three years only one quarter of the doctors have obtained a steady job (the lowest proportion for all university disciplines); and the unemployment rate is the highest (32 per cent, as compared with an average of 22 per cent). They are also the worst placed in terms of wages.[69] *France* gave no information in its contribution, but is probably among those countries where the situation is not very favourable.

The situation is often not so clear-cut and a distinction has to be made between the position of the various disciplines or the different levels of training. In *Australia,* doctors and dentists after qualifying and five years later have the highest wages, whereas the pharmacists, while they have best access to employment, are in 23rd and last place for wages, both initially and five years later. In the *Netherlands,* where the employment prospects are mediocre for university graduates, more or less good according to specialisation at HBO level, the wages of university graduates are among the highest, behind the economists, at 20 per cent above the average, whereas those from the HBO have the lowest wages for their level, 25 per cent below the average. The *Belgian* report states that employment prospects in the paramedical sector are excellent, while the higher levels are saturated. The *French* report on the other hand states that recruitments, running at a very high level in the 1970s, started to decrease during the 1980s and that the sector is now saturated until at least the year 2000. In *Switzerland,* where the situation is still favourable for the medical professions as a whole, although 39 per cent of graduates stated that they had encountered difficulties when looking for a job, the field where the difficulties are the most severe is human medicine (as distinct from veterinary medicine, pharmacy and dentistry); geographical mobility is something which young doctors are obliged to accept.

Several reports refer to temporary jobs for young graduates. This was already the case in Germany in 1983, where 39 per cent had access only to jobs which were without any future, even though they were of the correct level. A good part of this percentage may be explained by these people having trainee status in specialised branches. The Italian figures are explained above all by the difficulty in obtaining a job. Those given by Belgium are very high for doctors (45 per cent, though the average is already 42 per cent) and market saturation is perhaps not the only explanation. Similarly, there is an increasing proportion of part-time jobs: this may be due to the increasing proportion of women in these professions, but on the other hand it may also be a form of disguised unemployment. A particularity of the higher level medical professions (as well as those of architect, lawyer, etc.) is that by definition there is no deskilling: market saturation can be expressed only through other combinations of parameters.

Other authorities are better placed than the OECD for carrying out a study of employment in the health sector. We shall therefore not try to go any deeper into the question here, while regretting that we have no more detailed information on the ISCED 5 level and paramedical training, which do represent, or did in the past, especially for women, an important path for access to semi-professional technical jobs.

III. THE DISPARITIES

A. The difficulty of taking stock

At the beginning of the previous section we pointed out the difficulty of taking stock of the situation of young graduates at national level. In many countries there is not yet sufficient information: while the number of surveys has increased and they have become more reliable, they still often lack coherence, do not cover the entire field or refer only to a single year. It is obviously even more difficult to make a synthesis on the international level. The main problems are discussed here.

In this chapter we have used the material in the national contributions more or less as it came. A reading gives rise to three main criticisms:

i) the detailed analysis by field of study does not always bring out the overall trends, because we have to use the information available, which often refers to a specific period. Drawing on Section II.A of this chapter and Chapter 4, which describe the context, we can see the broad trends but when it comes to a particular discipline the analysis often remains imprecise;

ii) the same concern with using all the information available leads, if not to mixing the findings of surveys on entry to working life with those of follow-up or career surveys, at least to not making the best use of the career surveys carried out in several countries. We thus have a fragmented and incomplete picture of the transition from education to employment and sometimes run the risk of unjustified generalisation;

iii) lastly, there are still gaps in the synthesis as in the basic information. One concerns the ISCED 5 level, where we know that there are great disparities; and we have not always been able to describe the situation at ISCED 7 level either. An important gap concerns the situation of women, a subject on which we have often only general ideas (which may perhaps be sufficient); often the information exists, but it is not presented in order not to make the tables too complicated.

There are also difficulties which, without necessarily being specific to international comparisons, are particularly marked at this level. The first is naturally the diversity of post-secondary education systems and social and cultural differences in the conception of the relationship between training and employment in different countries. These differences can have a great influence on the form of the transition. This is not the place to compare the practices in Japan, Germany and the United States, but we can give a specific example: that of the length of studies. Saying that the employment conditions have become such that graduates are employed in the place of young people from secondary education – whether we judge it positively or negatively – has an entirely different meaning depending on whether the qualification was obtained after three years of general study or after six or seven years of specialised training. It is therefore necessary to always take account of this factor in interpreting the information, but this is often impossible.

Another difficulty is concerned with the extent of deskilling. The surveys use very different criteria, some more or less subjective, others referring to job classifications or wage levels. If we take only the most objective, we can see the difficulty of interpreting and comparing at the international level results that are already somewhat unreliable at national level. Deskilling is a complex concept which can assume different meanings depending on the occupations concerned, the sectors of employment and the regions, and one has to be careful about assuming a one-way or two-way relationship between training and employment.

Another term whose meaning is somewhat fuzzy and to which we have already drawn attention is that of temporary employment. At one extreme there are obligatory training periods for access to the public service or a teaching post with tenure, additional training for doctors who want to become specialists, etc. At the other extreme there are odd jobs as waiter, temporary postman, labourer, etc. referred to by the figures in the United Kingdom surveys. In this chapter we have simply quoted the rapporteur's judgement or presented only the extreme cases which, though perhaps not the most significant, are the least disputable.

B. The balance sheet

The overall picture is generally positive. The challenge of the 1980s was the slowing of public recruitment and the necessary reorientation towards the private sector. We might have expected a clear deterioration in the situation of young graduates, but the transformation of supply, a favourable trend in employment and also greater flexibility on both sides has enabled graduates to maintain or even improve their position, though it must be said that this was sometimes at the expense of young people of a lower educational level. The recent trend seems to be above all in favour of the highest levels (ISCED 6 and 7).

However it has to be admitted that the slowing of recruitments in the public sector was less rapid than expected and that the economic upturn enabled private services to take over from the public services, so that the scale of the adjustment was diminished to this extent. There are however great disparities in the transition conditions and for certain categories access to employment is very difficult.

The question arises of the real extent of this breakdown in the relationship between education and employment, the mismatch between supply and demand. This is a very difficult question, because as we have seen the judgement has to be made on the basis of a combination of parameters. The German rapporteur estimates the proportion of young graduates in a difficult situation at between 10 and 15 per cent and the Belgian at 15 per cent, while other countries would probably give a much higher figure, especially taking into account specialised tertiary training at ISCED 5 level. What is more, separate estimates are required for men and women, the figures for the latter being likely to be fairly high in some cases.

The data examined in this chapter show that the difficulties are far from being equally distributed between the different levels and disciplines: on the contrary, they tend to concern the lower levels of qualification and are concentrated on certain fields, where there are often a large number of students and a high proportion of females, though the fields concerned are not necessarily the same in different countries. Among the "high risk" scientific disciplines we can mention biology and chemistry, except for those with higher degrees, but the problems are mainly in disciplines like psychology and sociology. Facing the same difficulties, however, we also find graduates in economics, management and law, despite the fact that these disciplines are vocational in character. In most countries the overall situation for these graduates is favourable, but it is less so in the case of those with lower level qualifications, women and graduates from less prestigious institutions. Another category affected are graduates in arts subjects who do not have access to the teaching profession.

Table II–38. **France**

Destinations of graduates: proportion of graduates employed at lower levels

1987 jobs of 1984 graduates, percentages

		Teachers without tenure	Intermediate occup. Technicians	White/blue-collar workers
BTS	Secondary	–	–	10.1
	Tertiary	–	–	57.3
	Total	–	–	40.5
IUT	Secondary	–	–	9.1
	Tertiary	–	–	38.2
	Total	–	–	25.8
LM	Sciences	20.9	18.8	3.8
	Economics/law	7.6	31.3	14.1
	Arts, social sciences	33.1	16.7	15.5
	Total	20.4	23.5	12.8
DEA	Sciences	13.6	12.6	2.7
	Economics/law	4.1	25.3	9.4
	Arts, social sciences	22.7	23.9	5.7
	Total	11.4	21.7	6.9
Schools	Commerce	0.8	16.2	5.1
	Engineering	3.5	3.3	0.9

BTS: *Brevets de Techniciens Supérieurs* (Advanced technicians diploma).
IUT: University Institutes of Technology.
LM: *Licence* or *Maîtrise*.
DEA: *Diplôme d'études approfondies* (Diploma of advanced studies).
Source: F. Pottier and A. Charlot, French report, Table II–4.

Table II–39. **Finland**

Destinations of graduates by level and discipline: proportion of white- and blue-collar workers, 1985

Stock, percentages

		Total	Men	Women
"Arts"	B	25	15	27
	M	6	4	6
Social sciences	B	23	21	23
	M	11	8	16
Psychology	B	26	36	22
	M	3	3	4
Management	B	29	11	47
	M	15	10	22
Law	B	30	25	33
	M	5	4	9
Sciences	B	11	9	13
	M	6	5	7
Technology	B	–	–	–
	M	8	8	8
Agriculture	B	–	–	–
	M	8	4	14

B: Bachelors Degree.
M: Masters Degree.
Source: A. Haapakorpi, "Graduates' destinations on the Finnish labour market", Helsinki, 1989.

Table II–40. **United Kingdom**

Employment difficulties encountered by holders of a first degree: proportion unemployed or having only a temporary job as a percentage of those entering the labour market, 1989

Percentages

	Universities M	Universities W	Polytechnics M	Polytechnics W	Colleges T	HND T
Economics	9	10	30	25	42	–
Management	9	8	14	15	19	22
Accounting	3	1	7	8	10	–
Law[a]	15	11	34	27	25	–
Arts[b]	20-37	16-25	19-35	20-36	17-49	–
Social sciences	20-25	15-23	31-39	20-28	25-39	–
Total	12	13	16	18	20	15

a) Excluding those in post-graduate training.
b) Excluding those in teacher training.
Source: J. Tarsh, United Kingdom report.

Tables 38, 39, 40 and 41 contain data for France, Finland and the United Kingdom clearly showing the differences between levels and categories. Table 38, relating to France, shows the striking difference between secondary sector (technological or industrial) training and tertiary sector training at ISCED 5 level. The deskilling rates for the university institutes of technology (IUT) are 9 and 38 per cent respectively, for higher level technicians (BTS) 10 and 57 per cent. If we keep the same criteria (proportions of white- and blue-collar workers) for university graduates, the differences between the sciences and the other disciplines are very marked: 6 per cent as against 14 per cent for economics and law at *licence/maîtrise* level, 3 per cent as against 9 and 6 per cent at higher degree level (DEA-DESS). There is also a significant difference according to level: at *licence/maîtrise* level, 43 per cent obtain higher level jobs, while at DEA-DESS level the figure rises to 60 per cent. Graduates in psychology and sociology are nevertheless in a much less favourable position. Graduates from the *grandes écoles* have very little risk of deskilling, especially the engineers. It should however be mentioned that, at least in France, while the concept of deskilling is relatively clear-cut in the case of industry, where there is a relatively strict ranking of jobs, it is far more vague in the service sector, where most people are simply classified as "non-manual workers".

Table 39 refers to Finland; the criterion used is the proportion of graduates in white- or blue-collar jobs. In the first place there are considerable differences according to the level of degree, as pointed out above. The difference is already clear for the sciences (6 per cent for Bachelors, 11 per cent for Masters) and becomes very

Table II–41. **United Kingdom**

Destination of holders of a first degree: proportion of white-collar workers and secretaries as a percentage of those entering the labour market, 1989

	Universities	Polytechnics	Colleges	HND
Economics	4	4	–	–
Management	3	2	4	12
Accounting	1	1	3	–
Law[a]	9	9	–	–
Arts[b]	7-19	6-14	8-17	–
Social sciences	5-13	6-11	14	–
Total	5	4	9	8

a) Excluding those in post-graduate training.
b) Excluding those in teacher training.
Source: J. Tarsh. United Kingdom report.

considerable for psychology (3 and 26 per cent), the arts (6 and 25 per cent) and law (5 and 30 per cent). The differences are greater for women, except in psychology where the reverse is true. But as regards management and the social sciences, the differences (by level and sex) remain but are cumulated with a very marked speciality effect which leads to a deskilling rate of 47 per cent for women with a Bachelor's degree in management.

For the United Kingdom we present two tables, 40 and 41, where the criteria are the unemployment/temporary job rate and the proportion of white-collar workers and secretaries. They call for two remarks: the very difficult situation of art graduates (who do not enter teaching), social science graduates and to a lesser extent law graduates (who do not go on to further legal training). The second feature is the very marked hierarchy between universities, polytechnics and colleges: it is in economics that the difference is most striking, the unemployment/temporary employment rate ranging from 10 to 42 per cent. A third remark can be added: the unemployment/temporary job rate for women is generally lower (or very much lower) than that of men. The data on the proportion of white-collar workers and secretaries in Table 41 shows the same disparities. These two tables present more or less a cross-sectional picture. While data are given on the HND, below degree level, there is none on higher degrees. The United Kingdom report[70] suggests there is a good deal of substitution between Masters and Bachelor level, which leads to the conclusion that there is, in a slightly different form, a level effect in the United Kingdom similar to that demonstrated for France.

These examples suffice to show that certain types of higher education have made it possible to respond to a social demand for education, but without always succeeding in giving young people qualifications they can use for access to employment. Two factors combine to increase the risk of employment difficulties for graduates: the discipline and the level of the degree, on top of which or instead of which there may be the relative prestige of the higher education establishment from which they graduate.

Notes and References

1. Bruce Williams, Australia, Volume I; Y. Coppens, Netherlands, Volume III.
2. A. Casanueva, Volume II.
3. Jason Tarsh, Volume IV.
4. M. Tessaring, Germany, Volume I.
5. *Ibid.*
6. B. Williams, Australia, Table 7, Volume II.
7. L. Lassnigg, Austria I, Volume I.
8. A. Bonte, Belgium, Volume I.
9. R. McDowell, Canada, Tables 6, 9 and 10, Volume II.
10. H. Traberg, Denmark, Volume II.
11. E.S. Hunt, United States, Table II.7, Volume II.
12. A. Haapakorpi, Finland, Table 1, Volume III.
13. F. Pottier and A. Charlot, France, Volume III.
14. F. Bussi, Italy, Table II.13, Volume III.
15. P. Aamodt, Norway, Table A2, Volume III.
16. I. Coppens, Netherlands, Tables 2.4 and 2.5, Volume III.
17. S. Fornäng, Sweden, Volume IV.
18. J. Tarsh, Figures 2 and 3, Volume IV.
19. T. Ogay, Switzerland, Volume IV.
20. Dan Andersson, Swedish contribution to the project on the humanities and social sciences.
21. B. Williams, Australia, Tables 7, 8, and 9, Volume I.
22. I. Coppens, Netherlands, Table 3.3, Volume III.

23. M. Tessaring, Germany, Table 17, Volume I.
24. L. Lassnigg, Austria, Table 9, Volume I.
25. J. Tarsh, United Kingdom, Table A.1, Volume IV.
26. P. Aamodt, Norway, Tables A2 and A8, Volume III.
27. B. Williams, Australia, Tables 8 and 9, Volume I.
28. H. Traberg, Denmark, Table 17, Volume II.
29. J. Tarsh, United Kingdom, Annex 2, Table 12; Annex 3, Table 5, Volume IV.
30. I. Coppens, Netherlands, Table 3.4, Volume III.
31. M. Tessaring, Germany, Tables 17 and 18, Volume I.
32. P. Aamodt, Norway, Tables A8 and A9, Volume III.
33. F. Pottier and A. Charlot, France, Figures 27 and 28, Volume III.
34. *Ibid.*, Figure 2.
35. R. McDowell, Canada, Table 7, Volume II.
36. M. Tessaring, Germany, Table 17, Volume I.
37. H. Traberg, Denmark, Table 17, Volume II.
38. I. Coppens, Netherlands, Tables 3.3 and 3.4, Volume III.
39. A. Haapakorpi, Finland, Table 3, Volume III.
40. R. McDowell, Canada, Table 9, Volume II.
41. S. Fornäng, Sweden, Volume IV.
42. L. Lassnigg, Austria I, Table 9, Volume III.
43. P. Aamodt, Norway, Table 9, Volume III.
44. In this chapter we shall not be examining the situation of graduates from short-cycle non-university courses at ISCED 5 level, at which most countries do not distinguish between scientific and technical training, or else consider that there is no scientific training at this level.
45. R. McDowell, Canada, Tables 9 and 10, Volume II.
46. A. Haapakorpi, Finland, Table A1, Volume III; see also Table 38 below.
47. *Ibid.*, Finland, Table 3.
48. F. Pottier and A. Charlot, France, Figures 27, 29 and 30, Volume III.
49. *Ibid.*, Table 20; see also Table 38 below.
50. M. Tessaring, Germany, Tables 13, 15 and 17, Volume I.
51. L. Lassnigg, Austria I, Table 9, Volume I.
52. A. Bonte, Belgium, Tables 6.3 to 6.7, Volume I.
53. H. Traberg, Denmark, Table 17, Volume II.
54. F. Bussi, Italy, Table II.13, Volume III.
55. I. Coppens, Netherlands, Table 3.4, Volume III.
56. J. Tarsh, Table A1, Volume IV.
57. M. Tessaring, Germany, Table 15, Volume I.
58. F. Bussi, Italy, Table II.13, Volume III.
59. I. Coppens, Netherlands, Tables 3.3 and 3.4, Volume III.
60. F. Bussi, Italy, Table II.13 and II.17, Volume III.
61. A. Bonte, Belgium, Table 6.3 and 6.4, Volume I.
62. R. McDowell, Canada, Tables 13 and 15, Volume II.
63. H. Traberg, Denmark, Table 17, Volume II.
64. P. Aamodt, Norway, Tables A2 and A8, Volume III.
65. F. Pottier and Alain Charlot, France, Table 12, Volume III.
66. P. Aamodt, Norway, Tables A9 and A2, Volume III.
67. A. Haapakorpi, Finland, Tables 1 and 3, Volume III.
68. L. Lassnigg, Austria I; K. Schedler, Austria II, Table 3, Volume I.
69. F. Bussi, Italy, Tables II.13 and II.17, Volume III.
70. J. Tarsh, United Kingdom, Annex II, Volume IV.

Chapter 6

DESTINATIONS

I. INTRODUCTION

In this study, we have chosen to concentrate on entry to working life, considering that in the present situation this would give us more precise indications of the evolution of employment prospects and the disparities in the situations of different categories of graduates. Behind this choice there is also the hypothesis that the conditions of insertion reflect the general state of the market, as pointed out by the author of the Australian contribution. This hypothesis may be open to criticism, but it must be admitted that this is how we can obtain direct information on the evolution of openings, a major preoccupation for young graduates and of growing importance for those responsible for higher education.

In fact, it must be borne in mind that analysing the conditions of insertion, to which university orientation services attach particular importance, gives only a partial view of the problem. It is obviously necessary to take account of the general labour market situation and certain more or less permanent features of the transition between higher education and employment. In the preceding chapters we have been able, for example, to assess the consequences for the Norwegian economy of the fall in oil revenues and its immediate repercussions as regards openings for young graduates. We have also seen that in Italy, where unemployment weighs particularly heavily on young people, graduates have great difficulty in obtaining a steady job. Lastly, we have seen that the normal modalities of access to certain professions imply certain disparities, notably in terms of wages and stability of employment and in these cases we need look no further for the explanation.

In addition, sufficient account is not always taken of the fact that young graduates are not the only source of manpower for employers, whether it is a matter of replacing people going into retirement, filling new posts or filling posts that now require higher qualifications. Employers can also resort to the internal market or recruit experienced managers on the external market. We know that practices here vary considerably between countries and between occupations. The French contribution shows how the market "segment" of interest to young graduates has changed. During the 1970s, the number of recruitments into high level and upper middle level jobs was greater than the supply of young graduates, for whom the labour market was therefore very favourable. During the 1980s, the situation reversed, which implies a certain amount of deskilling for young people from post-secondary education.[1]

Neither must we underestimate the significance of the analysis of the conditions of insertion into the world of work. There is sometimes a tendency to think that higher education graduates, whatever their initial difficulties may be, finish up by obtaining steady and well-paid jobs. Since the Second World War this has been substantially true, thanks to the strong demand for high level professionals, managers and executives, first of all in industry, then in public services. This assumption is now not so justifiable as it was, and the French example shows that the overall equilibrium between the increase in the number of high level jobs and the supply of young graduates may change in the space of a few years. However, it is not the overall trend that gives rise to the greatest concern: in a few years' time, as pointed out by the author of the Danish contribution, students and young graduates may revise their aspirations and aim at jobs of a more modest level than their predecessors. It is the scale of the disparities of situation between the different categories that is at the centre of the debate, because these disparities reflect the extent of the mismatch between the graduate supply and changing requirements on the demand side. Our analysis of the transition conditions therefore needs to be completed by an analysis of the destinations, more closely associated with the structural changes.

In the introduction to Part Two, we pointed out that we used the term "destinations" in a more limited or stricter sense than that found in some of the national surveys: it is first of all a matter of describing the "place" of employment: sector or branch of economic activity, public or private sector, size of enterprise, etc.; then the nature of the job, by level and type of function.

This distinction is found in most countries, but we generally have much less systematic and complete information about the destinations than about the transition conditions. Some countries are concerned solely with the insertion conditions, using the variables generally found in labour market studies and an idea of the destinations can be obtained only through the analysis of stocks, *i.e.* through using other sources. Data on the functions are even less rich, and what is more they are difficult to use in an international study, mainly because of differences in classifications.

We saw in the preceding chapter that as regards the sector of employment, the main question that arose during the 1980s, notably in the European countries, was the decline in recruitment in the public sector and education and the reorientation of flows to new destinations in the private sector. This is what we shall try to document in this chapter. In Chapter 5, we already used data relating to the function and nature of jobs, the proportion of deskilling having been considered as one of the parameters of insertion into working life. In this chapter, we consider above all the trend of the correspondence between the training received and the job held.

II. SECTOR OF EMPLOYMENT

In Chapter 4, we examined the employment trend during the 1980s. We saw that, despite the intentions announced at the beginning of the decade, few countries succeeded in halting the expansion of the public sector (Table 7), but there was nevertheless a significant slowing of the growth of employment in this sector. We saw a considerable expansion in employment in private services, notably in "banking, insurance, real estate and business services" (Table 5). Lastly, we saw that employment in industry began to grow again, earlier and more rapidly in the United States, Australia, Canada and Japan, later and less rapidly in Europe. It is against this background that we shall situate the trends affecting graduate employment.

A. Employment in the public sector and education

In this report, as in that of 1981, great importance is attached to public sector employment, to which we attach employment in education, considered to be a "public function" even when it is partly a matter of private education. This is not the case with all the analyses. First, where enrolment rates in higher education are high, as in Canada, the United States and Japan, the proportion of graduates entering this sector is not so high, so that a reduction in public recruitment has much less severe effects. In the United States, the notion of a career in the public service is itself fairly vague. In many countries, the privatisation of certain public services has shown how close the nature of public sector jobs can be to that of private sector jobs, while conversely it is sometimes pointed out how similar employment in a large enterprise can be to employment in the public sector.

However, the distinction between public and private is not simply a matter of statistical convenience (the data showing a difference in status). In most countries, at least until recently, the methods of recruitment into the public service were very special, and in addition there was a "concentration" effect: many graduates, notably in humanities and the social sciences, but also in the sciences, preferred deskilling in a "familiar" sector of employment to reorientation towards new jobs. Above all, as pointed out by the author of the Belgian report, there is no limit to deskilling in the public sector, whereas in the private sector the employers and also the unions and the entire staff of enterprises are opposed to recruitments that are likely to be a source of frustration and internal conflict, notably as regards promotions.

Chapter 4 showed that with the exception of Austria and Spain, the tendency was for the diminution of the concentration of *university graduates* in the public sector. In *Austria,* where the proportion of graduates entering the public sector and teaching (flows) were still 60 per cent in 1986, there was still an increase in the proportion of graduates (stock) employed in this sector: 57 per cent in 1971, 65 per cent in 1981, 69 per cent in 1987.[2] In *Spain,* the proportion of graduates employed in "Education, research, culture and health" rose from 45.9 per cent in 1987 to 46.6 per cent in 1989. In *Canada,* the breakdown of the flows of university graduates was the same in 1984 and 1988. In *Sweden* too, the proportion of young graduates entering the public sector was virtually the same in 1980 and 1985, but it is true that employment in the public sector did not begin to decline until 1985.[3] In *Japan* (approximate figures because of the classification), the proportion of graduates rose from 33 per cent in 1975 to 41 per cent in 1985 before dropping back to 38 per cent in 1990.[4] In *Norway* on the other hand, the percentage, which had fallen from 65 to 60 between 1981 and 1987, was back up to 65 per cent in 1989. In the case of these two countries the trend corresponds to that of total employment in this sector. In *Belgium* the proportion fell from 62 per cent in 1970 to 49 per cent in 1978 and 41 per cent in 1987. In *Denmark* it fell from 71 per cent in 1981 to 54 per cent in 1987. In these two countries the decline has been very marked. In *France* in

1984 the proportion was still 51 per cent, but the public sector went on growing until the end of the decade. In *Germany* the proportion had fallen to 38 per cent.

As regards the destination of university graduates, it can be seen that the trend corresponds fairly closely to the trend in total employment in the public sector and on the whole it is declining, but whether the decline has been sufficient is open to question (Table 42). In *Germany*, we have seen that the concentration of graduates employed in the public sector (stock) fell from 74 to 66 per cent between 1976 and 1989, but at the same time the proportion of graduates in this sector increased from 21 to 26 per cent, a rise of 24 per cent, but lower than the rise in the proportion of graduates in total employment (39 per cent).[5] This increase could therefore be justified by the increased skill requirements of jobs. However, it is pointed out that over half of the young graduates entering the public sector still did not have a permanent job 18 months after qualifying.[6] Similarly, the *Belgian* report stresses the high proportion of temporary contracts in public services, in the context of various special schemes to reduce unemployment. Thus in one of the countries where the diminution has been most marked, to the point of bringing a real conversion as regards university education, the proportion of young graduates trying to enter the public sector is still too high and the adjustment insufficient.

Employment in education was always one of the main openings for university graduates. Recruitment here declined significantly for various demographic reasons, but there has recently been a tendency for it to increase again, for example in France, because of the higher enrolment rates in upper secondary education. In *Australia*, there was a slight decline between 1984 and 1988, from 30 to 27 per cent for the men and from 46 to 44 per cent for the women.[7] In *Austria* in 1986, employment in education accounted for 28 per cent of graduate recruitments, 33 per cent if we add research and culture.[8] In *Belgium*, during the 60s, employment in secondary and higher non-university education accounted for over one-third of recruitments; in 1987 it accounted for no more than 16.5 per cent. If we add university jobs, the proportion fell from 52 to 29 per cent.[9] In *France* in 1987, education accounted for 40 per cent of the recruitments for holders of the *licence* or *maîtrise*. This proportion is relatively stable, but the university is not the only form of higher education and it leads above all to this type of job. In *Italy*, 50 per cent of graduates entered education in 1970. The three surveys carried out in 1977, 1981 and 1986, show that the proportion had fallen to 21, 16 and 15 per cent respectively.[10] In *Japan* (where education is included with "other services and transport"), the overall figures show no variation, but those for women show a reduction from 60 to 47 per cent.[11] In *Switzerland*, a university degree is not the route followed by primary teachers, who undergo a separate form of training, which explains why teaching does not figure as a primary outlet for graduates. On the other hand, almost one out of four graduates remains connected with the university after having obtained a degree, this being partly due to the number of graduates who stay on to take the teacher training course for secondary teachers. However, it should be noted that the number of graduates employed in the service sector and in industry is on the increase.

There are many similarities in the destinations of university graduates according to the field of study. Everywhere it is graduates in the *humanities and social science,* and naturally those from teacher training courses in those countries where these are separate, who enter the public sector and education in the greatest numbers. Table 43 shows that for graduates in *education* the proportion varies between 74 per cent in *Belgium* and 95 per cent in *Australia:* it is connected with the operation of mechanisms regulating admission to this type of training. The destination of *arts* graduates is more varied. In countries where there is a diploma in education, such as Australia, Canada and Japan, it ranges from 42 to 55 per cent. The proportions are higher in *Belgium,* and above all *Austria* with 59 and 88 per cent respectively. This difference is partly explained by the fairly large proportion, very large in *Austria,* of people entering public services. In countries where there is no distinct teacher training at

Table II–42. **Trend in the proportion of university graduates entering public sector jobs**

Percentages

Belgium	55	(1973)	49	(1978)	41	(1987)
Spain[a]			50	(1987)	52	(1988)
France			51	(1984)		
Norway	65	(1981)	60	(1987)	65	(1989)
Sweden	57	(1976-80)	56	(1981-85)	52	(1986-89)
Switzerland	59	(1981)	54	(1985)	52	(1989)

a) Total graduates, stock.
Source: National reports

Table II-43. **Proportion of university graduates entering jobs in education (E) and public services (P), by field of study**

Percentages

		Education	Arts	Economics	Law	Science	Technology
Australia	E	88	19	3	3	18	2
1987	P	7	36	20	23	28	24
	T[a]	95	55	23	26	46	26
Austria	E	84	39	10	9	49	27
1986	P	6	49	12	42	9	12
	T	90	88	22	51	58	39
Belgium	E	45	41	20	3	60	18
1990	P	29	18	7	22	10	8
	T	74	59	27	25	70	23
Canada	E	71	32	3	–	15	5
1986	P	5	10	11	–	11	8
	T	76	42	14	–	26	13
France	E	–	56	10	10	46	5
1987	P	–	6	26	26	8	3
	T	–	62	36	36	54	8
Germany 1985	T	74	68	25	39	55	27
Italy 1986	E	–	47	9	3	18	6
Japan	E	75	40	11	11	37	16
1990	P	6	7	20	20	4	4
	T	81	47	23	23	41	20
Norway	E	–	67	14	3	70	42
1989	P	–	6	17	72	8	11
	T	–	73	31	75	78	53
Switzerland	E	–	55	16	9	57	24
1989	P	–	30	65	72	6	3
	T	–	85	81	81	63	27

a) T = total.
Source: National reports.

this level, the proportion ranges from 47 per cent in *Italy* to 73 per cent in *Norway,* naturally with a higher concentration in education.

In 1981 it was considered that graduates in law and economics were split fairly evenly between the public and private sectors. As regards *law,* there are very great differences, probably corresponding to different traditions. The proportion entering the public sector is about one-quarter in Australia and Belgium, one-third in France, half in Italy and three-quarters in Norway (where it had been as high as 80 per cent in 1981). The overall trend is thus a reorientation towards the private sector. As regards *economics* and *management,* there is a very clear orientation towards the private sector. The proportion entering the public sector ranges from 14 per cent in Canada to 31 per cent in Norway.

In many countries, degrees in *science* traditionally lead to teaching. Although the sharing of responsibilities between science and technology varies considerably from one country to another (in certain countries, such as France, there is still a fairly marked distinction, whereas in others, like the United States, is has virtually disappeared), it can be seen that young scientists are finding jobs in the private sector to a much greater extent than in the past. Australia, Canada and Italy are the countries where they have the least tendency to go in for teaching (18, 15 and 18 per cent respectively). For the whole of the public sector and education the lowest figures are in Canada and Japan (26 and 41 per cent respectively); the highest in Norway and Belgium (78 and 70 per cent). France, Austria and Australia are in an medium position. The general trend is for the proportion to fall. Graduates in *technology* are generally not very numerous in the public sector. With the exception of Austria (39 per cent) and of Norway (53 per cent) the proportion is at most one-quarter, as in Australia and Belgium, and frequently very much less, the lowest figure being that of France (8 per cent). Here again the general trend is downwards.

It is much more difficult to identify a general trend in the case of *non-university training*. At university level there is in some countries a clear division of tasks between the university proper and other institutions such as engineering schools, one being traditionally more oriented towards the public sector and the other towards the private. At non-university level the dichotomy is even sharper and training tends to lead to very distinct areas. In Part One, we saw that this specificity was a determining factor for the expansion – or decline – of enrolments in this sector. It also dominates the analysis of employment.

In *Australia,* for example, it is pointed out that the growth – relatively rapid since it concerns the period 1984-1988 – of the employment of young university graduates in the public service from 18 to 22 per cent (15 to 21 per cent in the case of women) is connected with the replacement by graduates of holders of lower level qualifications formerly recruited into the paramedical sector. In the education sector there are changes that can be explained only by the raising of the educational level of recruits in primary and pre-primary teaching or the elevation to the rank of post-secondary or higher education of teacher training colleges for these levels. On top of this first factor, which is of the nature of a break in classification, there are two others. The first, well known, that of the rapid diminution in the recruitment of primary teachers, which has been fairly general throughout the OECD countries, the saturation (probably only apparent in many cases) of the paramedical professions (also fairly generalised, with the exception of Belgium and Canada) and lastly, the effect of budget restrictions on public service recruitment, for example in social work. The second factor was, in Australia, not the closure but the transformation of primary teacher training colleges into institutions of a more general nature, in which curricula have been modified by adding an accounting component, a computing component, etc. so that students can aim at jobs other than teaching, notably in the private sector.

Under these circumstances, the statistics tend to show the respective situations and policies of the different countries rather than trends in employment. In *Austria,* the "*Akademien*" have virtually only public sector openings, while in *Italy* non-university training, still in its infancy, serves the private sector only. In *France,* the proportion of teachers having received short-cycle post-secondary training (IUT-BTS) is in the order of 7 per cent, as against 80 per cent in *Denmark*. In *Canada* on the other hand, the proportions coming from the colleges and the universities are within a few per cent of one another. In *Japan,* the main destination for those from the Junior Colleges (which take almost exclusively women) is that of "other services and transport", which includes teaching (36 per cent of those qualifying in 1980).

The data for *Denmark,* corresponding to three levels of studies shown in Table 44, provide another example of the interplay of these different factors. Those from short courses mainly go, as we have seen, into public service jobs, pre-primary teaching, social work, nursing, etc.; however between 1981 and 1987 we nevertheless see a certain diminution, from 77 to 71 per cent. Those from training of medium duration entering the public sector declined in the space of a few years from 74 to 50 per cent, which is partly explained by the rapid increase in the number of graduates in management and commerce, leading to the expansion and transformation of supply. The decline of the proportion of graduates from long courses, from 71 to 54 per cent over the same period, is explained by the reduction of public recruitment, the increase in the number of students in courses leading to private sector jobs and also to increased recruitment by the private sector of the type of graduates who formerly went into the public sector. The data for *Germany* also show the dominant effect of the orientations of the different types of course: in 1985, the public sector employed only one-quarter of the young people from technical schools, as compared with half those from the *Fachhochschulen* and two-thirds of the university graduates.

Table II–44. **Denmark**

Proportion of graduates entering public employment, by type of course

Percentages

	Short courses	Medium courses	Long courses
1981	76.7	73.4	70.5
1987	70.9	49.9	54.3

Source: H. Traberg, Danish report, Table 14.

The highly specialised nature of non-university training thus defies global analysis. A series of analyses by field of study or professional orientation would be required in order to identify the trends, and the national studies generally provide little information of this type. A general impression is that there has no doubt been an increase in recruitments into the public sector, either through "substitution" or due to the needs of technical services, but that by far the greater part of the expansion is in the private sector, secondary or tertiary.

While it is difficult to draw any clear-cut conclusion on the international level concerning the future of non-university higher education, it is clear that in the case of university graduates there has been a significant reorientation of flows towards private sector jobs. It is necessary to bear in mind however that this global trend is made up of several components, or has several explanations, the relative weights of which may vary from country to country:

  i) purely and simply the expansion of higher education: with the absolute number of graduates entering the public sector remaining virtually unchanged, the "additional" graduates go into the private sector. The absorption by the private sector of an increased number of graduates in economics or management would have such a statistical effect;
  ii) a new structure of flows from higher education, which under the influence of an invisible hand or that of the authorities, has adapted in time to the changes in employment opportunities. In France for example, the proportion of arts graduates entering teaching has remained the same but the overall number of arts graduates has greatly diminished;
  iii) in each discipline (and hence overall) an increasing proportion of young graduates has sought a new orientation. We can cite the example of science and law graduates. It is likely that this also corresponds to shifts within each group of disciplines: from general economics towards management; from public law to private;
  iv) lastly, there has not always been sufficient adjustment and the mismatch results in temporary jobs, lower status and deskilling, notably for graduates in education, the arts, social sciences and psychology.

B. Employment in the private sector

There is no point in returning to the global trend, which is the complement of that discussed above and for which the figures for university graduates were presented in Tables 42 and 43. It remains to describe how these graduates are distributed between the private tertiary sector, industry, and where the data are available, the liberal professions. These data are presented in Table 45.

In the countries examined, few graduates in *education* enter the private sector: in the order of 4 per cent in Australia, Canada and Denmark, but with a much higher proportion in Japan and Belgium (19 and 27 per cent respectively). Together with Australia and France however these last two countries are those where the proportion of arts graduates entering the private sector is also among the highest: 38 per cent in France, 45 per cent in Australia, 51 per cent in Japan. The author of the Japanese report points out that it was during the first half of the 1970s and the second half of the 1980s that there was an influx of arts graduates into the private sector, notably in banking and insurance: these were two periods of rapid economic expansion and a shortage of graduates. One may nevertheless ask whether this in all cases reflects a real demand or is simply a matter of "absorption" by expanding sectors. In France in 1987, of the 34 per cent of arts graduates employed in the private sector, only 9 had management posts three years after graduating, while 15 were in white- or blue-collar jobs. It is curious to note that in Austria, where the proportion of arts graduates in the private sector is fairly low (10-12 per cent), only a quarter of these are employed in banking, and almost half in the chemical industry; this proportion even increased from 44 to 49 per cent between 1985 and 1990.[12]

We have seen above that the proportion of graduates in *law* and *economics* entering the private sector increased significantly during the 1980s. Starting from an "average" situation, in which every other graduate entered the private sector, the proportion was soon 2 out of 3 or even 3 out of 4, notably for graduates in economics and management, the legal careers having greater specificity. However, the percentages do not give a sufficiently complete picture of the trend: we need to take account of the very strong expansion of these disciplines over the same period and the substantial growth in employment in private services, precisely at the moment when these graduates arrived on the labour market. The author of the United Kingdom report situates this change during the 1970s, while Table 45 suggests at least that it continued during the 1980s, the banking and insurance sector in particular having experienced one of the highest growth rates in OECD countries up to 1990. In addition, the number of young graduates recruited in accounting and commerce increased by 35 per cent between 1982 and 1987 and by 72 per cent in financial services over the same period. In Japan, the trend varies from branch to branch: graduate employment in "commerce" expanded rapidly until 1980, then there was a certain regression during the 1980s. In the second half of the 1980s it was in the banking and insurance sector

Table II-45. **Proportion of university graduates entering the private tertiary sector (TE), the primary and secondary sectors (PS) and the liberal professions (LI), by discipline**

Percentages

		Education	Arts	Economics Management	Law	Science	Technology
Australia	LI	0	4	29	61	5	15
1987	TE	4	33	34	10	27	10
	PS	1	8	14	2	20	48
Austria	LI	5	5	22	25	6	6
1987	TE	2	5	29	17	6	1
	PS	3	2	25	6	26	52
Belgium	LI	1	2	2	34	1	4
1990	SP[a]	26	39	71	41	29	73
Canada	TE	2	8	30	–	29	23
1986	S[b]	1	8	10	–	13	34
Denmark	TE	3	1	43		18	36
1987	PS	1	6	5		10	53
France	LI	–	4	12	3	1	
1984	SP[a]	–	34	48	47	93	
Italy 1986	LI	–	9	22	25	11	36
Japan	TE	10	50	43	10	6	
1990	PS	9	21	25	46	73	
Norway	TE	–	3	47	21	10	20
1989	PS	–	4	14	2	9	25

a) SP = TE + PS
b) Manufacturing.
Source: National reports.

that graduate employment expanded most. However, the author of the Japanese contribution points out that this was not the only sector in which graduates found jobs; they are now more evenly distributed among the different sectors of activity than they were 30 years ago. The United Kingdom report raises the question of whether the scale of recruitment in these branches is due to an increase in the level of knowledge and skills necessary for this type of activity or whether employers are simply taking advantage of the opportunity provided by the reduction of public service recruitment to hire the graduates thus made available instead of taking young people from secondary education as before. It should be noted however that the lawyers virtually always head for liberal practice and the tertiary sector, while a substantial proportion of the economists go into industry.

The demand for scientific and technical staff was very strong during the 1980s: this is one of the reasons for the higher proportion of *science* graduates in the private sector, which in Japan for example increased from 46 to 56 per cent over the decade. In Japan and Australia they are often recruited into industry but generally they tend to go into the service sector. In several countries there is a growing tendency for *engineers* to be less concentrated in production and increasingly found in the tertiary sector. There are several reasons for this. One reason, put forward in Japan to explain the choice of banking and insurance by (a small number of) young engineers is simply that wages are higher here than in production. Another reason, cited by the author of the United Kingdom contribution, is that graduates in the "wrong" disciplines, such as chemistry, are recruited into the same types of posts as graduates in management or the social sciences: 24 per cent of the chemists are recruited into financial functions and 21 per cent into commercial or management functions. More generally, certain highly technical functions have been contracted out by enterprises and are now classified as services; some of these, computer services for example, require highly technical staff. The fact is that as pointed out by the author of the Australian report, the distribution between secondary and tertiary is increasingly fuzzy, notably when it is a matter of employing highly qualified staff, and the very diffusion of the technology means that for example engineers are found, as are accountants, in all branches of activity, both public and private.

Similar remarks also naturally apply to people from *non-university education*. However, as we have seen this type of training has a very marked vocational orientation. This results in a greater specificity of the correspondence between training and destination and, as pointed out in the French report, a strong relationship between the speciality of the training and that of the job. The destination results from it: those with diplomas in tourism head for the corresponding sector, those with electronics qualifications go into engineering consultancy firms or electrical and electronic maintenance. The result is that men and women head for different destinations to a greater extent than at university level.

III. TYPES OF JOB

The nature of the jobs is unfortunately an area in which we have much less information that can be used for the purposes of the analysis. What is more, that presented in the national contributions often refers only to a single year, hence the impossibility of identifying trends. However, in view of the increasing fuzziness of the boundaries between branches and sectors, these trends would be useful for defining the desirable "profiles" for graduates. Three questions merit discussion here:

i) the level of the job and its correspondence with the level of training, the segmentation of professional structures;
ii) the job speciality and its correspondence with that of the training, the question of generalist training and generalist jobs;
iii) lastly, the identification of areas of growth or of uncertainty, such as research and development, information technology, etc.

A. Job level

We have already touched upon this question on several occasions: in Chapter 4 where we examined the evolution of employment structures; in Chapter 5, where we studied the disparities in the labour market situation using as a measure the proportion of deskilling or displacement; lastly, in the present chapter when we showed the link between the overall scale of this deskilling and the trend in the number of high level (or upper medium level) jobs open to young graduates.

Several countries have employment classifications that are largely based on differences in hierarchical level. These classifications are not pure, to the extent that they also take into consideration status, but it is true that levels are also frequently defined in terms of status. A French study[13] indicates that management executives are considered as such because their employer has so decided and they contribute to the retirement fund for this category. The French contribution points out that hierarchies are fairly well defined in industry, but that in the tertiary sector (or in tertiary jobs) the definitions are much more vague, so that it is difficult to determine the difference, for example between "white-collar workers" and "intermediate professions" and hence to measure the extent of any deskilling. In Italy, the very size of the "*impiegati*" category (50 per cent of graduate employment in 1982, but only 23 per cent in 1989) suggests that it is a definition by exclusion, or that it refers to a status rather than to a well-defined level of function; the increase in the number of graduates choosing a liberal profession or self-employment may possibly be connected with the difficulty in obtaining a stable job as an employee; on the other hand, when we see the considerable increase in the number of "higher executives" we may ask whether this is a real evolution or simply the extension of this status to a greater number of employees. In Sweden, in the surveys and censuses the level of the job is defined as a function of the educational level "normally" required which can also make interpretation difficult.

These classifications can nevertheless provide a useful framework for discussion, to the extent that data are available from which it is possible to identify the trends. Lacking such data, we shall limit ourselves here to asking two questions: at what level of job are the greater part of the needs of the economy situated, notably in the private sector? Does the tendency (which is by no means new) to extend the duration of studies and accumulate diplomas correspond to real needs or is it because of the competition for access to "professional" jobs which are scarcer than the statistics would imply?

B. Breakdown by type of function

Several countries have adopted more "horizontal" classifications for their surveys, and their national contributions discuss the distribution of the different categories of graduates. This is the case of the *United*

Kingdom[14] where it is pointed out that employment is expanding most rapidly in finance and information technology, but that the majority of those entering these fields do not have any corresponding training (56 per cent for information technology, 62 per cent for finance). The *Canadian* contribution points out the marked correspondence between training and employment in medicine, education, science and technology, and to a lesser extent management, but little such correspondence for graduates in the humanities and social sciences. A similar conclusion is to be found in the *Swedish* contribution. In the *Norwegian* contribution, four broad categories of function are used (research and development, relations with clients, administration, white- and blue-collar worker)[15], making it difficult to draw conclusions; facts that stand out are the remarkable number of agricultural engineers in administration (24 per cent) and of economists in white- or blue-collar jobs (31 per cent) which probably reflects a marked deskilling for graduates in these fields. *Germany* uses a fairly detailed classification for identifying graduates by level;[16] worthy of note are the high proportion of *Fachhochschule* graduates and even people from technical schools in management, planning and research and development jobs (even taking account of their low representation in advisory and teaching functions). *Finland* uses a very detailed classification that shows a fairly strong relationship between type of discipline and job, with the degree of concentration varying according to the type of study.

It would be desirable to have more comparable series and possibly classifications in order to identify the trends. We have simply used these data as insertion parameters. Another question of broader significance arises however. It is touched upon in several reports and concerns the very nature of the correspondence between training and employment: the question of the distinction between generalist and specialist training (and jobs).

Certain commentators simply mention the more or less strong concentration of graduates in certain jobs: these are the very terms of the *Canadian* contribution to which we have just referred. The *Swedish* report speaks of "target occupations" and notes that according to the type of training the market is more or less open. Doctors and architects have very few openings outside their profession and planning therefore has to take care to avoid surpluses. Engineers and scientists have a broader market and adapt (horizontally and vertically) to different jobs, thus avoiding unemployment in the case of recession. The report mentions teachers as having a specialised training and a very narrow market, while other countries assimilate them to generalists. There is no mention of the humanities and social sciences. The conclusion remains that certain types of training with a very narrow market give no horizontal flexibility, so that if no corresponding job is found the graduate is reduced to unemployment or considerable deskilling.

The French report mentions a certain adaptability for higher level mechanical engineering technicians in the context of a similar analysis. A distinction can be made between dispersion associated with the adaptability of the training and that connected with its generalist character. The risk of deskilling is very much greater in the second case. By and large, the French report points out that despite the substantial changes on both the supply and demand sides, the correspondences have been maintained.

The United Kingdom and Australian reports describe a very different situation, in which a distinction is made between generalist and specialist jobs. The UK report indicates that the generalist jobs (where the graduate's discipline does not have to correspond with the speciality of the job) represent 52 per cent of recruitments and cites a publication in which 35-40 per cent of job vacancy notices did not mention any specific discipline. *De facto* correspondences are obviously found between these jobs and the training, even if such subjects as chemistry are found, and there is also a good deal of deskilling and underemployment. Lastly, it can be pointed out that studies leading to a degree in the United Kingdom are quite short (three and a half years on average). The degree is thus seen more as an indication of good general ability (an indication that might be reinforced by the prestige attached to the higher education establishment, as we saw in Chapter 5), than as a qualification or indication of specialist competence. There is more critical comment in the United Kingdom report than in the Australian one.

If nothing else, this somewhat broad divergence at least prompts two questions. First of all, that of the validity of the analysis in each case: are generalist jobs in the United Kingdom as general as current practice seems to suggest, and does the description not conceal implicit correspondences and processes of selection and training? Conversely, is the more strict correspondence observed in Continental Europe not a reflection of recruitment criteria or methods of placement, rather than of the skills that are actually required? The correspondence between training and employment is the result of both the conceptions regarding the aims and objectives of education and the characteristics of the labour market for graduates. It therefore can vary enormously depending on national contexts.

However, national practices – and one might even add national philosophies – which emerge from the studies that have served as the basis for this analysis, could evolve substantially with the diversification and expansion of the various forms of higher education, as is already beginning to happen in a number of countries. The second question that needs to be addressed, therefore, is the changing structure of employment. The way in which these correspondences are perceived is still often coloured in some countries (and particularly in higher education circles) by the situations of comparative scarcity that existed some twenty or thirty years ago. In Part One it was shown that the pressure of social demand was likely to increase substantially in the coming years: what this means is that the range of jobs into which graduates from the various forms of higher education will go is likely to broaden considerably, and we are moving towards a situation where these various forms of higher education will "produce" most of the skilled workers required in the advanced economies.

Notes and References

1. F. Pottier and A. Charlot, France, Table 3.2, Volume III.
2. L. Lassnigg, Austria I, Table 6; K. Schedler, Austria II, Table 1, Volume I.
3. S. Fornäng, Sweden, Table 7, Volume IV.
4. M. Kaneko, Japan, Table C.1, Volume III.
5. M. Tessaring, Germany, Table A.3, Volume I.
6. *Ibid.,* Table 14.
7. B. Williams, Australia, Table 6, Volume I.
8. L. Lassnigg, Austria I, Table 6, Volume I.
9. A. Bonte, Belgium, Table 8, Volume I.
10. F. Bussi, Italy, Table II.6, Volume III.
11. M. Kaneko, Japan, Table C.3, Volume III.
12. K. Schedler, Austria II, Table 10, Volume I.
13. D. Blondel, *Les cadres de gestion,* CEREQ, Paris, 1990.
14. J. Tarsh, United Kingdom, Tables A6, A7, A9, C5 and Table 11, Volume IV.
15. P. Aamodt, Norway, Tables A6 and A7, Volume III.
16. M. Tessaring, Germany, Table A4, Figure 8, Volume I.

ISSUES FOR THE FUTURE

The preface to this study drew attention to the change in climate which was noted in most Member countries between the end of the 1970s, when the tendency was to pessimism, and the present period with its return to some degree of optimism despite the lingering recession. The analysis provides some explanations for this phenomenon and at the same time leads to a more balanced view.

There was good reason for the malaise at the end of the 1970s. The economy had suffered the effects of two successive shocks. These needed to be offset by productivity gains, and growth in public spending had to be limited. In this context some suspicious looks were cast at all the activities of a constantly expanding public sector which in most countries attracted the majority of university graduates. Were so many of them to go on being trained? The idea that universities were a breeding ground for unemployment was obviously wildly exaggerated, but it did express an intuitive perception of a structural imbalance.

Today, when unemployment rates are much the same if not higher, the emphasis is mainly on the high demand for qualified staff, particularly in science and technology. The current optimism, which is probably based on the pace of employment growth during the early 1980s, could also be questioned. It might simply reflect the convergence of interests among various parties who would have us believe that higher education has a new basis for expansion with its task of preparing students for employment in the private sector; that employers are grateful for the plentiful supply of qualified staff, and that in countries where higher education is to a large extent financed by the government they accordingly receive a kind of indirect subsidy. This optimism therefore is perhaps not so justified as is thought. The change of climate can, however, be welcomed, if it creates a new momentum.

This report went back to an argument used in the 1980 study which stressed the extent of the adjustments that would be required of higher education by the slowdown if not the standstill in recruitment for the public services and teaching. It is in fact somewhat oversimplified as an argument, because it gives no more than a partial view of the situation of university graduates during the late 1970s and is of limited relevance to some countries outside Europe, notably Japan and the United States. It was, however, a good basis for discussion, particularly because it went beyond generalities on the situation of graduates seen as a whole and made it possible to show and often explain the change.

Given the range of higher education systems and labour markets, is it justifiable in an international study to look for trends common to all OECD countries or to groups of countries? The analyses presented in this report have in fact revealed many similarities as regards not only major trends but also subtler changes in a particular field of education or employment. Obviously there are lags or delays in adjustment, for which the causes are sometimes known. On the other hand, the many differences between countries in fact make it possible to throw more light on the action of cyclical and structural factors and the changes they bring about in each national context.

The wealth of material contained in the national contributions has made it possible to illustrate in detail most of the issues that were to be studied. It has been shown that, by and large, graduates have benefited more than most from the upturn in economic activity, since the effects of growth have been compounded by the rise in the level of skill requirements. Yet unemployment persists among young graduates, and it is to be feared that skills inflation and deskilling have increased. The overall picture is therefore very positive, although the differences in situation between the various categories of graduates are striking.

We hope we have given a fairly comprehensive picture of the 1980s. Not that this makes the forecasts for the coming years any easier. The general prospects for an economic recovery are still very uncertain, as are the effects on employment of technological development and structural adjustment. Nor can we foresee what the consequences of internationalisation will be: should we expect increased mobility on the part of science and technology graduates and, in particular, an influx from Central and Eastern European countries? As regards the future relationship between higher education and employment, there is scarcely any clear trend. In 1980 it was possible to give a general forecast (at least with regard to university graduates), but it was difficult to do more than this. Today, forecasts can be made for particular categories (doctors or teachers, for example), but it is risky to attempt an overall forecast. We therefore confine ourselves here to highlighting certain issues that will need to be faced in the future, either in employment or in higher education.

A. Employment prospects

1. Supply and demand

In the coming years there is likely to be a further substantial increase in the outflows from higher education systems. These outflows have been practically unaffected by population trends and, except perhaps in the United States, will in all probability not be influenced by them in the 1990s. In most countries, these flows will soon represent *half of each generation*. By comparison, the proportion of graduates in the labour force (stocks) is about 10 to 15 per cent.

Higher education graduates will maintain their position on the labour market. If the occupational structure remains unchanged, they are likely to see a decline in their *average level of employment* and in their salaries; in each generation the "same" young people will move into the "same" jobs, but with higher qualifications. There is nothing new in this, except for the range of jobs, and hence skills, that will be affected. However, after a period of overheating of demand – given a plentiful supply, a number of countries have tended to recruit too many young people (rather than adults) and to be too demanding with regard to educational qualifications – employers, particularly in industry, might go back on this policy, especially if they are more in need of highly skilled operatives and technical staff. Employers are not necessarily in favour of longer and longer studies and are more interested in real skills than formal qualifications.

There is still often a tendency to consider – although major differences exist from country to country on this point – that a separate labour or jobs market exists for higher education graduates (or at least university graduates). This attitude may have been encouraged not only by the actual existence of a segmentation of this kind but also by the fact that graduates are employed in quite specific sectors and are scarcely to be seen in others, especially in industry. This view, of course, no longer holds true. In many countries, some industries already employ high proportions of graduates; young people also know that if they do not obtain a high-level qualification in a good special field from a major university, they will be eligible only for medium-level jobs. The purpose of many kinds of post-secondary education is precisely to prepare them for such a qualification.

The main risk in the increase in outflows is that the *conditions governing access to employment may be* disrupted. In the 1980s young graduates still benefited from a combination of factors: general growth in employment, an increase in the proportion of "high-level jobs", and also the fact that there were not enough qualified adults to meet this increased demand or that, for various other reasons, young people were preferred. But in most countries the ratio of graduate outflows to stocks will, for a number of years, be considerably changed if not reversed. Nor would it seem that this situation will be altered by the population trend: the advantage in employing young people will therefore mainly be that their training is recent and up-to-date and that they accept lower salaries.

This obviously raises the question of whether the proportion of high-level jobs will continue to rise. There are rival theories on this point: deskilling, "polarisation", *i.e.* an increased proportion of high-level and low-level jobs, or an increase in the number of medium-level jobs. Each of these theories corresponds to actual, observable trends. It is now generally agreed that the *rise in the level of qualifications* is the predominant trend, although the possibility that this may be partly a supply-side effect cannot be ruled out. The position adopted in this report is that, in advanced democracies, this trend is the only one which can reconcile economic needs and social and cultural aspirations.

2. Directions of growth

The 1980 analysis highlighted the saturation of public services and teaching. It has been pointed out that this was responsible for the most pronounced change in the relationship between higher education and employment during the 1980s. Demand for higher education shifted on a massive scale, either spontaneously – sometimes belatedly but sometimes, oddly enough, prematurely – or as a result of measures taken by the authorities, away from training for jobs in the public service or teaching, to management and business training. At the same time, governments were not always able to control growth in the public services, so that the extent and particularly the pace of the necessary adjustments were reduced accordingly. Another factor was that the sector to develop most in that decade was the financial and business services sector. It was therefore not too difficult for the private sector to absorb this influx of young graduates.

There is nothing to suggest that the changes of the 1980s, the extent of which we have shown, will continue in the coming years; there is nothing to suggest either that there will be a return to the earlier situation. Admittedly a need for more teachers is emerging as a result of the increase in the number of upper secondary pupils and especially the need to replace the many teachers recruited in the 1960s: this trend reversal will give a new boost to the institutions responsible for their training. But when related to the present volume of flows, these openings are proportionately no longer so important. Information is in fact available on employment prospects in some sectors, but by and large these sectors will not provide openings for the vast majority. It will therefore be necessary to try to identify the directions of possible growth in employment for young graduates.

The analysis suggests that graduates tend to focus on and seek jobs in the same sectors. Obviously this may mainly reflect primarily the pattern of demand. The tendency is then magnified by the form taken by recruitment procedures. Lastly, when a certain kind of job has become the usual choice following certain types of training, some young graduates prefer downgrading, deskilling or even unemployment rather than opt for other sectors of activity or other categories of jobs. This trend is compounded by another which narrows their focus still further: it seems that there are no limits to deskilling in the public sector, whereas in the corporate sector social constraints are often a barrier to the recruitment of graduates for lower-level jobs. As a result, further divisions are created.

The aim is not to revert to a planning system based on the forecast demand for graduates (although this is essential in some sectors), for this approach is based on a scarcity concept; conversely, neither is it to see which sectors are tending towards saturation, for it would be very difficult to define the relevant criteria. But it seems that what is necessary is to monitor the trend in occupational structures in the various branches of economic activity, taking into account not only needs but also the social pressures or constraints that may facilitate or hinder the employment of young graduates, and to have appropriate means of observing this trend.

In this respect, what is striking is the low proportion of graduates employed in industry where the level of technical know-how is much higher than in many services. While the proportion of graduates may amount to as much as 50 per cent in sectors such as teaching and cultural activities, it is often no more than 5 per cent in industry. The proportions obviously vary greatly from one industry to another (between electronics and public works for example). It is also necessary to take into account the tendency to contract out some of industry's skilled technical activities, with the result that some jobs which are in fact industrial are counted under services. The lowness of the figures, however, not only suggests that their trend needs to be monitored but that the underlying technical and social factors need to be analysed.

3. *Underemployment and skills inflation*

The concept of underemployment and skills inflation is an extremely complex one and to a large degree subjective. In this report we have been careful not to take a normative approach to the subject. We have confined ourselves to noting that some categories of graduates – especially women – are, more than others, forced to accept jobs, conditions and salaries far below the average. We have simply suggested that, if underemployment, skills inflation and deskilling were due to the fact that these graduates did not wish to venture outside a traditional employment sector (such as the public service), then it was hardly possible to talk about of "positive" adjustment.

We have come back to this concept here simply in order to see things from an economic angle. Without entering into a discussion of the actual level of employment, as defined by statisticians or as emerges from surveys, or the actual level of education as measured by formal qualifications, there may be grounds for concern at the economic cost of skills inflation – *i.e.* the cost of education and lower productivity – at a time when the emphasis is on the need for qualifications and the higher general standard of skills required by the economy. This is a paradox or contradiction which cannot simply be explained by the factors influencing the pattern of flows. It can obviously sometimes be the result of temporary situations, the effect of personal choices, and cyclical phenomena, but it may also be the outcome of a structural imbalance between supply and demand.

One of the questions which needs to be analysed in greater detail is the exact nature of this general tendency to require higher qualifications. The concept of a high-level job is quite vague and unquestionably differs widely from one country to another. Given the frequency and extent of underemployment and skills inflation, there are two hypotheses that can be advanced. The first is a qualitative one: it is possible that the sometimes very high level knowledge and skills acquired cannot be used because they are too theoretical or too academic. In that case higher education paradigms would only partially correspond to a large proportion of the skills requirements. Another hypothesis is that the concept of high-level employment should be defined more carefully and the steady increase in the proportion of such jobs analysed in greater detail. It is often considered, for example, that the highest growth is in intermediate or "upper-medium-level" jobs. Without necessarily suggesting that training should be tailored to employment, this could be an important aspect for further consideration with a view to defining priorities in initial training.

4. Education and the labour market

Young people with a post-secondary education will soon represent half of each generation: what are the implications for labour market policies? The business world now fully realises the need for higher-level skills and the initial and ongoing training that this calls for. In this respect it would seem that labour market policies are somewhat behind the times, that they are still based on the idea of an underskilled and substitutable labour force, or that the social function of these policies is simply to help the least skilled and most vulnerable.

The way in which those responsible for labour market policy view education and training has changed considerably over the years. It should be said that initially, in the 1960s, it was considered as having a structural role: this was the era not only of "investment in education", but also of an "active labour policy". The aim was to provide a professional qualification for young people who had completed their compulsory schooling or for adults who had been forced to abandon declining, labour-intensive, low-skill sectors. With the 1970s and the offensive against unemployment, the only reason why any interest was shown in education was that the other temporary measures had achieved only a limited impact; training seemed to be a more positive approach than certain community service jobs or simply paying unemployment benefit. Nonetheless, it was still regarded as a partial and temporary solution. By contrast, by the 1980s, initial or continuing training was once again being looked upon as a major instrument in structural adjustment, and a skilled labour force as a "strategic resource".

Nonetheless, the 1960s had a fairly clear vision of the role of training: any improvement in the level of general training and any acquisition of a professional skill in this period of relative scarcity were seen as an advance and an investment. The operational implications for the ministries of education and those responsible for labour market policy stemmed from this concept. Today it does not seem that we have arrived at such a clear view of the role of education. If it is sometimes associated with unemployment, the reason is that unemployment is also seen as structural, but it is obvious that there is no direct relationship between the two and that the association has no obvious operational implications. The quantitative aspect is still important, since too many young people or adults still have no qualifications or only insufficient skills. But the issue today is more the nature and quality of training. Higher education, and in particular post-secondary non-university education, could well be at the centre of thinking and discussion about the new relationship between education and the economy.

B. Higher education's responsibilities

1. Volume of demand

Without doubt the central issue in higher education is its current dimension, and at the same time, its ability to meet the increasing and changing needs of the economy and to respond to the substantially greater social pressures, particularly from young people. In recent decades, higher education has seen unprecedented expansion and diversification, and yet it does not seem that today's institutions have been designed or are in a position to meet the very wide range of employers' needs or cope with the diversity of the interests and aptitudes of their new intakes. The unsolved problems of first degree university education (particularly in the social sciences), the exponential growth in forms of education and training on the fringe or outside the formal system, and the never-ending debate on entrance requirements all point to a mismatch between supply and current needs.

But a further increase in social demand must be expected. A number of countries in the 1980s feared that population trends would lead to less demand for higher education. With few exceptions, this has not at all been the case and a strong surge in demand is generally expected in the next few years. This is connected with a sharp increase in the number of children going on to upper secondary education, a trend which has been greatly encouraged by the authorities but which also reflects new social standards. This increase in numbers is compounded by a shift in demand within secondary schools away from vocational-type training to broader forms of education that naturally lead to higher education. Lastly, it must be considered that, in the more advanced countries, young people with "only a secondary education" have difficulty in finding jobs; often their only choice is to go on with their studies. The first step is therefore to measure the volume of demand and to analyse its implications. It must, of course, be borne in mind that the demand is partly due to the internal logic of the system and the shortcomings of secondary education and post-compulsory training: the answer does not always lie simply in the expansion of higher education. But this demand also reflects real requirements, which have to be catered for.

The authorities need to take a wider view of the economic and social demand for higher education, whether or not this demand is to be met by recognised higher education institutions or by other public sector establishments. Far too often the debate focuses on the management and internal organisation of existing institutions rather than the needs of young people or employers. This in itself is not surprising. The prime concern is for the students who have been accepted or enrolled, for whom the educational institutions are responsible, and not for those who have left or have not been accepted; the country contributions give striking examples of this point. In the recent past – the 1970s – when the intention was to satisfy the increase in demand, the emphasis was on the development of "new forms" of higher education: the analysis shows this debate should be continued and new paradigms considered.

2. *Efficiency and output of higher education*

What emerges from an examination of the country contributions is the need to take a close look at the efficiency and overall output of higher education. Considering demand as a whole, this need is connected, it would seem, with three main aspects: the selection and streaming process; the duration or extension of studies; and the high proportion of failures and dropouts in higher education, particularly in the initial stages.

The first question we might consider is the duration or extension of studies. There are differing opinions on this. The one most frequently heard is that of the higher education authorities, who point to the increasing length of studies compared with their theoretical duration or the tendency of students to enrol for additional courses and to collect diplomas. The authorities are concerned at the increase in costs. Another opinion is that expressed by employers – or society as a whole – pointing out that the constant extension of the time spent in education does not necessarily result in a proportional increase in the level of skills of those entering the labour market. Some studies have shown that this trend was partly due to employment difficulties and that, when prospects improved, students behaved more "rationally" and completed their training quickly.

The problem is, however, wider than this. It concerns not only the time needed by students to complete a course of study but also the broader issue of the lengthening of the time spent in education. We noted above that this could be partly explained by the system's own internal logic and the inadequacy of the training provided at the post-compulsory level. But it is also necessary to consider all the selection and streaming mechanisms which, from secondary school through to entry into post-secondary education, are intended either to weed out some of the students or, on the contrary, oblige others to continue their studies, without however this process being related to employment needs or social aspirations. The following two examples illustrate this point: on the one hand, the uncontrolled flow of young people into the humanities and social sciences, in some countries, most of whom will not obtain useable qualifications and, on the other, the successive selection processes which often bar a number of young people from science and technology courses.

Another concern is the number of failures and dropouts, which is seen by some observers as a consequence of open access to higher education and its flexibility, but might be considered by others as a social evil, notably by young people and their families, and by employers who have to recruit among the successful and unsuccessful alike, the latter in many cases representing over half those going into higher education. Is it acceptable that institutions should consider the proportion of failures and dropouts as a measure of the quality of their teaching? The situation varies from one country or type of institution to another, and prior elimination is to be observed in some cases, and dropouts and failures in others. The issue of overall efficiency is therefore a complex and controversial one, but it warrants greater attention, particularly from a human and social viewpoint.

3. *The pattern of supply and the role of short training courses*

The expansion of higher education over the past 20 or so years has been made possible by its diversification, as many OECD studies have shown. Two sets of questions a rise here: has diversification achieved its objectives, and what is currently the place and role of these new training courses or institutions? To what extent has this diversification been sufficient, considering the spread of new types of training that are often based on private initiatives?

The answer to the first set of questions will probably differ greatly from country to country. Inadequate development of short training courses and excessive development of university courses is often noted with regret. In a number of countries, some non-university institutions prepared students mainly for careers in the public sector: as they lost their outlets, they sometimes also lost their students or had to switch to other objectives. In other cases the relationship between university and non-university education is the subject of fresh debate. Is non-university training in such a strong position as was thought ten or so years ago?

Conversely, it may be asked if diversification has been sufficient to meet the volume of demand and its expansion. An examination of the country contributions makes it quite clear that most countries have some types of training which are not yet recognised or integrated in the higher education system, are not yet subject to its constraints and are expanding exponentially. This may be the case of a faculty which is not yet subject to a *numerus clausus,* private sector training courses (mostly in management, computers or accountancy), or local initiatives into which the excess demand plunges.

It therefore seems that fresh consideration needs to be given to the structure of the supply, as part of a broader concept of higher education functions and their diversity. It has been noted that a number of countries considered they had a unified or extended system of higher education, although in fact it was rather one to which institutions deemed worthy of higher education status were co-opted, since the extended system often took only a fraction of the flows going into post-secondary studies. An essential factor in this respect is that the administrative "split" of education levels no longer corresponds to the structure of demand.

4. Vocationalisation

In response to the increase in the needs of firms and the decline in recruitment for the public service and teaching, the authorities in a number of countries have endeavoured to "vocationalise" higher education. This process has taken widely differing forms with the creation of new streams and new diplomas and curriculum reform, but the question has mainly concerned the humanities and social sciences, and generally speaking courses leading to "service" jobs.

Young graduates with qualifications in the humanities or social sciences, and also in other fields such as economics, law or even management, especially if their qualification is not a high-level one, not only have great difficulty in finding jobs but, in addition, have to accept long-term deskilling. This runs counter to the widespread idea that these broader types of training are an advantage on the labour market; it probably is, but not for everybody. Conversely, it may be felt that, if young graduates who have taken certain programmes of an explicitly vocational character obtain jobs easily, this is due rather to the network of contacts that the institutions have been able to build than to the course content: their salaries and their career prospects are not necessarily any better.

A theory that might seem attractive is that the issue is not one of vocationalisation but of an imbalance in the structure of the training supply. According to this theory, as a result of a negative selection process, some "surplus" students enter streams where they are readily accepted and where entrance requirements are far less demanding. The upturn in the recruitment of arts teachers might give some credence to this idea, but it corresponds to a necessarily restrictive concept of higher education as a whole and of its relationship with employment. The vocationalisation issue does not in fact seem to have been resolved.

5. Management of an extended and diversified system

The 1980s were marked by a dual trend: greater decentralisation and an increase in the amount of private funding received by higher education institutions. There are features common to most countries, however, in the management of higher education systems: first, the concept itself of a "system", however broad, however diversified or however circumscribed, from which parallel and competing types of training are by definition excluded; second, management methods that often differ greatly with the type of institution. The authorities generally manage certain types of non-university training directly (at central or regional level), whereas the universities enjoy greater autonomy and other types of training develop independently, sometimes without any government supervision.

Since preparations have to be made to absorb an even wider range of students and much greater diversification must be envisaged, how can such a system be run as an entity? Should the focus continue to be on the management of institutions as is the case in countries where higher education is mainly a public service, or should an attempt be made to ensure quality and transparency in the system, for example by defining educational standards or criteria which public or private institutions should conform to? One of the problems in this context is to achieve a proper balance between the general training component and its long-term objectives and the more immediate objectives of vocational training and adjustment to employment needs.

Another major question in the case of an extended system is the channeling of flows between the various streams of higher education. Recognising the character of higher education as vocational training, a number of countries decided at the end of the 1970s to manage flows through entrance requirements or a *numerus clausus*; many are now moving away from this approach, as this kind of planning is appropriate only where there is an obvious connection between training and employment, not in today's extended systems. Other countries have applied this method only to certain specialities, such as medicine or teacher training. This has often led to excessive growth in social science studies, the repercussions of which in terms of employment we have seen. At the same time, many initiatives have been taken concerning courses leading to tertiary jobs; they are far less costly and often profitable; but they do not provide job openings for all that. Many issues which will be assuming greater importance in the coming years are therefore still pending.

The main impression from this vast study covering 19 of the 24 OECD countries, is that in the coming years we must expect major changes in the relationship between higher education and employment. The number of students in higher education is continuing to rise and will soon represent half of each generation. Just as, in the world of work, it will no longer be possible to consider the employment of young graduates as a distinct and separate problem, the requirement in higher education, despite the marked changes in the institutional context in some countries, will no longer be to think in terms of adjustment, flexibility or even diversification, but to adopt new concepts.

Such changes will probably arouse some misgivings. The main one might be due to individual conceptions of higher education. In the preface and in the introduction to the four volumes of country contributions, we drew attention to the very broad definition which had been adopted, one that has perhaps ruffled certain feelings: it is possible to have a more restrictive and even elitist conception of higher education, and keep this term for institutions such as universities, and see others only as ‘‘post-secondary’’ or ‘‘tertiary’’ bodies. We have shown that these terms themselves, which refer to a wider but well-defined series of training courses, are often not sufficient to define supply in its entirety, not to speak of demand. It may be asked if this shortcoming is not at the root of some of the difficulties encountered not only in the relationship between higher education and employment, but in higher education itself.

Annex

AUTHORS OF THE NATIONAL REPORTS

Australia

Sir Bruce Williams,
National Board of Employment, Education and Training, GPO Box 9880, Canberra ACT 2601.

Austria

Dr. Lorenz Lassnigg,
Institut für Höhere Studien, Stumpergasse 56, A-1060 Wien.

Dr. Klaus Schedler,
Institut für Bildungsforschung der Wirtschaft, Rainergasse 38, A-1050 Wien.

Belgium (Flemish Community)

André Bonte,
Université de Gand, Duifhuisstraat 14, B 9000 Gent.

Canada

Ramona McDowell,
Analyste de recherche, Secrétariat d'Etat du Canada, K1A OM5 Ottawa (Ontario).

Gilles Jasmin,
Secrétariat d'Etat du Canada, 25, rue Eddy, 10H19 Hull (Québec).

Denmark

Hanne Traberg,
Poul Bache,
Directorate for Further and Higher Education, Ministry of Education, Frederiksholms Kanal 26, DK 1220 Copenhague K.

Finland

Arja Haapakorpi,
University of Helsinki, Helsinki.

France

Alain Charlot,
François Pottier,
Centre d'études et de recherches sur les qualifications (CEREQ), 9, rue Sextius-Michel, 75015 Paris.

Germany

Manfred Tessaring,
Institut für Arbeitsmarkt- und Berufsforschung (IAB), Regensburger Strasse 104, 8500 Nürnberg.

Italy

Federico Bussi,
Centro studi investimenti sociali (CENSIS), Piazza di Novella 2, 00199 Rome.

Japan

Motohisa Kaneko,
Research Institute for Higher Education, Hiroshima University, Higashi Senda Machi, Naka Ku, Hiroshima Shi, 730.

Netherlands

Ivonne Coppens,
Ministerie van Onderwijs en Wetenschappen, Europaweg 4, Postbus 25000, 2700 LZ Zoetermeer.

Norway

Per Olaf Aamodt,
Terje Naess,
Institute for Studies in Research & Higher Education, Munthes gate 29, 0260 Oslo 2.

Portugal

Luis Valadares Tavares,
Gabinete de Estudos e Planeamento, Ministério da Educação, Av. Miguel Bombarda 20, 1093 Lisboa Cedex.

Margarida Abecassis,
Manuel Carmelo Rosa,
Comissão Interministrial para o Emprego, Avenida da República 62, 1000 Lisboa.

Spain

Antonio Casanueva de Luis,
Jefe del Servicio de Documentacion, Consejo de Universidades, Ciudad Universitaria, s/n, 28040 Madrid.

Sweden

Stig Forneng,
Dan Anderson,
National Board of Universities & Colleges, Box 45501, S-10430 Stockholm.

Switzerland

Tania Ogay,
Office fédéral de l'Education et de la Science, Wildhainweg 9, 3001 Bern.

United Kingdom

Jason Tarsh,
Department of Education & Science, Sanctuary Buildings, Great Smith Street, Westminster, London SW1P 3BT.

United States

E. Stephen Hunt,
Office for Educational Research and Improvement, OERI, United States Department of Education,
555 New Jersey Av., N.W., Washington D.C. 20208-5647.

MAIN SALES OUTLETS OF OECD PUBLICATIONS
PRINCIPAUX POINTS DE VENTE DES PUBLICATIONS DE L'OCDE

ARGENTINA – ARGENTINE
Carlos Hirsch S.R.L.
Galería Güemes, Florida 165, 4° Piso
1333 Buenos Aires   Tel. (1) 331.1787 y 331.2391
                    Telefax: (1) 331.1787

AUSTRALIA – AUSTRALIE
D.A. Information Services
648 Whitehorse Road, P.O.B 163
Mitcham, Victoria 3132   Tel. (03) 873.4411
                         Telefax: (03) 873.5679

AUSTRIA – AUTRICHE
Gerold & Co.
Graben 31
Wien I   Tel. (0222) 533.50.14

BELGIUM – BELGIQUE
Jean De Lannoy
Avenue du Roi 202
B-1060 Bruxelles   Tel. (02) 538.51.69/538.08.41
                   Telefax: (02) 538.08.41

CANADA
Renouf Publishing Company Ltd.
1294 Algoma Road
Ottawa, ON K1B 3W8   Tel. (613) 741.4333
                     Telefax: (613) 741.5439
Stores:
61 Sparks Street
Ottawa, ON K1P 5R1   Tel. (613) 238.8985
211 Yonge Street
Toronto, ON M5B 1M4   Tel. (416) 363.3171
Les Éditions La Liberté Inc.
3020 Chemin Sainte-Foy
Sainte-Foy, PQ G1X 3V6   Tel. (418) 658.3763
                         Telefax: (418) 658.3763

Federal Publications
165 University Avenue
Toronto, ON M5H 3B8   Tel. (416) 581.1552
                      Telefax: (416) 581.1743

CHINA – CHINE
China National Publications Import
Export Corporation (CNPIEC)
16 Gongti E. Road, Chaoyang District
P.O. Box 88 or 50
Beijing 100704 PR   Tel. (01) 506.6688
                    Telefax: (01) 506.3101

DENMARK – DANEMARK
Munksgaard Export and Subscription Service
35, Nørre Søgade, P.O. Box 2148
DK-1016 København K   Tel. (33) 12.85.70
                      Telefax: (33) 12.93.87

FINLAND – FINLANDE
Akateeminen Kirjakauppa
Keskuskatu 1, P.O. Box 128
00100 Helsinki   Tel. (358 0) 12141
                 Telefax: (358 0) 121.4441

FRANCE
OECD/OCDE
Mail Orders/Commandes par correspondance:
2, rue André-Pascal
75775 Paris Cedex 16   Tel. (33-1) 45.24.82.00
Telefax: (33-1) 45.24.85.00 or (33-1) 45.24.81.76
                       Telex: 640048 OCDE
OECD Bookshop/Librairie de l'OCDE :
33, rue Octave-Feuillet
75016 Paris   Tel. (33-1) 45.24.81.67
              (33-1) 45.24.81.81

Documentation Française
29, quai Voltaire
75007 Paris   Tel. 40.15.70.00

Gibert Jeune (Droit-Économie)
6, place Saint-Michel
75006 Paris   Tel. 43.25.91.19

Librairie du Commerce International
10, avenue d'Iéna
75016 Paris   Tel. 40.73.34.60
Librairie Dunod
Université Paris-Dauphine
Place du Maréchal de Lattre de Tassigny
75016 Paris   Tel. 47.27.18.56
Librairie Lavoisier
11, rue Lavoisier
75008 Paris   Tel. 42.65.39.95
Librairie L.G.D.J. - Montchrestien
20, rue Soufflot
75005 Paris   Tel. 46.33.89.85
Librairie des Sciences Politiques
30, rue Saint-Guillaume
75007 Paris   Tel. 45.48.36.02
P.U.F.
49, boulevard Saint-Michel
75005 Paris   Tel. 43.25.83.40
Librairie de l'Université
12a, rue Nazareth
13100 Aix-en-Provence   Tel. (16) 42.26.18.08
Documentation Française
165, rue Garibaldi
69003 Lyon   Tel. (16) 78.63.32.23
Librairie Decitre
29, place Bellecour
69002 Lyon   Tel. (16) 72.40.54.54

GERMANY – ALLEMAGNE
OECD Publications and Information Centre
Schedestrasse 7
D-W 5300 Bonn 1   Tel. (0228) 21.60.45
                  Telefax: (0228) 26.11.04

GREECE – GRÈCE
Librairie Kauffmann
Mavrokordatou 9
106 78 Athens   Tel. 322.21.60
                Telefax: 363.39.67

HONG-KONG
Swindon Book Co. Ltd.
13–15 Lock Road
Kowloon, Hong Kong   Tel. 366.80.31
                     Telefax: 739.49.75

ICELAND – ISLANDE
Mál Mog Menning
Laugavegi 18, Pósthólf 392
121 Reykjavik   Tel. 162.35.23

INDIA – INDE
Oxford Book and Stationery Co.
Scindia House
New Delhi 110001   Tel.(11) 331.5896/5308
                   Telefax: (11) 332.5993
17 Park Street
Calcutta 700016   Tel. 240832

INDONESIA – INDONÉSIE
Pdii-Lipi
P.O. Box 269/JKSMG/88
Jakarta 12790   Tel. 583467
                Telex: 62 875

IRELAND – IRLANDE
TDC Publishers – Library Suppliers
12 North Frederick Street
Dublin 1   Tel. 74.48.35/74.96.77
           Telefax: 74.84.16

ISRAEL
Electronic Publications only
Publications électroniques seulement
Sophist Systems Ltd.
71 Allenby Street
Tel-Aviv 65134   Tel. 3-29.00.21
                 Telefax: 3-29.92.39

ITALY – ITALIE
Libreria Commissionaria Sansoni
Via Duca di Calabria 1/1
50125 Firenze   Tel. (055) 64.54.15
                Telefax: (055) 64.12.57
Via Bartolini 29
20155 Milano   Tel. (02) 36.50.83
Editrice e Libreria Herder
Piazza Montecitorio 120
00186 Roma   Tel. 679.46.28
             Telefax: 678.47.51
Libreria Hoepli
Via Hoepli 5
20121 Milano   Tel. (02) 86.54.46
               Telefax: (02) 805.28.86
Libreria Scientifica
Dott. Lucio de Biasio 'Aeiou'
Via Coronelli, 6
20146 Milano   Tel. (02) 48.95.45.52
               Telefax: (02) 48.95.45.48

JAPAN – JAPON
OECD Publications and Information Centre
Landic Akasaka Building
2-3-4 Akasaka, Minato-ku
Tokyo 107   Tel. (81.3) 3586.2016
            Telefax: (81.3) 3584.7929

KOREA – CORÉE
Kyobo Book Centre Co. Ltd.
P.O. Box 1658, Kwang Hwa Moon
Seoul   Tel. 730.78.91
        Telefax: 735.00.30

MALAYSIA – MALAISIE
Co-operative Bookshop Ltd.
University of Malaya
P.O. Box 1127, Jalan Pantai Baru
59700 Kuala Lumpur
Malaysia   Tel. 756.5000/756.5425
           Telefax: 757.3661

NETHERLANDS – PAYS-BAS
SDU Uitgeverij
Christoffel Plantijnstraat 2
Postbus 20014
2500 EA's-Gravenhage   Tel. (070 3) 78.99.11
Voor bestellingen: Tel. (070 3) 78.98.80
                       Telefax: (070 3) 47.63.51

NEW ZEALAND
NOUVELLE-ZÉLANDE
Legislation Services
P.O. Box 12418
Thorndon, Wellington   Tel. (04) 496.5652
                       Telefax: (04) 496.5698

NORWAY – NORVÈGE
Narvesen Info Center – NIC
Bertrand Narvesens vei 2
P.O. Box 6125 Etterstad
0602 Oslo 6   Tel. (02) 57.33.00
              Telefax: (02) 68.19.01

PAKISTAN
Mirza Book Agency
65 Shahrah Quaid-E-Azam
Lahore 3   Tel. 66.839
           Telex: 44886 UBL PK. Attn: MIRZA BK

PORTUGAL
Livraria Portugal
Rua do Carmo 70-74
Apart. 2681
1117 Lisboa Codex   Tel.: (01) 347.49.82/3/4/5
                    Telefax: (01) 347.02.64

SINGAPORE – SINGAPOUR
Information Publications Pte. Ltd.
41, Kallang Pudding, No. 04-03
Singapore 1334　　　　　　Tel. 741.5166
　　　　　　　　　　　　　Telefax: 742.9356

SPAIN – ESPAGNE
Mundi-Prensa Libros S.A.
Castelló 37, Apartado 1223
Madrid 28001　　　　　Tel. (91) 431.33.99
　　　　　　　　　　　Telefax: (91) 575.39.98

Libreria Internacional AEDOS
Consejo de Ciento 391
08009 – Barcelona　　　Tel. (93) 488.34.92
　　　　　　　　　　　Telefax: (93) 487.76.59

Llibreria de la Generalitat
Palau Moja
Rambla dels Estudis, 118
08002 – Barcelona
　　　　　(Subscripcions) Tel. (93) 318.80.12
　　　　　(Publicacions) Tel. (93) 302.67.23
　　　　　　　　　　　Telefax: (93) 412.18.54

SRI LANKA
Centre for Policy Research
c/o Colombo Agencies Ltd.
No. 300-304, Galle Road
Colombo 3　　　Tel. (1) 574240, 573551-2
　　　　　　　Telefax: (1) 575394, 510711

SWEDEN – SUÈDE
Fritzes Fackboksföretaget
Box 16356
Regeringsgatan 12
103 27 Stockholm　　　Tel. (08) 690.90.90
　　　　　　　　　　Telefax: (08) 20.50.21

Subscription Agency-Agence d'abonnements
Wennergren-Williams AB
Nordenflychtsvägen 74
Box 30004
104 25 Stockholm　　　Tel. (08) 13.67.00
　　　　　　　　　　Telefax: (08) 618.62.36

SWITZERLAND – SUISSE
Maditec S.A. (Books and Periodicals - Livres et périodiques)
Chemin des Palettes 4
1020 Renens/Lausanne　Tel. (021) 635.08.65
　　　　　　　　　　Telefax: (021) 635.07.80

Librairie Payot S.A.
4, place Pépinet
1003 Lausanne　　　　Tel. (021) 341.33.48
　　　　　　　　　　Telefax: (021) 341.33.45

Librairie Unilivres
6, rue de Candolle
1205 Genève　　　　　Tel. (022) 320.26.23
　　　　　　　　　　Telefax: (022) 329.73.18

Subscription Agency - Agence d'abonnement
Naville S.A.
38 avenue Vibert
1227 Carouge　　　　Tél.: (022) 308.05.56/57
　　　　　　　　　　Telefax: (022) 308.05.88

See also – Voir aussi :
OECD Publications and Information Centre
Schedestrasse 7
D-W 5300 Bonn 1 (Germany)
　　　　　　　　　　Tel. (49.228) 21.60.45
　　　　　　　　　　Telefax: (49.228) 26.11.04

TAIWAN – FORMOSE
Good Faith Worldwide Int'l. Co. Ltd.
9th Floor, No. 118, Sec. 2
Chung Hsiao E. Road
Taipei　　　　Tel. (02) 391.7396/391.7397
　　　　　　　Telefax: (02) 394.9176

THAILAND – THAÏLANDE
Suksit Siam Co. Ltd.
113, 115 Fuang Nakhon Rd.
Opp. Wat Rajbopith
Bangkok 10200　　　　Tel. (662) 251.1630
　　　　　　　　　　Telefax: (662) 236.7783

TURKEY – TURQUIE
Kültur Yayınları Is-Türk Ltd. Sti.
Atatürk Bulvari No. 191/Kat. 13
Kavaklidere/Ankara　Tel. 428.11.40 Ext. 2458
Dolmabahce Cad. No. 29
Besiktas/Istanbul　　　　Tel. 160.71.88
　　　　　　　　　　　Telex: 43482B

UNITED KINGDOM – ROYAUME-UNI
HMSO
Gen. enquiries　　　　Tel. (071) 873 0011
Postal orders only:
P.O. Box 276, London SW8 5DT
Personal Callers HMSO Bookshop
49 High Holborn, London WC1V 6HB
　　　　　　　　　　Telefax: (071) 873 8200
Branches at: Belfast, Birmingham, Bristol, Edinburgh, Manchester

UNITED STATES – ÉTATS-UNIS
OECD Publications and Information Centre
2001 L Street N.W., Suite 700
Washington, D.C. 20036-4910 Tel. (202) 785.6323
　　　　　　　　　　Telefax: (202) 785.0350

VENEZUELA
Libreria del Este
Avda F. Miranda 52, Aptdo. 60337
Edificio Galipán
Caracas 106　Tel. 951.1705/951.2307/951.1297
　　　　　　　Telegram: Libreste Caracas

Subscription to OECD periodicals may also be placed through main subscription agencies.

Les abonnements aux publications périodiques de l'OCDE peuvent être souscrits auprès des principales agences d'abonnement.

Orders and inquiries from countries where Distributors have not yet been appointed should be sent to: OECD Publications Service, 2 rue André-Pascal, 75775 Paris Cedex 16, France.

Les commandes provenant de pays où l'OCDE n'a pas encore désigné de distributeur devraient être adressées à : OCDE, Service des Publications, 2, rue André-Pascal, 75775 Paris Cedex 16, France.

12-1992

OECD PUBLICATIONS, 2 rue André-Pascal, 75775 PARIS CEDEX 16
PRINTED IN FRANCE
(91 92 05 1) ISBN 92-64-13825-0 - No. 46225 1993